The Popperian legacy in economics

The Popperian legacy in economics

Papers presented at a symposium in Amsterdam,
December 1985

Edited by

NEIL DE MARCHI

Department of Economics
Duke University and
University of Amsterdam

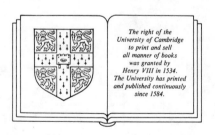

The right of the
University of Cambridge
to print and sell
all manner of books
was granted by
Henry VIII in 1534.
The University has printed
and published continuously
since 1584.

CAMBRIDGE UNIVERSITY PRESS

Cambridge
New York   New Rochelle   Melbourne   Sydney

Published by the Press Syndicate of the University of Cambridge
The Pitt Building, Trumpington Street, Cambridge CB2 1RP
32 East 57th Street, New York, NY 10022, USA
10 Stamford Road, Oakleigh, Melbourne 3166, Australia

First published 1988

Printed in the United States of America

Library of Congress Cataloging-in-Publication Data
The Popperian legacy in economics : papers presented at a
symposium in Amsterdam, December 1985 / edited by Neil de
Marchi.
p. cm.
Papers from a symposium sponsored by the University of Amsterdam
held Dec. 17–18, 1985.
Includes index.
ISBN 0-521-35576-1
1. Popper, Karl Raimund, Sir, 1902–   – Views on Economics –
Congresses.   I. de Marchi, Neil.   II. Universiteit van Amsterdam.
HB103.P66P66   1988
330.1–dc1988–1519

British Library Cataloguing in Publication Data
The Popperian legacy in economics : papers presented at a
symposium in Amsterdam, December 1985.
1. Economics. Theories of Popper, Karl R.
(Karl Raimund), 1902–
I. Title
330.1

ISBN 0 521 35576 1

To Joop Klant

Contents

Preface

This volume had its origin in a desire on the part of Joop Klant's colleagues at the University of Amsterdam to mark his retirement from the Chair of History and Philosophy of Economics. That desire translated into an attempt to focus scholarly effort on some of the themes that have informed his work over the past quarter-century.

Those themes are clearly evident in his own chapter, "The Natural Order," and are also spelled out in his contribution to the Discussion. They have to do with the nature of economics and with certain implications for being an honest practitioner in that discipline. First of all, economics is not value-free. That means that the choices we make about theories and policies in economics inevitably reflect our preferred notions of how the world is constituted. Furthermore, because we do not have natural constants in the world of economics and because our theory in economics is often so general (for instance, "agents optimize") that only specific versions can be tested, this leaves the basic theories themselves immune to test results. In our efforts at self-criticism, therefore, we have to go beyond mere testing for falsifying instances. This does not mean that striving after falsifiable theory is unimportant. It does mean that we must acknowledge and identify, as far as possible, the role of "vision" (perceived natural order) and art – the art of the good practitioner – in our economic "science."

Klant, it should be said, is a novelist of some repute in the Netherlands and also an artist in his own right, and was for years an analyst and adviser in a major commercial bank before taking up his chair at the University of Amsterdam. His perspective on economics bears the marks of one familiar with the various ways of engaging and persuading others that go beyond the empirical core that he too would acknowledge lies at the heart of his methodological writing.

The initiative for a conference came from Wim Driehuis, Professor of Macroeconomics at the University of Amsterdam. We agreed that such a gathering should pick up on the doubts that lay behind Klant's study on "the logical structure of economic theories," which is the subtitle to his *The Rules of the Game*. These were, as he wrote in the preface, "doubts . . . about how we, economists, can prove our theories. How do

ix

we take the decisions to accept or reject theories? Have we a right to put on scientific faces?" And so on. Answers to these questions, as he also pointed out, have a lot to do with the falsifiability of economic theories. For Popper at least, falsifiability is a logical affair; but the logical structure of economic theories is, after all, the subject of Klant's book. It was decided, therefore, that the conference should leave this aside and instead take a critical and historical look at the role played by Popper's demarcation criterion and his insistence on falsifiability as these have affected economists and their work.

We met for two days, December 17 and 18, 1985, at the Grand Hotel Krasnapolsky in Amsterdam. This two-day symposium was made possible by the generous financial support of the Dutch Foundation for Pure Economic Research (ZWO), the Foundation for Economic Research of the University of Amsterdam (SEO), and the Faculty of Economics, University of Amsterdam. An organizing committee comprising Wim Driehuis, Corien Sips, and Neil de Marchi formulated the plans. Special thanks are due to Corien Sips and Hugo Keuzenkamp for attending to the myriad practical details that went into making the gathering a success.

Thanks are due, too, to those participants whose invited commentaries and comments from the floor have made it possible to present an edited version of the discussion.

The manuscript was typed by Forrest Smith and Sharon Packer, to whom I am grateful.

Colin Day and Andrew Schwartz at Cambridge University Press sought readings from several outside reviewers that yielded helpful comments; and their wise counsel and patient guidance have been a boon at every stage of getting the manuscript into print.

N. de M.

August 14, 1987

Contributors

Doctorandus J. Birner, Department of Economics, University of Limburg, Maastricht, The Netherlands

Professor Mark Blaug, University of London, Institute of Education, 56/59 Gordon Square, London, England

Professor Bruce J. Caldwell, Department of Economics, University of North Carolina at Greensboro, Greensboro, N.C., U.S.A.

Professor J.S. Cramer, Stichting voor Economisch Onderzoek, University of Amsterdam, Jodenbreestraat 23, Amsterdam, The Netherlands

Professor Wim Driehuis, University of Amsterdam, Vakgroep Macro-economie, Jodenbreestraat 23, Amsterdam, The Netherlands

Doctor Bert Hamminga, School of Economics, Social Sciences and Laws, Tilburg University, Tilburg, The Netherlands

Professor D. Wade Hands, Department of Economics, University of Puget Sound, Tacoma, Washington, U.S.A.

Professor Daniel M. Hausman, Department of Philosophy, Carnegie-Mellon University, Pittsburgh, Pa., U.S.A.

Professor Terence W. Hutchison, 11 Clark Road, Woodbridge, Conn., U.S.A.

Doctorandus T.J. Kastelein, Department of Economics, University of Groningen, Padepoel, Groningen, The Netherlands

Professor Arjo Klamer, Department of Economics, University of Iowa, Iowa City, Iowa, U.S.A.

Professor J.J. Klant, Keizersgracht 405^1, Amsterdam, The Netherlands

Professor Donald N. McCloskey, Department of Economics, University of Iowa, Iowa City, Iowa, U.S.A.

Professor Neil de Marchi, Department of Economics, Duke University, Durham, N.C., U.S.A.; and University of Amsterdam, Jodenbreestraat 23, Amsterdam, The Netherlands

Doctor Mary Morgan, London School of Economics, Houghton Street, Aldwych, London, England

Professor E. Roy Weintraub, Department of Economics, Duke University, Durham, N.C., U.S.A.

Introduction

NEIL DE MARCHI

1

Economic methodologists and historians of economics have begun to find common ground in studying the actual practices of economists. Ironically, this has come about partly because both have sought and found inspiration in the philosophy of science. Ironic because, in its early days, philosophy of science was the captive of the philosophy of Logical Positivism, whose overriding concern with meaning, rather than with knowledge, made it remote from the activity of scientists. Thus the alleged connection between philosophy of science and the methodology and history of economics may seem unlikely, and a brief history of the interaction seems called for.[1] Sir Karl Popper's views and reactions to them are central to the story.

In the heyday of Positivism the authority undoubtedly due to science was thought of as being intimately linked with the properties of statements. So-called elementary statements were deemed to capture in a quite direct way elements of reality. Hence the logical relation of such statements to nonelementary statements, and the verifiability of a statement (by observation), became the central concerns of philosophy of science. Apart from analytic propositions, only empirically verifiable statements were judged meaningful (cf. Ayer 1946). But after all, it is statements not about particular instances or observations but about general classes of experience that interest scientists. Thus, as Popper noted in *The Logic of Scientific Discovery* (1959, ch. 1, sect. 4), the philosophy of logical empiricism inevitably led to a search for a modified logic of induction. Popper himself firmly believed the problems of induction to be insoluble, and he imparted to the phrase "the logic of scientific discovery" the very special sense of a logic of deductive testing.

My thanks to Roy Weintraub, Bob Coats, and Bruce Caldwell for helpful comments on earlier drafts of this introduction.

[1] What follows is in no sense a complete history. Essential complements are the introduction to Hausman (1984) and the editorial commentaries in Caldwell (1984), together with their respective bibliographies.

1

The insoluble problems of induction could be eliminated, Popper asserted, without putting new problems in their place, by restricting epistemology to a deductive analysis of what he took to be its central problem, the growth of knowledge; in particular, of "scientific," or empirical, knowledge. Growth implies discovery, but Popper did not mean that the actual process of discovery should form the province of this redefined philosophy of knowledge. The study of such a process falls more naturally under empirical psychology. What the philosopher of scientific knowledge could and should investigate, however, is that which is distinctive about the world of experience, namely, that "it has been submitted to tests, and has stood up to tests" (ibid., p. 39). In Popper's hands, then, "the logic of scientific discovery" became the analysis of the logic of testing. Testing, in his system, takes the place of verification in the Positivists' approach to what is known to be knowledge. Popper pointed out that universal statements (those generalizations that scientists seek to identify) cannot be derived from singular statements, but can be refuted by singular statements; hence the appropriate way to demarcate "empirical science" from, say, metaphysics (or nonscience in general) is not by applying a criterion of verification but a criterion of falsifiability: "I shall require [of a scientific system] that its logical form shall be such that it can be singled out, by means of empirical tests, in a negative sense: *it must be possible for an empirical scientific system to be refuted by experience*" (ibid., p. 41).

Popper is quite willing to take responsibility for having killed Logical Positivism; that is, he claims to have sown the seeds of its destruction. At the same time, he notes that the problems to which he pointed were inherent and that the real cause of death was "insuperable internal difficulties" (1976, p. 88). From the outside it doesn't much matter; Positivism matured into a more moderate logical empiricism, which in turn died a lingering death of a thousand qualifications in the 1950s and 1960s (well chronicled by Suppe, 1977, introduction; see also Caldwell, 1982). It is doubtful whether many practicing economists mourned its passing. What took its place, however, was very attractive to economists, and even more so to economic methodologists and historians of economics.

Positivism was succeeded by what many have come to call the "growth of knowledge" tradition (e.g., Caldwell, 1982, ch. 5). Popper's redefined epistemology – a skeptical (critical) rationalism, with its distinctive program of deductive testing – was its progenitor, though it evolved in directions that left Popper less than satisfied (see Newton-Smith 1981, for a thorough treatment of the issues). A major new element was Thomas Kuhn's rejection of the idea that the historian of science must be able to determine exactly the "when" and "by whom" of every discovery, and must necessarily view the history of a discipline as a process of error replacement (1970, p. 2). In rejecting these caricatures Kuhn was distancing himself from Positivism; but he also differed substantively – large areas of agreement notwithstanding – from Sir Karl Popper. One central disagreement was over the role of "normal science." Kuhn argued that Popper's sort of testing does not occur during nonrevolutionary phases of science; normal scientists simply do not question their premises, yet normal science or research is "an enterprise which accounts for the overwhelming majority of the work done in basic science" (1970, p. 4). A similar emphasis on the fundamental importance of unchallengeable (by fiat) "hard core" propositions – those that identify a program of research – is to be found in the work of Imre Lakatos. This emphasis contrasts sharply with Popper's insistence that the only uncriticizable statement should be something like "all of my views must be subject to criticism and possible rejection" (Caldwell's characterization of Popper's position: op. cit., p. 64, n. 3). A third strand in the new growth of knowledge fabric was woven by Paul Feyerabend, whose historical studies led him to conclude that the variety and subtlety of processes at work in producing scientific knowledge "defies analysis on the basis of rules which have been set up in advance and without regard to the ever-changing conditions of history" (cited in Caldwell, 1982, p. 8).

But to go back to Popper, what did his own message about refutability and testing in *The Logic of Scientific Discovery* hold for economists? Since the 1930s there had been two methodological beliefs exercising economists in the English-speaking world. One was the belief that a meticulous study of the facts will eventually issue in good theory. Much of the work done at the National Bureau of Economic Research under Wesley Clair Mitchell was of this sort – for example, Frederick C. Mills's *The Behavior of Prices* (1927). This was not exactly measurement without theory; it was more an insistence that we must first find out about the nature of the facts and what there is to explain. This contrasts strongly with the other methodological belief: not deductivism but, as Klant more appropriately calls it, empirical a priorism. This was espoused by Lionel Robbins, according to whom true knowledge could be deduced from premises that a moment's introspection would show to be true. These two views more or less divided up the field, although the increasing mathematicization of economic theory in the 1950s had strengthened the Robbins position, a position that made fact gathering and measurement seem not just difficult and tedious, but beside the point.

Popper changed the nature of this debate. His anti-inductivism weakened the claims of the Mitchell–Mills approach, but at the same time his insistence on testing opened up the deductivist position to criticism.

Quite apart from what he had to say viewed as matters of logical relations and of the properties of statements, he represented an *attitude*–to be critical. Neither fact nor theory is more than an element in the process of identifying error. This was liberating for economists in a special way. Popper's balanced insistence on empirical content *and* on the epistemological priority of theorizing might have been tailored to appeal to practitioners in a discipline where experimentation is difficult and inconclusive and theory seems more solid, yet where numbers are seen to be essential to adapting theory to yield advice for policy making. His stress on methodological conventions–rules of the game–was helpful to a group of social scientists anxious to be useful and to explain themselves to a somewhat reluctant public, yet conscious of the fallibility of their pronouncements. In short, in contrast to much writing in the philosophy of science, Popper's work was not only accessible to economists but seemed relevant.

Economic methodologists and historians of economics took to Popper with avidity. Some methodologists–Hutchison (1964, 1968, 1977, 1981, in addition to his pioneering 1938) and Blaug (1975, 1980a, 1980b) in particular, but also Klant (1979) and Boland (1982, 1985)–used Popper's methodological rules to criticize economic practice. Historians of economics, encouraged by Popper's attention to historical episodes in science and to "problem situations," began trying to elucidate episodes in their own parent discipline with the aid of Popper's rules and perspective (Blaug, 1968, ch. 16; de Marchi, 1970; Latsis, 1972). Both groups, however, quickly ran up against what might seem to be a fundamental difficulty: Economists pay lip service to notions like empirical content and falsifiability and deductive testing but do not actually put the Popperian rules for strenuous testing into practice (see esp. Blaug 1980b).

This caused no widespread consternation, however, both because it had always been known in some sense and because the Kuhn, Lakatos, and Feyerabend alternatives to Popper were being developed and made available. Kuhn gave a place to actual practice and real history that Popper's and Lakatos's "rational reconstructions" could not. On the other hand, Lakatos's methodology of scientific research programs, with its uncriticizable hard core, offered a seductive way to rationalize the very failure of economists to apply the Popperian conventions of good science. In this sense it, too, came closer to actual economic practice. Feyerabend's "anarchism," for its part, served to render inquiry into all kinds of methods and all kinds of subgroups among economists free from the judgments of "scientific" acceptability or its opposite, which seemed to be part of every attempt to apply Popper's demarcation criterion.

Preliminary attempts to apply Kuhnian and Lakatosian schema quickly showed that they held problems of their own. How many paradigms are there in the history of economics – one or many? Is there predictive force to the notion that revolution is preceded by an accumulation of anomalies, or is Kuhn's framework primarily useful for writing history? Is it damaging if we cannot reach precise agreement on the elements of the hard core of a research program? What exactly is a novel fact? How should one describe testing between noncomparable but supposedly competing paradigms or research programs? And so on. These sorts of questions led historians of economics to wonder about the usefulness of the grand visions of Kuhn and Lakatos. Both of these frameworks and more traditional philosophy of science rested heavily on studies of physics and astronomy and, in the case of Lakatos, mathematics. The difficulties that arise in trying to transfer the results to economics have also led a few philosophers to examine economics and its literature afresh as a distinct area of inquiry (Rosenberg, 1976, on the nature of microeconomic laws; Mackay, 1980, on Arrow's Theorem; Hausman, 1981, on capital theory; Nelson, 1984, 1987, on the reduction of macroeconomic phenomena to microfoundations; Bicchieri, 1987, on rationality, information, and equilibrium). The growing skepticism about grand visions and the new-found interest in economics as a subject of philosophical investigation have given rise to increasingly detailed examinations of how economists actually go about their work (Wong, 1978; Hamminga, 1983; Klamer, 1983; Diesing, 1985; McCloskey, 1985; Weintraub, 1985; Hirsch and de Marchi, 1986; also, for econometrics, though with a slightly different motivation, Hendry, 1980, 1983, 1986).

Two further elements that have been moving things in this direction, though at the same time away from traditional philosophical concerns, are the work of philosophers such as Richard Rorty and of adherents of the so-called Strong Program in the sociology of science at Edinburgh University. The early response of Popper and Lakatos to Kuhn was that he was replacing rational history of science with the history of science as social psychology and sociology. Rorty (and others, in complementary ways) have challenged this kind of criticism by pointing out that it confounds explanation and justification, and presumes that the rational account of knowledge is in some privileged position. An " 'account of the nature of knowledge'," Rorty points out, "can be, at most, a description of human behavior" (1979, p. 182). Aiding and abetting these philosophers have been literary critics, such as Stanley Fish (1980), who are intent on dethroning structure and text as touchstones of truth (or at least meaning). Klamer and McCloskey independently have embarked upon research involving the rhetorical analysis of economic writing and a close look at the discourse that takes place among economists and between them and other audiences. This reinforces the efforts of a group of philosophers and social thinkers linked to the Strong Program to construct a social theory of knowledge (Bloor, 1983; see also Barnes and Edge, 1982, and Knorr-Cetina and Mulkay, 1983).

Historians of economics and economic methodologists might find much in the new "rhetorical" and "social" approaches that is attractive. These approaches at least claim to relieve them from having to engage in demarcation disputes. Nor need they spend time rationalizing the discrepancy that exists between the lip service economists pay to falsifiability and testing and their very different practices. They are free to examine just what counts as supporting evidence without fear of dismissal by anti-inductivists. And they can begin to attend to the actual "conversations" that take place among economists, and between economists and their audiences, without expecting to find debate being closed by some criterion of truth or adequacy imported from outside.

2

That is the point at which we have arrived after a quarter-century of debate over the ideas of Popper and of Kuhn, Lakatos, and Feyerabend. The prospect is like a glimpse of the promised land to some. To others it seems that we are threatened by the abandonment of all standards. The symposium reported in this volume brought together a group of historians of economics and economic methodologists to reflect on what we have learned from recent philosophy of science; more particularly, what we have gained from the philosophy of Karl Popper, whose work was the first radical departure from the Logical Positivist tradition. The discussion fully reflects the current mixed sense of anticipation and reticence.

3

Why Popper? Proximately because Klant's *The Rules of the Game* drew inspiration from Popper's philosophy. More basically, however, because, as should be clear by now, Popper is the one philosopher from the years of dominance of the Positivists who, to many economic methodologists, has seemed to convey a clear and simple set of guidelines for exposing the self-indulgence of economists who cared little about the empirical world. Simply put, Popper made it clear that this self-indulgence could not be tolerated if economics was to be counted among the sciences. It is important to note that this reading of Popper is regarded by some methodologists as a travesty. Lawrence Boland has consistently urged that Popper aims to be critical, not to offer rules for providing a "sound" *foundation* for our knowledge (1982, esp. ch. 10). The fact remains, however – as Boland also acknowledges – that Popper's economics audience has tended to read him in the way suggested. It would be a useful exercise, not undertaken here or elsewhere in this volume, to trace the course of this divergence between the intended and the received message. Popper's demarcation criterion was first brought to the attention of economists in the 1930s by Terence Hutchison, who used it to show just how much of what then passed for economic analysis was tautology masquerading as substantive propositions. Popper himself used the criterion and the notion that we cannot establish truth, but can only identify error, in the fight against fascism. His ideas were put to similar use by followers such as Hans Albert and Imre Lakatos in the ideological struggles that wracked European universities in the 1960s. Economic methodologists came to share the conviction that if their discipline is not value-free, it – and they – can at least strive after falsifiability. That has been Klant's persistent plea.

The idea of positive (i.e., nonnormative) economics, meanwhile, was given a new lease on life by Milton Friedman – consciously influenced by Popper, but no Popperian – when he linked it to the Popperian ideal of science as conjecture and refutation. In Friedman's version the conjectures need not be realistic, provided only that they give rise to anticipations that check out against the facts. This provided generations of university teachers with a handy rationalization for the apparent irrelevance (unrealism) of much economic theory. More importantly the formula, substantive hypothesis followed by empirical test, became the international standard for acceptable Ph.D. dissertations. By the 1970s this bowdlerized message had become established in the minds of many economists as the contribution of Sir Karl Popper.

In setting up the symposium, the organizers saw it as one of their tasks to reexamine what Popper really did have to say to economists on matters of methodological import. Further, in light of the debate of the last twenty-five years in philosophy of science, it seemed appropriate to ask, how much of the original message, in its English-language version just three years older than Kuhn's book, is worth retaining?

4

There is much in Popper that need not be rejected along with rationalist views on the way science develops, or should develop. Those elements that can be retained stand out more clearly in the oral tradition surrounding Popper's London School of Economics teaching than they do in his writings, though they are there too.[2] The oral tradition stresses that he was very concerned with imparting to students a sensitivity to evolving problem situations, and to the creative element in formulating discriminating hypotheses, and that he did not place too much emphasis on falsifiability and testing, except in the sense of testing the real mettle of a particular solution to a problem. That is to say, his instructional concern was with the *history* of science – albeit a "rationally reconstructed history" (Popper's phrase, before it was popularized by Lakatos) – as a lead-up to criticizing current theories. Thus criticism (of proposed solutions to problems) was important, as were modeling and things like the the rationality principle (or logic of the situation); but none of these depended upon the strict dictates of *logical,* as distinct from conventional, falsificationism. As noted previously, they reflected an attitude rather than faith in rules or methods.

If we can accept this, it actually puts Popper much more in line with the limitations to which economists know they are subject. Moreover, we see a Popper who at one level is by no means out of place alongside Rorty, for whom, too, "there are no assertions which are immune from revision" (1979, p. 181). Indeed, as Klant points out, although parameter inconstancy and the generic nature of our underlying theories in economics make it pointless to try to apply a sharp demarcation line based on falsifiability, the role of criticism is thereby actually enhanced. Curiously, however, the symposiasts in Amsterdam were not taken with the idea of seeing how much of Popper could be retained, but spent a great deal of time discussing – inconclusively – the need for and possible alternatives to Popper's demarcation criterion. This preference may reflect the current confusion about standards noted already.

5

Four positions emerged in the course of the two days of discussion. First, Klamer and McCloskey identified themselves from the outset as fanciers of the – to most still somewhat exotic – Rorty–Fish agenda. The majority response to this was that advocacy must be backed by evidence of superiority, and that accepting the "rhetorical" as *one* approach to understanding the way economics has evolved ought not preclude others. Some of the promise of rhetoric, it should be said, has since been made actual in a fascinating book by Don McCloskey, *The Rhetoric of Economics* (1985).

---

[2] For a comprehensive introduction to Popper's philosophy, see O'Hear (1980). I am indebted to Jeremy Shearmur for comments on the oral tradition.

Second, a rearguard action was fought by Hutchison and Blaug, both of whom argued that some standard is indispensable. Moreover, it should be one that is less question begging than "do what successful scientists have done in the past" and stronger than "be critical" or "follow the rules of good conversation."

A third stance – what might be called "critical pluralism" – was enjoined by Bruce Caldwell. Caldwell's view amounts to a dual plea to allow many methods to flourish and to submit each of them relentlessly to criticism. It is unique in that Caldwell wants to change not the practice of economists, but those of methodologists.

Finally, the remaining four authors of papers (Hands, de Marchi, Weintraub, Morgan) identified behaviors by practicing economists that drew attention to the limitations of trying to understand economics using Popper's guidelines for good science. These forays into what economists do reveal that it is not easy to find consistent ways to apply the Popper–Lakatos criteria of "progress"; that the notion of testing in (Popperian) philosophy of science and in econometrics is not the same; that would-be empirical falsificationists among economists soon discover that there are special limitations imposed by the material they work with; and that the focus of inquiry in applied economics is not some imagined confrontation between theory and facts but a middle ground where both interact in complex ways and where (in Weintraub's phrase) "evidence is developed to appraise excess content." The position implicitly adopted here is that questions of standards and epistemological questions generally need to be sorted out in an applied context if the answers are to be useful to those who study and practice economics.

6

So much for the general tone of the discussion at the symposium. To enable the reader to follow its flow, it has been placed en bloc before the collection of papers, reversing the usual order. Although some editing has been undertaken, every effort has been made to respect the variety of styles and the extempore nature of the discourse. The discussion is meant to be self-contained. To that end, it includes brief summaries of the papers and of prepared responses by commentators. But the summaries are no substitute for the papers themselves, and a brief indication of how they hang together is in order.

The motivation behind the form given the symposium was that Popper and his philosophy constitute a puzzle for workers in economic methodology or the history of economic thought. Popper's ideas are known (albeit imperfectly), referred to, often appealed to in disputes about "right" practice, yet not deferred to in the actual doing. Why not? If they are of little use, why even refer to Popper? If they are of genuine value, why only pay lip service?

The first two papers, those by Hausman and Klant, ask, in effect, what can we conclude if we take seriously both Popper and the limitations under which real economists do their work? Hausman concludes that logical falsificationism is artificially narrow because so much more than simple "basic statements" is taken as established background knowledge in actual practice. Worse, Popper's anti-inductivism distracts us from examining how we produce the support for those things we do accept. Klant reminds us that Popper himself backed away from applying strict demands for falsification to economics. That is in accord with the lack of numerical constants in the economic environment. Even rational criticism, however, entails values and commitments, and is strictly on the wrong side of Popper's demarcation criterion. Klant infers that if we take Popper seriously we must acknowledge that falsifiability is only an ideal and that economics is some mix of science (à la Popper), "philosophy," or vision (à la Schumpeter) and art (as in J.M. Keynes's famous dictum: "Economics is a science of thinking in terms of models joined to the art of choosing models which are relevant to the contemporary world" (*Collected Writings,* vol. XIV, p. 295).

What really happens when economists take Popper seriously and when they do not? Hands's study of how economists use notions of ad hocness shows that economic theorists at least, in defining non-ad hocness, tend to prefer Lakatos's idea of program continuity to Popper's notion, which has to do with declining to adopt defensive stratagems. De Marchi's paper examines the way Popper was taken up by a group of young economists at the London School of Economics in the 1950s and 1960s. They found his views helpful in what was really (in part, anyway) a struggle to accelerate the quantification of economics. That the encounter was convenient and superficial, however, is suggested by the fact that as soon as problems appeared in applying logical falsification – as in qualitative comparative statics and probabilistic models – the economists quickly abandoned Popper rather than explore his own efforts to deal with the difficulties, some of which he had recognized.

If these two case studies and the preceding papers by Hausman and Klant imply that the Popperian legacy in economics is insubstantial, or survives only if we are prepared to modify substantially his logical falsificationism, balance is provided by Terence Hutchison's restatement of the case *for* falsifiability. His argument will be familiar to students of his writing: He protests that hubris and mystification flourish where standards are lax, and although falsifiability has its limitations in economics, no better alternative standard has been adumbrated. Mark Blaug's study seems to confirm Hutchison's most pessimistic expectations. He examines the work of J. R. Hicks with the aim of discovering whether a coherent methodological position informs Hicks's writing. Hicks, of course, is well known for rejecting falsificationism, and Blaug is unable to find any other coherent methodological stance in his work. That, it need hardly be added, is no conclusive argument for falsificationism.

One of the ironies of economists' preoccupation with Popper is that he has so little to say about the problem of testing in economics. A major exception to that is his concession in *The Poverty of Historicism* that because economic parameters "are themselves in the most important cases quickly changing variables [, t]his clearly reduces the significance, interpretability, and testability of our measurements" (p. 143). Another is the remarks he makes in *The Logic of Scientific Discovery* about the rules governing the *use* of (strictly nonfalsifiable) probability statements as if they were falsifiable statements (e.g., p. 204). None of this, however, comes close to dealing with the problems that econometricians routinely face in bridging the gaps between data and economic theory. Two authors were invited to reflect on this complex of issues.

Mary Morgan's paper is a valuable survey of the ways in which econometricians have understood their task over the past fifty years, none of which turn out to be very close to Popper's general view of hypothesis testing. Roy Weintraub's complementary study of a sequence of papers on household behavior holds a double lesson. On the one hand, it suggests that general equilibrium analysis can issue in empirically progressive applied research. On the other hand, it raises the question of whether the relationship between theorist and empirical worker should continue to be regarded as that between proposer and disposer. That view implies that there is more independence about theory and more givenness about "facts" than is true of either. As Weintraub sees it, data gathering is, of course, theory driven; but it is not so simple a matter as punching out shapes in dough with a cookie cutter. Appropriate data gathering involves many interactions between analysis and evidence. In the end, what good applied economics is about is not well described as confronting a conjectured hypothesis with a widely accepted empirical basis by means of a neutral method. It is more a matter of designing evidence so as to put one in a position to appraise excess content (itself not a straightforward notion, as Hands pointed out in the discussion). This looks very much like what Ian Hacking calls "the creation of phenomena" in the process of experimentation (Hacking 1983, ch. 13).

The final three papers look beyond the sorts of things that Popper is able to contribute. In varying degrees they take up the challenges posed by Kuhn, Feyerabend, and Rorty. Caldwell has argued at length elsewhere that no useful resolution of the post-Positivist confusion is emerging in the works of philosophers of science. At the same time, he is unwilling to abandon methodology merely at the insistence of McCloskey (Caldwell and Coats, 1984). In his contribution here he argues for toleration and criticism of diverse methods and supplies reasons, based on the practices of scientists, why we need not fear anarchy. McCloskey again calls for the study of rhetoric to replace "modernism" and "Methodology," urging that the range of questions to which epistemological concerns confine one is simply too narrow, leaving out as it does any serious interest in how economists present arguments and try to persuade each other. Klamer pursues the same general point by showing that the logical structure of theories and properties of statements–the domain of Popper's philosophy of science–cannot begin to capture the rich interactions possible between the sender and receiver/interpreter of messages.

7

The papers at the Amsterdam symposium were not specifically designed to contribute to current philosophical debates. They did, however, serve to lay some ghosts to rest and to clarify issues of concern to economic methodologists and historians of economics. There was agreement, for example, that Popper's view of testing was too narrow–he does not adequately consider supporting evidence–and that he knew too little of the peculiar difficulties of economics for his guidelines concerning scientific practice to be readily transferable to our discipline. The value of a demarcation criterion based on empirical falsifiability, and of injunctions against immunizing stratagems, as even the neo-Popperians among the symposiasts acknowledged, lies in their capacity for "keeping us honest." Economists may choose to respond to the invitation to be critical, but for that they do not need to adhere to logical falsificationism or squeeze economics into a physical or astronomical mold.

Although a minority of the symposiasts might disagree, it seems fair to conclude that for most, and for a variety of good reasons, there is no very substantial Popperian legacy in economics. That comment does not apply to the critical attitude of mind that Popper sought to inculcate, but refers to his rules for the practice of "good" science. The rules, of course, are meant to give expression to what is involved in being critical; but if they cannot be used in economics as more than ideals, or to identify examples of good past practice, then we are left with the attitude itself, and not much more. Karl Popper's philosophy of science proved highly instructive to a generation of economic thinkers. But its main lesson was to disabuse economists of the idea that they could establish truth and could rest content with criteria for theory acceptance such as plausibility based on introspection, or logical consistency. Quantification, rigor in formulation, explicitness in establishing conditions for rejection – these things were given a fillip in economics by Popper. Those prescriptions having become widely accepted, however, it is entirely appropriate that a new generation of students of the evolution of economics occupy itself with detailed efforts to find out *how* economists use theory, view their models, discuss causation, advance arguments, go about testing, and so on, as necessary first steps toward constructing a methodology of economics that is more than a borrowed philosophy of physics.

References

Ayer, A.J. (1946). *Language, Truth and Logic*. London: Gollancz.

Barnes, B., and Edge, D., eds. (1982). *Science in Context: Readings in the Sociology of Science*. Cambridge, Mass.: MIT Press.

Bicchieri, C. (1987). "Strategic Behavior and Counterfactuals." Mimeo.

Blaug, M. (1968). *Economic Theory in Retrospect,* rev. ed. Homewood, Ill.: Irwin.

(1975). "Kuhn versus Lakatos, on Paradigms versus Research Programmes in the History of Economics." *History of Political Economy* Winter:399–433. Reprinted in Latsis (1976).

(1980a). *A Methodological Appraisal of Marxian Economics*. New York: North-Holland.

(1980b). *The Methodology of Economics: Or, How Economists Explain*. Cambridge: Cambridge University Press.

Bloor, D. (1983). *Wittgenstein: A Social Theory of Knowledge*. New York: Columbia University Press.

Boland, L.A. (1982). *The Foundations of Economic Method*. London: Allen & Unwin.

(1985). *A Methodology for a New Microeconomics*. London: Allen & Unwin.

Caldwell, B.J. (1982). *Beyond Positivism: Economic Methodology in the Twentieth Century*. London: Allen & Unwin.

(ed.) (1984). *Appraisal and Criticism in Economics. A Book of Readings*. Boston: Allen & Unwin.

and Coats, A.W. (1984). "The Rhetoric of Economists: A Comment on McCloskey." *Journal of Economic Literature* 22:375–8.

de Marchi, N. (1970). "The Empirical Content and Longevity of Ricardian Economics." *Economica* n.s. 37:257–76.

Diesing, P. (1985). "Hypothesis Testing and Data Interpretation: The Case of Milton Friedman," in W. Samuels, ed., *Research in the History of Economic Thought and Methodology,* Vol. 3. Greenwich, Conn.: JAI Press, pp. 61–89.

Fish, S.E. (1980). *Is There a Text in This Class?* Cambridge, Mass.: Harvard University Press.

Hacking, I. (1983). *Representing and Intervening.* Cambridge: Cambridge University Press.

Hamminga, B. (1983). *Neoclassical Theory, Structure, and Theory Development: An Empirical-Philosophical Case Study Concerning the Theory of International Trade.* New York: Springer-Verlag.

Hausman, D. (1981). *Capital, Profits and Prices: An Essay in the Philosophy of Economics.* New York: Columbia University Press.

——— (1984). *The Philosophy of Economics: An Anthology.* Cambridge: Cambridge University Press.

Hendry, D.F. (1980). "Econometrics: Alchemy or Science?" *Economica* n.s. 47:387–406.

——— (1983). "Econometric Modelling: The Consumption Function in Retrospect." *Scottish Journal of Political Economy* 30:193–220.

——— (with N. Ericsson) (1986). "Assertion without Empirical Basis: An Econometric Appraisal of *Monetary Trends in . . . The United Kingdom* by Milton Friedman and Anna Schwartz." International Finance Discussion Paper No. 270, Federal Reserve Board of Governors, Washington, D.C.

Hirsch, A., and de Marchi, N. (1986). "Making a Case When Theory Is Unfalsifiable: Friedman's Monetary History." *Economics and Philosophy* 2:1–21.

Hutchison, T.W. (1938). *The Significance and Basic Postulates of Economic Theory.* London: Macmillan.

——— (1964). *'Positive' Economics and Policy Objectives.* Cambridge, Mass.: Harvard University Press.

——— (1968). *Economics and Economic Policy in Britain, 1946–1966.* London: Allen & Unwin.

——— (1977). *Knowledge and Ignorance in Economics.* Chicago: University of Chicago Press.

——— (1981). *The Politics and Philosophy of Economics: Marxians, Keynesians, and Austrians.* New York: New York University Press.

Keynes, J.M. (1973). *The Collected Writings of John Maynard Keynes,* Vol. xiv. *The General Theory and After.* Part II: *Defence and Development,* ed. Donald Moggridge. Cambridge: Macmillan for the Royal Economic Society.

Klamer, A. (1983). *Conversations with Economists.* Totowa, N.J.: Rowman and Allenheld.

Klant, J.J. (1979). *Spelregels Voor Econmen,* 2nd ed. Antwerp: Stenfert Kroese.

——— (1984). *The Rules of the Game: The Logical Structure of Economic Theories.* Trans. by Ina Swart. Cambridge: Cambridge University Press.

Knorr-Cetina, K.D., and Mulkay, M. (1983). *Science Observed: Perspectives on the Social Study of Science.* London: Sage Publications.

Kuhn, T.S. (1970). *The Structure of Scientific Revolutions,* rev. ed. Chicago: University of Chicago Press.

Latsis, S. (1972). "Situational Determinism in Economics." *The British Journal for the Philosophy of Science* 23:207–45.

(ed.) (1976). *Method and Appraisal in Economics.* Cambridge: Cambridge University Press.

Mackay, A.F. (1980). *Arrow's Theorem: The Paradox of Social Choice.* New Haven, Conn.: Yale University Press.

McCloskey, D. (1985). *The Rhetoric of Economics.* Madison, Wisc.: University of Wisconsin Press.

Mills, F.C. (1927). *The Behavior of Prices.* New York: National Bureau of Economic Research.

Nelson, A. (1984). "Some Issues Surrounding the Reduction of Macroeconomics to Microeconomics." *Philosophy of Science* 51:573–94.

(1987). "Average Explanation." Mimeo.

Newton-Smith, W.H. (1981). *The Rationality of Science.* London: Routledge & Kegan Paul.

O'Hear, A. (1980). *Karl Popper.* Routledge & Kegan Paul.

Popper, K. (1959). *The Logic of Scientific Discovery.* London: Hutchinson.

(1957). *The Poverty of Historicism.* Boston: Beacon Press.

(1976). *Unended Quest: An Intellectual Autobiography.* London: Fontana.

Rorty, R. (1979). *Philosophy and the Mirror of Nature.* Princeton, N.J.: Princeton University Press.

Rosenberg, A. (1976). *Microeconomic Laws: A Philosophical Analysis.* Pittsburgh: University of Pittsburgh Press.

Suppe, F., ed. (1977). *The Structure of Scientific Theories.* Urbana, Ill.: University of Illinois Press.

Weintraub, E.R. (1985). *General Equilibrium Analysis: Studies in Appraisal.* Cambridge: Cambridge University Press.

Wong, S. (1978). *The Foundations of Paul Samuelson's Revealed Preference Theory: A Study by the Method of Rational Reconstruction.* New York: Methuen.

Discussion

Hausman paper

Summary remarks

My thesis is that Popper's philosophy of science is a mess, and that Popper is a very poor authority for economists interested in the philosophy of science to look to.

I am not concerned with all of Popper's philosophy of science. My focus is on falsifiability, the idea that what distinguishes science from nonscience is that scientific claims are falsifiable and that there are certain rules of procedure which one can derive from the notion of falsifiability, which characterizes how a scientist should go about his business.

Popper employs two contradictory notions of falsifiability. *Logical* falsifiability is logical inconsistency with some set of basic statements. This gives rise to the asymmetry between verification and falsification and to Popper's insistence that we can never have reason to believe that theories are correct. All we can find out is that they are incorrect. In other passages, however, Popper maintains that we can only decide whether we are dealing with an empirical science by examining the methods the supposed scientists employ.

A serious difficulty with logical falsifiability is that any test requires background knowledge as well as basic statements. If we could rely on nothing but relations between theories and basic statements, no science would be possible.

Popper knows this and allows that we must combine our theories with auxiliary hypotheses, and from these larger "test systems" derive predictions which involve basic statements. The problem with this is that we can no longer falsify *theories,* only whole system amalgams. To insist that it be possible to embed a theory in a logically falsifiable test system is, moreover, terribly weak. Virtually nothing is, in this sense, unfalsifiable.

So, logical falsifiability gets us nowhere. If we insist that theories be logically falsifiable, there'll be no science, while if we insist merely on the falsifiability of whole test systems, we are demanding almost nothing.

17

When we turn to Popper's rules of scientific procedure, we find that they are arbitrary and unjustifiable. Popper insists that science should aim at falsifications only, not verifications, because (as the problem of induction supposedly shows) we can never have good confirming evidence. But, in fact, though we can never falsify theories, we *can* sometimes verify them. To falsify individual theories, we need background knowledge as well as basic statements as premises. But with such expanded premises, one can also make valid arguments for theories. Supporting evidence can thus be had, which is lucky, for we cannot have good reason to regard a theory as falsified by the data unless the necessary auxiliary assumptions are well supported.

Discussion

de Marchi: If Hausman is right, why did we ever take Popper seriously? I suspect one part of the answer is that economists, like other scientists, have found in Popper's rules of procedure both an encouragement to be specific about what they are claiming and a feeling of freedom from an obligation to be right. There is a challenge to be tough with oneself and a sense of liberation.

But that aside, once we move away from *logical* falsification and in the direction of "conventional" falsification, then there's not very much to distinguish Hausman's position from the sorts of things McCloskey argues for. "Shared background beliefs" puts one in mind of Kuhn. What then is the unit of analysis? Whose beliefs? Who decides what is well established? There are genuine difficulties here. We want a certain amount of clarity about grounds for belief. The empirical study of the sociology of science tends to abstract from this. Nor does McCloskey deal adequately with the problem in telling us simply that we *know* when the conversation is "good." Dan Hausman encourages us to prospect in this old epistemological territory in a new way, but we desperately need a map.

To mention just one specific element that troubles me: It is not clear that the alternative to logical falsification is conventional falsification. "Plausibility" and "warranted belief" seem to be rich in content, and both merit further exploration. Surprisingly, though, we seem to have been caught up for several decades with matters of justification, and not very much has been done on how economists actually explain. I would like to see a shift in emphasis, but also to have Hausman tell us about some of the next steps that should be taken.

McCloskey: What would Hausman make of the assertion that Popper's arguments aren't so much arguments in epistemology as in ethics? If true, what is wrong with Popper is that he isn't "thick" in his ethical argumentation. He doesn't use the long Western tradition of discussion of ethical issues to help him understand why one might want to be a *good* scientist.

Hausman: Popper is absolutely explicit that he is engaged in a normative endeavor, in telling scientists how to behave. He stipulates the goals of science and probably would defend these on ethical grounds, though this is not something he has done well and at great length. Once we have a stipulation of the goals of science, as a search for truth or knowledge, though, the argument for his methodology comes directly from epistemology. The basic argument why we ought only to seek falsifications, as to why we should only accept propositions as worthy of further critical discussion and never as well supported . . . the basis for this is his epistemological claims.

Now I think there are many interesting things to be said about the goals of science, but the central difficulties in Popper's philosophy of science would remain regardless of how well specified and how well justified his account of the goals of science is. They stem from a mistaken epistemological thesis.

McCloskey: I think you have made a very persuasive case that the epistemology is not as helpful as he claims, but I'm trying to agree with Neil de Marchi that there are other questions to be considered. In particular, it's not enough, as ethical conversation, to simply specify the goals for science. That sounds an awful lot like the economist's discussion of a similar question, when we decide what our goal for public policy should be and then pursue the goal. It's in deciding what the goal is that the ethical conversation of Western philosophy might be helpful. Popper doesn't address this.

Hausman: On the contrary, Popper is terribly concerned about this. He thinks knowledge is important, not just for its own sake, but because it is important to combat all sorts of evils. I certainly agree that in the justification of the whole scientific endeavor, ethics is going to be crucial.

Caldwell: I have a simple question for Hausman. It's really what Neil de Marchi was asking, but he got no answer: "Where do we go from here?"

Hausman: I think there is a struggle on two fronts to understand better the nature of science, and I believe that there's a useful division of labor here between philosophers and economists. We can be helped by more detailed studies of how theories are supported – and they *are* supported – in economics. That's not to say that, having examined economics more carefully, we won't find that the sorts of arguments economists give are very bad arguments. But to understand better what sorts of arguments they do give is likely to be helpful. Philosophers really have a very, very difficult task, to understand the nature of knowledge acquisition. There are some complicated and not very well established systems which economists would be crazy to *rely* upon in attempting to understand and judge the work of other economists, but which may be useful in some cases. I don't see why it should be *simple* to map out what the proper rules of procedure are to understand the world. And it shouldn't be surprising that some quite simple account like Popper's turns out to be terribly inadequate.

Caldwell: But you do feel that we should look for rules of procedure?

Hausman: Implicitly . . . In any institution, and science is obviously an institution, there are and always will be implicit accounts of how one should do one's work. I don't see why they should be worse for being made explicit.

Blaug: As a neo-Popperian, I find Hausman's position, while at first sight seeming to be an onslaught on Popper, is, on second viewing, much less controversial. What he says about Popper has been said by a lot of Popperians. The strong asymmetry between verification and falsification largely disappears once Popper in *The Logic of Scientific Discovery* takes on board the Duhem–Quine thesis that we can never conclusively falsify a theory, because any test involves not just the theory but also auxiliary assumptions. So, one can never attribute the blame exclusively to the theory. Popper is aware of this. That's why he introduces the set of rules forbidding immunizing stratagems. That means he was perfectly well aware that falsification is "conventional" falsification. It is also true that he later goes on making statements that suggest that he believes that the strong asymmetry is somehow maintained.

Now once you've appropriated the idea that falsification in Popper involves a whole set of rules forbidding immunizing stratagems, and that what he is laying down is a set of rules for good conduct, then you're left at the end of the day asking, well, what then is Popper's contribution to the philosophy of science? I'm inclined to say that what does survive is a normative prescription, the idea that *strong* testing of theories implies that the most desirable theories are those which involve a falsifiable prediction. If you ask what states of the world does this theory really forbid, you get a much greater insight into the true discriminating empirical strength of the theory than if you ask what states of the world will corroborate it.

Hausman: No one denies that we aren't interested in merely multiplying confirming instances. This is not controversial. The critical thing to avoid is to go from Popper's straw man account of inductive logic to any of the strong theses of his philosophy of science. The notion that we really want theories that forbid lots of states of affairs does not imply that we reject confirming evidence or that we should only accept falsifying evidence.

One other thing that one might read into Mark Blaug's comments. To interpret the claim that economic theory is unfalsifiable in terms of some sort of criticism of economists, as being too willing to employ immunizing stratagems, is unfair to economics and stresses too much a difference in behavior where there is a real difference in the theory. It is not that economists are weak-willed in always being ready to make excuses for their theories. The problem is that their excuses are such *good* excuses. In analogous circumstances in physics the excuses wouldn't be such good excuses, because the other hypotheses we need to derive the test predictions are well supported. My big emphasis is that we really have to look at the extent to which claims are supported. I don't think that this should be regarded as a problem that exists only within a neo-Popperian tradition, because the same difficulty infects, for example, Lakatos's philosophy of science. He stresses that we must make all kinds of decisions along the way, but there is no room in there for the decisions being based upon how well *supported* various hypotheses are. The notion of *support* is the crucial problem for a philosopher of science – to figure out just what support is. One cannot just say, as Popper does, that there isn't such a thing, because then you really can't have rational growth of knowledge.

Klant paper

Summary remarks

I am interested in what economists *do* and in what they *say* they do, that is, their pretensions.

One pretension that we economists have is that economics is objective, or value free. Nobody, however, including Popper, has solved the objectivity problem in economics.

There are similarities and differences between physics and economics. Three are relevant to the objectivity problem.

1. Any science is likely to contain elements of a preconceived natural order.
2. The natural order in economics and social science affects not only what we see, but also what we want to do.
3. Contrary to physics, economics does without universal numerical constants.

As to (1), since hypotheses cannot be tested independently (as Hausman properly points out), it is inevitable that science contains preconceptions of a natural order.

Under (2), let me reaffirm the truth that in economics and other social sciences we are more than outside observers. But if the scientific objectivity that allegedly determines our choice of scientific theories cannot be fully complied with, then the choices we make are *more* sensitive to our other, subjective reasons for being attached to certain views of the world.

Finally, as to (3), the influence of subjective values is reinforced further by the fact that our domain changes more and is less stable than that of physics. We have never found the relevant natural constants in economics. This means that our basic theories – the ones out of which specific, falsifiable models are built – are not themselves interpretable within a narrow enough range to be testable. If test results are negative, it is never clear whether a specific *model* is at fault or its underlying [basic] *theory*.

Popper considers it worthwhile to submit every theory, whether scientific or philosophical, to rational criticism. It is this kind of criticism that occurs in economics. But such discussion, which takes place more or less on the other side of Popper's demarcation line, cannot proceed free of values. Economics, therefore, has the character of being a mixture of science, philosophy, and art – the art which Keynes called "the art of choosing models which are relevant to the contemporary world."

Discussion

Kastelein: I want to challenge Klant's use of the term "plausibility" and its meaning and function as a methodological concept. Klant's "plausibility" has the same meaning as Popper's "assessment." Consequently, Klant writes in terms of "justification," "acceptance and rejection," and "choice." In the end, however, economists are said to defend their positions and to try "to convince each other of the plausibility of their point of view."

Now everyone is free to use the words he wants; I am simply not very happy with Klant's choice of the term "plausibility" as a substitute for "assessment of an irrefutable theory." It sounds like a transcription of Popperian terminology into the language of positivist and coherence theorists. It is confusing rather than enlightening. "Plausibility" is not a term that has a place in the vocabulary of Popper's meta-language.

There is an escape from this conclusion. If we accept Klant's interpretation of Popper's convictions about the social sciences, in which falsifiability is not a logical criterion for scientificity, then we are beyond the "Logic of Scientific Discovery," but we are still "in Popper." All our discussions as economists about Popper's "Logic," "Conjecture," "Refutations," and so on were understandable; nevertheless, these discussions were based on a wrong reading of Popper on the social sciences.

Does such a position make any sense? Can we maintain Popperian ideals of methodology and accept, although *contre coeur,* that Popper's methodology is not only inadequate as a description of the methodological behavior of economists but basically is not applicable and thus cannot be recommended?

Klant: I tried to demonstrate my thesis by using Popperian tools. Popper himself is ambiguous on the subject. If he had been a true Popperian he would have accepted my view, at the risk of starting a big row at the LSE! By the way, to me, as an economist-methodologist, Popper is not my authority. He is my servant. I use him as I use other philosophers, to solve methodological problems in economics. The solutions to our problems should not crack when neopositivism or critical rationalism collapses.

The general theories which we cannot corroborate in a Popperian way, but which we nevertheless do accept, I call "plausible"–plausible to the acceptants, of course. Theories which are rejected are "implausible" to the rejecters. These theories may all be subjected to criticism in the same way that, according to Popper, philosophical theories are criticizable. Ideas are considered to be plausible if they cannot be corroborated but are nevertheless accepted, because they meet the acceptant's requirements of consistency with other accepted ideas, problem solving, etc.

I cannot see why Kastelein thinks that I use "plausibility" as a substitute for "assessment of an irrefutable theory." "Plausible" designates a quality, "assessment" designates a process. I am afraid he misread my sentence: "I call a critical discussion [etc.] a rational discussion on plausibility, meaning the same as what Popper calls to assess [etc]." Discussion = assessment.

Does discussion about plausibility imply that we are using "plausibility" as a criterion? No. When I discuss the beauty of a painting, I use criteria relating to color, composition, expression, brush stroke, etc. If, on common grounds, we apply the same "hypothetical prescriptions" there is a great chance of reaching agreement, but we can discuss the whole matter without ever using a term such as "beauty." In the same way, you need not use the word "plausibility" when discussing the plausibility of a theory. Economists hardly ever do. They consider things to be true, natural, obvious, in fact so, etc. What they actually do we should learn from McCloskey [1985], Klamer [1980, 1984], and Hamminga [1982]. Their investigations produce ideas about economists' discussions on the plausibility of their theories.

Pen: I have my own particular demarcation problem. We have in economics a great number of particular statements which are not altogether true, but "respectable"; some which are less so, but still "acceptable"; and some which are clutter, hokum, bogus. How do we draw the line?

Klant: Don't worry, truth is not the property of a statement.

Nooteboom: I would like to suggest a way to reconcile Klant and Hausman. Hausman insists that for falsification we need more than just basic statements. We need background knowledge. But this is an argument relating to plausibility. Cannot Klant agree with this?

Klant: Popper insists that *falsifiability* is necessary, not *falsification*. For the rest, I don't disagree with that attempt at reconciliation.

Hausman: There is indeed no sharp distinction between falsifiability – logical, sharp – and plausibility arguments.

McCloskey: Why are we interested in a demarcation line? Klant supposes, as I would not, that conversations among social scientists are sharply distinguishable from conversations among physicists or artists. There is no point in the long surveying expeditions that have produced various demarcation lines. In answer to Jan Pen, I *don't* think the demarcation line is of *any* help in choosing between respectable and bogus statements. Who here will defend the usefulness of the demarcation line?

Hutchison: Well, there *is* a division between theories which have been submitted to some sort of tests – strenuous attempts to falsify – and those which haven't. It doesn't matter if we call this science and nonscience, but the distinction is important.

I agree very much with Professor Klant's reformulation of Popper.

What alarms me is that we are not building on the advances of the 1930s. In some respects, we are going back to the 1930s. The barbarians really *were* at the gates then, and in some ways they still are.

Hands paper

Summary remarks

I wanted to find a particular issue, with the aid of which I could relate the responses of three groups of individuals: Popperian philosophers, economic methodologists, and economic theorists. The issue I chose is that of ad hocness, the modification of an economic theory in an "ad hoc" manner. How does each of the three groups use this term?

In general, ad hoc modification of a theory means a patching up. The patching up may be merely specifying exceptions so as to protect or preserve the theory. Such modification may be acceptable, of course, but on Popper's terms would be so only if it increased the falsifiability of the theory or hypothesis. Otherwise it is to be classed among immunizing stratagems.

Lakatos takes a somewhat different line. He was, in addition to the above sense of ad hoc, concerned with the continuity of a research program. His ad hocness has to do with some breach of this continuity.

A look at the literature turns up some surprises. Economic methodologists seem to complain about ad hoc moves in Popper's sense. Economic theorists, however, frequently use more the Lakatosian notion of ad hocness. This emerges very clearly in the rational expectations literature, though not only there.

The literature also contains some confusion between the problem of the independent testability of hypotheses and the notion of novel facts. One way to interpret independent testability is to say that a hypothesis which *is* independently testable should predict something we have never thought of before – a novel fact. It's not clear whether this is a sufficient or only a necessary condition for independent testability. The issue is important given that Lakatos's views on theoretical and empirical progress make much use of "novel fact."

I have been surprised too by the importance of the idea of heuristic progress in the Lakatosian program, or *non*-ad hocness. Much of what economists do that looks to be immunizing, however, is *consistent* with what Lakatos calls "heuristic progress." Weintraub's paper shows that you *can* find empirical progress in economics, but we all know that you have to work hard to find it. On the other hand, heuristic progress, or changes in the theory to avoid ad hocness, is something that happens all the time.

Discussion

Nooteboom: It seems to me that the distinction between the two types of ad hocness – the Popperian and the Lakatosian – is close to the old, well-worn distinction between empiricism and rationalism. Seen in this light, Professor Hands's observation that most (neoclassical) economists are preoccupied with heuristic rather than empirical progress ties in with our knowledge of a priorism as a traditional and still very strong tendency in economic thought.

What I miss in Hands's paper, however, is a clear normative judgment. In the actual conduct of neoclassical economists, program continuity has prime or even exclusive priority. But is this good or bad? To what extent and when is priority of program continuity justifiable? I would like to provide a basis for normative judgment.

We must recognize, firstly, the need for a wider basis for criticizing both core assumptions and subsidiary assumptions. I propose that such a widening of the basis for criticism is provided by considerations of plausibility. They are not by themselves sufficient, but we cannot do without them.

Ad hocness, in the Lakatosian sense, is the acceptance of patched-up explanations that do not follow from basic principles. Heuristic progressiveness requires coherence with basic principles. But why stop at the boundaries of one program? Why coherence only within a program and not between programs? If it is ad hoc, within a given program of economics, to accept explanations that do not follow from some established conception of economic rationality, isn't it also ad hoc, in a wider perspective, to accept economic conceptions of rationality that are in conflict with common sense, direct observation, and psychology? I propose that implausibility is also a form of ad hocness. It is lack of coherence, a patching up, the acceptance of something which does not tie in with some important part of knowledge. The concept of implausibility is thus an extension of the concept of ad hocness. If ad hocness is lack of coherence with the basic principles of a theory or program, implausibility is lack of coherence with background knowledge. Should we perhaps call this its "ad hoc$_4$-ness"?

What normative judgments result from all this? To arrive at methodological prescriptions that are realistic and useful, we should consider theories not just as finished products, but we should look also at their life cycles and at the underlying processes of invention, development, and use. A theory is a program in development.

The methodological rules we choose should reflect this fact of stage of development. As an epistemological basis for this stage approach to methodological rules, I favor using the "genetic epistemology" of Jean Piaget. To illustrate, novel infant explanatory principles deserve protection. The principles may be considered implausible for a considerable time, and a benign neglect of falsifiers is justifiable.

As a theory develops, it is bound to accumulate problems and to become more and more patched up. This is no cause for shame. The anomalies are useful to indicate where and why explanatory principles fail and in what direction alternatives should be sought. It *is* a cause for shame to stick blindly to the program and pretend the problems are not there. Program continuity is too easy when there are no clearly identifiable forbidden events, when empirical anomalies can be circumvented and implausibilities are not considered.

Methodological rules here are rather loose guidelines that cannot be reduced to one simple, rigorous rule, and may be conflicting. But normative order need not be logical order, and my claim is that the question, Which rules deserve priority? is a matter of judgment. The judgment must reflect, in part, the stage of development of a theory.

Member of the audience: The notion of fact in Hands's paper is similar to the idea in physics, where we mean by "fact" not just an observation but also a phenomenon that can be repeated in some kind of experimental setup. Economic methodologists, in discussing novel facts, also seem not to be talking only about some prediction as to these or those data but about how a new phenomenon has been predicted. But are there really any novel facts in this sense in economics – phenomena that have been discovered by economic theory?

de Marchi: In macroeconomics the proposition that policies will tend to be neutralized by the reactions of the individuals comprising the collective on which they are supposed to work – this is a novel phenomenon, identified for us by the incorporation of rational expectations into macroeconomic models.

McCloskey: My own candidate would be the so-called Modigliani effect: Consumption is dependent not only on income but also on wealth. But I think what's important in the question is precisely that the ability to observe this fact is a theoretical event.

Hands: We can give such examples, but there *is* a problem. The type of novel fact discussed by Popper and Lakatos – physical novel facts, which provoke a response of "Ah ha! – are *not* as likely to occur in economics. That does not mean that we cannot discover a suitable sense of "novel fact" for economics, but we do have a translation problem.

Hausman: A comment on ad hocness. For Lakatos a theory has to be *non*-ad hoc in all three senses, not just in terms of preserving program continuity. Let me give an example to show how difficult it can be to apply Lakatos's requirement. The change from cardinal to ordinal utility involved a large *de*crease in content. It wasn't ad hoc in the third Lakatosian sense, but both Popper's and Lakatos's general account of ad hocness would describe it as an ad hoc theory modification, even though most economists regard it as an important piece of progress in economics.

Hands: If you have a case where more than one type of ad hocness surfaces at the same time, Lakatos is unclear as to which ought to be addressed first.

de Marchi paper

Summary remarks

Why is Popper so highly regarded, at least among some methodologically inclined economists, whereas most economists in their practice seem to pay him little heed? There is evidence, in the recent book by Paul Levinson [1982], that a similar situation exists in philosophy. Popper's following is devout but quite small. On the other hand, there is also a hint that practicing *scientists* find, or have found, Popper's views helpful. Sir John Eccles, for instance, recounts in the Levinson volume that Popper significantly shaped his own practice in two respects. Firstly, he found it helpful to be encouraged to express his working hypothesis as sharply as possible. This forced him to identify both what it ruled out and how it differed from rivals. Secondly, Popper's emphasis on falsifiability freed him from a felt obligation to speak only the Truth.

It is perhaps not surprising that scientists at this level of generality find Popper's views exciting and directly applicable. I suspect that a survey of practicing economists would yield similar responses. Indeed, some of the young economists at the LSE in the late 1950s seem to have found in Popper mainly a reinforcement of their desire to remake economics as a rigorous, empirical science. But take Popper's philosophy of science as quite specific rules of procedure, and the objections raised by Hausman and the reformulations made by Klant are unavoidable. My paper may be regarded as an illustration of that thesis.

I had long been vaguely aware that Popper exerted an unusual influence among a bright and articulate group of young economists at the London School of Economics in the late 1950s and early 1960s. This turned out to be a good episode to examine in detail, because it became clear that while Popper's influence was strong, it was also surprisingly short-lived. Why should that have been?

There appear to have been two specific technical reasons for it. [Firstly] the stochastic nature of economic propositions quickly posed a problem for the strong interpretation of falsifiability. Help from Popper himself was available in his writings – advice, such as to truncate distributions – to resolve the difficulty. But the economists, while practicing such commonsense methodology themselves, seem to have hoped for something more objective from *logical* falsifiability. Secondly, the paucity of unambiguous predictions from theory alone emerged in the course of trying to spell out the testable content of the theory of the firm in a qualitative, comparative statics framework. This seems to have been taken as a sign that a central part of economic theory has almost no testable content, and it produced disenchantment not only with the theory but also with falsifiability as a criterion.

I doubt whether these reasons adequately account for the group's turning away from Popper. It seems more likely that after a time, in the broader battles in which they were engaged, the methodological slogans they could take from Popper simply no longer served, because the issues were only partly methodological. In any case, after these two disappointments with *logical* falsifiability, the group retained a commitment to what we might call "testable content" but moved away from trying to apply Popper's philosophy as anything more than an ideal in economics.

Discussion

Blaug: Did Lipsey and Archibald give up on Popper? That seems to be hinted at in what you say, but it is surely false in the light of successive editions of Lipsey's *Introduction to Positive Economics.* Lipsey became a sophisticated falsificationist, but he always asks after he's presented a theory if there's any good empirical evidence for this theory. The book is entirely in a Popperian strain. Furthermore Lipsey has been working more recently on the problem of world inflation, and in a recent paper [1981], where he lays out his research program, his emphasis is on setting down sharp predictions that will discriminate between a monetarist position and various kinds of Keynesian positions. The same Popperian spirit is evident in his other recent work on location as a variable in the theory of the firm. I'm certain Lipsey and Archibald have never ceased to be Popperian, although, like all of us, they're probably not quite sure exactly what they mean by it.

I'm also puzzled by the two problems for the Popperian view of economics that de Marchi singles out for discussion. The first – virtually all problems in economics are probabilistic – is fair enough. These can never be unambiguously refuted. That is something Lipsey discovered – that's the difference between the first and second editions of the *Introduction to Positive Economics*. But the problem of unambiguous predictions troubles me more. This is introduced as the most daunting difficulty for economics. The question is the one Archibald discusses. If a parameter enters into more than one equation of a system, then we can no longer unambiguously sign our endogenous variables. Now I can see how this is a real difficulty in all second-best theorizing, but I doubt if this is really a general difficulty in all or virtually all economic theory. Both de Marchi and Professor Klant, in his discussion of the parametric paradox, seem to imply this. I would want to see many worked-out examples before I could convince myself that the parametric paradox is the Achilles heel of the notion of falsifiability in economics. I'd like to ask Professor Klant how one can go on advocating Popperianism, as he does in his book, if the parametric paradox really bites as deeply as he says.

Klant: The parameter paradox is not my crucial argument against the testability of economic theories. I raised it [1984, ch. 4, sect. 9] as an argument against Samuelson's analysis of the falsifiability of economic theories. It is applicable to a special type of theories, viz., those in which no stable relations are postulated. If you assume parameters to be variables, you imply that your theory is not falsifiable. I mentioned this special case in my paper because, judging from his example in the *Poverty*, Popper seemed to see it as typical of all economic theory.

If you postulate, as modern economists do, that parameters are "fairly stable," general theories can be applied by developing specific models which must be "augmented" because the general theories do not inform us accurately enough about the nature of the relations and because the supplementary general hypotheses needed for an adequate reconstruction of concrete events are deficient. The requirement of augmentation evolves from the lack of relevant universal numerical constants in economics. This prevents us from testing general hypotheses through "partial equilibrium analysis."

The parameter paradox is a matter of logic. The assumption of freely changing parameters logically excludes falsifiability. The lack of constants, on the other hand, is fundamentally a matter of experience. Because we have not discovered them, we must construct general theories which are not testable. We can, however, base specific models on those (less than general) theories which are testable.

Hands: I'd like to add something to Mark's comment on Neil's use of the Archibald problem. The paper by Archibald that you refer to ["The Qualitative Content of Maximizing Models" (1965)] is a specific paper on qualitative comparative statics under second-order conditions assumptions in a maximizing model. If all you assume are first- and second-order conditions for optimization, can you sign the inverse matrix that you need to sign in order to be able to do the comparative statics? The answer is no – not without knowing something about the cross-partial derivatives of the Hessian, in this case. But there are a number of cases where you *can* sign such things. In general equilibrium theory you have a very similar sort of case. If every good is a gross substitute, then you can change fifty-three parameters and still sign every term because the matrix that you're concerned with has all positive terms. My comment is that there is no global methodological significance in the one case that Archibald identified. It's a local technical result. The problem is narrow. Assuming only first- and second-order conditions, what can we say? I don't believe that empirically there's any reason to believe that the second-order conditions for a maximization problem are any more likely to hold than some other bit of information we might have – that the functions are Cobb–Douglas, for instance. It isn't an empirical problem, since the antecedent conditions governing the result may not be satisfied anyway. It is a methodological decision to make second-order conditions minimal. Empirically, it may require less information to know that the function has a particular form than it requires to know what you need to know about, say, bordered Hessians. What is called "minimal information" may only be minimal by methodological fiat. That's what concerns me.

de Marchi: I should clarify that the economists at the LSE did not abandon Popper, but they did experience deep frustration at the difficulties they encountered in trying to check whether economic theories had any testable content and in trying to fit *logical* falsifiability into a stochastic world. Popper and his group at the LSE did not help them deal with these difficulties (although Popper does discuss the difficulties for logical falsifiability posed by probabilistic propositions), and perhaps part of their frustration was that they felt a lack of interest by Popper.

They moved, as I said in my earlier remarks, to a less restricting form of Popperianism, looking for empirical implications of theory and asking whether theory is supported or refuted by the facts. But this hardly amounts to sophisticated or even conventional falsificationism. Lipsey went on in the same vein as he had begun, trying to quantify economic science and assess the evidence, but it should be stressed that this concern both preceded and outlasted his flirtation with Popperian ideas. Archibald turned away from writing on methodological issues and his last paper in this area, "Refutation or Comparison?" is an attempt at *replacing* Popper's demarcation criterion.

On Archibald's problem, which might be viewed as a variant of the parametric paradox, there really are two levels involved. One is Archibald's use of qualitative comparative statics and the signing of endogenous variables. I am not concerned to argue that this is of general significance as a demonstration that economic theory as a whole has little testable content. Klant's comment makes it clear that a logical lack of falsifiability only arises if you assume that parameters are variable. Indirectly that turns out to be the case in Archibald's analysis. But the larger significance of his paper is that it points to the importance and scarcity of necessary background knowledge – in this case, information on cross-partials – if we are to get theory to yield testable predictions. Do we have the necessary information? How could we get it? Archibald's "signing problem" – as we might perhaps more aptly refer to it – was not insignificant in the context of the then standard approach of qualitative comparative statics; *and* given the conviction that the information on cross-partials that would have allowed more specific predictions than he was able to squeeze out of microeconomic theory by itself was either not present or not obviously obtainable.

At a different level, the testability issue is joined when Klant points out that our basic theories are so loosely specified as to be consistent with many model interpretations. One of the frustrating things for Archibald and for Lipsey was to discover that fairly general formulations of our theories – surely that's what Archibald was trying to say – can turn out to have so little testable content.

Hutchison: I was rather surprised by the extent to which Neil de Marchi made the Lipsey–Archibald movement an anti-Robbins movement. Insofar as it's positive economics, one of the good points of Robbins's book was how he insisted on the normative–positive distinction. For me this Lipsey–Archibald thing was that they were *too* Robbinsian. In that they were proclaiming positive economics, they were being Robbinsian.

de Marchi: But they were concerned about what they took to be Robbins's antiempiricism and by his perceived use of nonquantitative theory to justify free market policies. Whatever the rights of the matter, Robbins was taken to be standing in the way of remaking economics as a quantitative and essentially empirical science, and he became the target to be attacked.

Klant: The mystery is, what was Popper thinking about economics? Did the LSE economists ever have contact with Popper?

de Marchi: I agree that Popper's views on economics are mysterious. In *The Poverty of Historicism* [p. 143], he made an exception of economics – because of parameter inconstancy and measurement problems – in the following way. He removed – at least implicitly – the requirement of testability from falsifiability for economics. This looks as if he suspended the rules of good science for economists without, however, abandoning the demarcation criterion. Where that leaves economics is not clear, and Popper doesn't clarify it any further for us.

As to contact between the LSE economists and Popper, there was none, because they smoked and he had an aversion to smoke.

Hutchison paper

Summary remarks

I thought I would offer a few supplementary remarks rather than summarize the paper, remarks arising partly out of what's been said at the sessions so far.

Over the years I've come to reject a good deal of Popper . . . not as much as Daniel Hausman [laughter]. Popper was not all that interested in economics. He didn't know much about it and it was indeed a brief encounter, as Neil described it, that he had with economics. I'd only add that Lakatos, similarly, was mainly interested in physics and mathematics.

Popper's *Poverty of Historicism* I'd largely reject now; in particular, his emphasis, which I at one time accepted, but feel much more reserved about now, on the close resemblances between the natural and social sciences. I think that on this a balanced view is necessary. One must recognize the historical dimension in economics, which Popper does, but doesn't really take into account.

I'd also reject, with Hausman, Popper's exclusively anticonfirmationist line. I think this is an attitude of somebody who takes physics as the ideal form of knowledge. We can't attain that in economics. Knowledge in economics of the kind you get in physics is a very rare, scarce thing. You use every method, no matter how suspect or unsatisfactory, to get whatever scraps of economic knowledge you can.

Though one may accept Popper's condemnation of induction as a "bad" method – you've got to be critical of what you get – I place more emphasis on what I take to be the basic principle of Popper's philosophy of science, which is almost semipolitical. It is based on fallibilism, critical fallibilism. All scientific theories are tentative, subject to testing and attempted falsification . . . to revision. This is against the *in*fallibilism which one meets with in and around the social sciences and in economics, in Marxism and Mises-ism, which claims propositions which are absolutely, apodictically certain.

I insist on – which I think follows Popper – the vital importance of the trichotomy: well-tested theories and propositions, testable but not yet very adequately tested, and completely untestable. As regards that very large second category, I'd simply hold – I don't know if Popper would insist on this so much – that economists have to withhold judgment on those which are not adequately tested.

Just a remark or two about my quotation from Hicks [p. 170]. I love that quotation. It seems to me to give the game away rather. What it says is that much of economic theorizing is simply a good game. That seems to state very frankly what others practice but do not always state so clearly – that much of economic theory is *pursued* for no better reason than its intellectual attraction. I would not for a moment legislate against games, but if that's what you're doing, you should say it bluntly and clearly. I think there's a great deal of confusion among students as to the relevance of this kind of theorizing. But also – I said it in the thirties, that the barbarians are at the gates; and there were a few around – but there are *within* the gates today the Hicksian obfuscators, or whatever you want to call them; and there are the dogmatists – Marxians, Mises-ists, infallibilists – who *claim* real-world relevance and apodictic certainty – that's the Mises phrase. That even seems to me *politically* very dangerous . . . that in a free society anybody should be able to claim absolute certainty for any nontrivial economic or political proposition.

So there is a lot of work for demarcationists to do. We've got to draw lines and demarcations. That's why I'm against "anything goes." People who reject the demarcation criterion seem to be saying, "We are critical too, only we reject the *Popper* criterion." But you must have some substantial standard or criterion for basing criticism on. I haven't heard another useful criterion propounded.

Discussion

Klamer: There is a great temptation to think in dualities . . . to divide the world in twos, into black and white; subjective and objective; irrational, rational; nonscience, science; values and fact. This dual thinking concurs with binary logic and is very tempting. However, I suggest that it is misleading and that thinking in threesomes may make more sense when we come to try and understand what economists do.

Economists as scientists strive to know the truth about economic relationships. We seek objective knowledge in the sense of a correspondence with the way things are. In principle, such knowledge should be independent of our intentions and our interests. In this striving, then, we turn against those who let intention and interest prevail. This striving is expressed in the discourse in which we partake. It is expressed in the talk about *statements,* the *logic* of statements, and the role of *empirical tests.* It all serves the purpose of giving us certainty, or at least something to hold on to. Logic and fact supersede intention and interest. But we've heard many times today that the authority of logic and fact is highly questionable. How do we react to that? One reaction is to think that if economic knowledge is not objective, it must be subjective. It must all be a matter of taste, class interest, ideology, or whatever. Anything goes, apparently. These, however, are not the only two alternatives. Both I and McCloskey are keen to suggest that this either-or thinking is misleading.

There is a third possibility: We may talk about what economists do in a way that allows a role for intentions and interests, *as well as* for the constraints under which they operate. This may mean that we become more sensitive to the intersubjectivity of what we say, and the context of conversations and the discipline of these conversations. This implies that not anything goes – there is a discipline; there are constraints on conversations.

Professor Hutchison's writing seems to fit more into the first way of talking – the "objective." But this paper actually brings him somewhat closer to my suggested third alternative. He does not maintain that it is logic and fact that rule our world. He does not grant explicitly that intention and interest are involved, but he does admit that any significant case for adopting or striving after a methodological principle must rest ultimately on some ethical, moral, or political argument. Both Hausman and Hands focus on logic and fact, and to them Hutchison provides a sort of counterweight. He stresses the desire of economists to go beyond form and [theoretical] structure and to intervene. Many even seem to have an axe to grind. This opens the way to take seriously intentions and interests and to study those things directly. That means, however, that rather than judging the desire to be involved . . . to intervene, we should look at motives very carefully. We should behave more like anthropologists, trying to understand rather than to render judgments.

McCloskey: As Klamer says, knowledge is social. I think we can suggest an alternative to Hutchison's epistemology demarcating good arguments from bad by rule. Our standard can be the good or bad quality of the scholarly conversation. There's a helpful analogy to natural languages here. To write down a complete grammar of any language is hard; it would make a very long book. By analogy, short methodological rules are probably going to be too simple. But we as competent speakers of a language *know* when a good conversation is happening. So too in the economic sphere.

Caldwell: Who are the barbarians? Are all theorists in that category? Are methodologists, who do no testing?

Hutchison: The barbarians in the 1930s that I was concerned about were the Nazis. They had a pseudo race science which I saw taught in German universities. Today there are dogmatists of a different sort – I've mentioned them – and there are obfuscationists who play games without admitting it.

Caldwell: My point is that the criterion you used against the Nazis can also be used against much of economic theory as well . . .

Hutchison: Then let it be so used.

Caldwell: But do you simply apply it less harshly against theories you happen to like? I'd like to see the criterion employed more equitably, and then there'd not be much of economics left.

Hutchison: I wouldn't say that. But if a lot has to go, then let it go.

McCloskey: I wonder how effective against a Hitler a narrowed range of argument would have been. Isn't it better to argue against a Hitler using every device of logic and grammar, not limiting ourselves to the demand that he speak falsifiabilities? How did falsification, in the historical event, help against Hitler?

Hutchison: No mere argument would have been proof against Hitler. But in the academic sphere, in dealing with Hitler's professors, a criterion like Popper's was important and relevant. Popper's philosophy grew out of that very situation and was designed to meet that situation intellectually, not via newspapers or in street demonstrations.

Hamminga: What does this have to do with the methodology of economics [laughter]?

Nooteboom: To answer Hamminga's question, the relevance is that we are discussing the nature of methodological order. We seem to fall into this trap of thinking that there is either a strict, rigorous order of universal claims or there is nothing. That is the fallacy of Feyerabend. I sympathize with discourse, but also with Hutchison, who asks, how do we bridge the gap and reach some sort of economic guidelines? I would allow Klamer a good deal of time to be an economic anthropologist, and discover how the discourse works, but ultimately this should issue in some guidelines which allow us to judge and say why we believe an economist rather than someone in the street. It is not enough to say merely that it is discourse. The important step is, can we learn from that about an order which is workable and relevant, and does it yield some guidelines? Without that one cannot find satisfaction in being an anthropologist.

Klamer: The importance of the work of literary critics is not that they finally issue some guidelines as to how to write a novel; it is that their talk gives us ideas which enable us to understand better what economics is all about. Knowing these things, the discussion practices of economists may be affected; but we – McCloskey and I – are not trying to suggest what is good and bad. We are trying to bend the methodological stick one way after it has been far too long bent in another. We have been too long preoccupied with rules. Just as in a dialectical moment in dialogue, we say, "let's forget about rules."

Blaug: Ah, so you *don't* mean what you say. Now we finally have it [laughter].

Blaug paper

Summary remarks

My paper is a case study of the methodological views of one of the most famous of all living economists, Sir John Hicks. Since he rejects Popperianism and falsifiability quite explicitly in a 1983 paper, "[Economics:] A Discipline not a Science," there is no question of applying to Hicks Popperian standards. This therefore is an attempt by a neo-Popperian to examine Hicks's methodological pronouncements, using the lower-order standard of coherence. Does Hicks have a coherent methodological position?

Hicks has written quite openly on methodology. The essay I just mentioned is a main source, as is his book *Causality in Economics* (1979); but there are numerous implicit references peppered throughout his writings.

There are two characteristic approaches among living economists who've written about methodology. One is that of Friedman, Kaldor, or the young Keynes, whose interest is largely that of an applied academic; they appraise economic ideas fundamentally in terms of their relevance to policy issues. The other is the position of the theoretical economists, like Samuelson, Hicks, or Frank Hahn, whose main concern appears to be to defend their pure theorizing by adopting a particular methodological stance. Now Hicks is peculiar in that he has one foot in each camp – and that is precisely why his methodological position is incoherent.

On the one hand, he tries to justify economic theorizing on its own terms, as a good game, as fascinating. On the other hand, he repeatedly says that economic theory is simply a handmaiden for economic policy; it has ultimately no other methodological justification. Hicks moves between the two positions: (1) that there is no such thing as decisive empirical refutation of economic theory and (2) that economic theory must guide policy. But how *can* it do the latter if it produces no substantive insights or predictions? How can it guide policy if testability is ruled out and – as emerges in the final chapter of the book on causality – if there can be no econometrics, because of pervasive Knightian uncertainty?

Hicks appraises theories in terms of the realism of their assumptions, rather than their predictive record. So he takes a strong anti-Friedman line. By contrast, he admires Keynes more than any other economist. It is impossible to discover in his work precisely the grounds for his admiration, but it appears to be that he finds in Keynes an essentially simple model which nonetheless contains dramatic conclusions for economic policy. This is what Schumpeter called the "Ricardian vice," but which Hicks finds the Keynesian virtue.

There is, for Hicks, no sense in which economics progresses; hence it is not a science. There are revolutions, but each must be judged against the historical circumstances in which it took place. He also is an extreme historical relativist. Each theory has its own merit in its own time, but we are given no basis for resolving contemporary conflicts or for comparing different theoretical traditions.

Hicks has much more to say, but I've indicated enough perhaps to convince you that we have here a methodological position which is totally incoherent. This is of considerable interest not only because of Hicks's eminence, or because he follows Keynes's methodological preferences so closely, but also because he is so anti-Popperian. The outcome of my study therefore gives point to Professor Hutchison's earlier comment that he has seen no satisfactory alternative to the principle of falsificationism enunciated. At the same time, Hicks and several other leading economists (including Kaldor), give the lie to one of the conclusions of my hastily written little book on methodology, to the effect that *most* economists are falsificationists, albeit with a small "f."

Discussion

Cramer: Let me complement Blaug's paper with a few remarks about this – may I say – desperate longing for empirical tests or falsifications of economic theory. I should like to stress that this business of testing or falsifying is a highly intricate, technical matter. It is very difficult to decide here, on the basis of some examples, whether economic theories are testable or not. I think this is insufficiently realized in the requests we have heard for a simple – or any – demarcation criterion. Nor do I think that it is altogether fortunate that we refer to "the barbarians at the gates." I do not think that macroeconomic theories, for instance, are in the same category as Marxism or psychoanalysis, even though they are difficult to falsify.

I want to illustrate my point with an example: the duration of unemployment. It is common knowledge that if you take a sample of people who are unemployed, you will find that those who have been unemployed for a very long time stand little chance of finding a job. The chance actually diminishes with the duration of unemployment. Why is this so? One hypothesis is that unemployment *itself* is the reason; that unemployment has a debilitating effect and that to be unemployed for a very long time renders one unfit for the labor market. Thus, for the *individual,* unemployment is the cause of further unemployment. An alternative view is that unemployment is not the cause, but that it is a *symptom* of ineptitude lodged in the individual; that he is simply an unsuitable individual from the point of view of the labor market. Such people are, of course, overrepresented in a sample of people who have been unemployed for a long time.

A distinction between these alternatives is relevant to policy, and it is an interesting question whether they can be falsified or not, on the basis of evidence that discriminates between them. Now it is easy to conceive of an experiment that would so discriminate, but such an experiment is not possible in fact. You could randomly fire people from their jobs and then prevent them from finding other jobs. But the fact that one can *think* of such an experiment . . . is that sufficient to render a proposition testable?

The interest of this particular example is that there is some hope that we need not go to such extremes. Some authors have quite recently argued that the issue can be decided without recourse to impossible experiments by intelligent sample design and other clever devices. This illustrates that it may be not so much a matter of having a demarcation line, or of deciding where it should be drawn, but rather that progress lies in shifting the boundary itself, in moving the line itself, or in moving propositions of this kind from one category to the other. The true inventors and the true servants of economics are then the people – the technicians – who think of new experiments, new sample designs.

Member of the audience: Hicks tells us that economics is on the edge between science and history. His point is that we can experiment, but only in time; we cannot repeat.

Blaug: Yes, that is one of his favorite sayings. But it leads to the question of whether there is something called "historical explanation" which is very different from scientific explanation. There are problems about testing historical retrodictions, not the least of which is that usually there is no control. Explanation and associated problems do not, however, enter into his book on economic history; so the saying, which sounds nice, tells us absolutely nothing.

McCloskey: There is a Ricardian vice. There's also a Hicksian vice, theorizing without reading. What is objectionable about Hicks's *A Theory of Economic History* (1969) is its unconversational character, its antisocial character. It is solipsistic.

Hutchison: I'm delighted to find McCloskey being so critical of Hicks, but I can't decide what his grounds are. You can't just say, "I don't like this stuff." That's not being critical. It's not good scholarly conversation? Well, that doesn't tell me very much either.

At one stage Arjo Klamer said that we must be like anthropologists, and not criticize. Yet he is very critical without having critical principles to put in place of Popper's.

Hausman: In Galileo's dialogues concerning the two chief sciences, he has his spokesman giving Simplicio, who represents the Aristotelians, a hard time. At one point, Simplicio says, "Well, if there are all these problems with Aristotle, who'll be our guide in philosophy? Name somebody!" And Galileo's spokesman, Salviati, says, "We need guides in deep forests, jungles and the like, but out on the plains we can use our own eyes." That's Don McCloskey's answer. I think I'm somewhere in between. In methodology I don't think we are on the open plain. We want some way of criticizing "bad" work. What we have, even without falsificationism, is a whole lot of detailed criteria, none of which are necessary or sufficient conditions; they are virtues, and vices, that adhere to particular theories. We have, using Don's grammatical analogy, short and simple rules that break down in lots of cases but that are not entirely useless. A more effective criticism of the claimants of apodictic certainty is not to dismiss them as crazy, but to criticize the basis on which they argue, to use the much more detailed criteria which each of us can make explicit if we take the time. This is also how I'd respond to Professor Pen's point of this morning [p. 24].

Klamer: The two worlds that you represent reflect the dualistic thinking that I regard as unfortunate – there is either the jungle or the open plain. I don't support the idea of "anything goes" . . .

Hausman: I really don't mean to imply that. The plain is where the rules are entirely clear, not where there are *no* rules.

Klamer: All right, but we are involved in conversations and this notion of standards has unfortunate connotations. I want to avoid it. There are, however, rules of conversation. The reason we avoid discussing them is because we are too used to studying the form and structure of theories. I argue that we should also look at discursive practice.

Morgan paper

Summary remarks

My paper is a fairly detailed discussion of two emerging econometric concerns in the 1920s and 1930s: finding an empirical model and the notion of what constituted a "satisfactory" model.

I argue from the perspective that the history of econometrics has to an important degree set present practice. Historically the aim of econometrics–dating from the 1920s and 1930s–has been to make economic laws concrete. I've used in my paper the notion of operationalization of theory, and this is a deliberate reference to Bridgman, who was influential in those two decades.

To the econometricians of the 1920s and 1930s, economic theories were generally true, though there was a problem in that they were not actually applicable. A set of approximations, it was thought, had to be added in order to make theory correct for any given situation. So when early econometricians developed an applied counterpart to theory which worked in some sense with reference to data, they called this "testing." Thus testing had a meaning which is not quite the same as refutation, confirmation, verification, or falsification.

Without repeating what is in the paper, perhaps this is the most relevant lesson from the detailed story told there: *Econometrics is mostly about getting together the right sorts of approximations to make a "good" empirical model.* In the process of this–doing their craft–econometricians are all the time trying to *prove* a hypothesis; they are all the time trying to make the model work, in the sense that maybe an experimental scientist tries to make an experiment work. They do not aim to refute; they aim to make the thing work. Thus the testing idea here is not really a notion of accept or reject; it is a testing of how good is the quality of the empirical model we've got. It is a quality control mechanism. When econometricians talk about testing–even when they speak of rejecting–this does not have Popperian overtones. What they are doing in fact is testing in the form of looking for something better or worse–a quality scale–not something that is right or wrong.

Discussion

Driehuis: I find myself comfortable with Mary Morgan's view that econometricians have been concerned primarily with translating economic theories into empirical or measurable models, and not with trying to prove theories incorrect or correct. Econometricians make economic theories concrete. They try to operationalize general ideas for a specific period and for a specific political, social, and technical context. The aim of the econometrician is modest: [to answer the question] "How well does the empirical model work with reference to the data?"

The central issue in Mary's paper is whether satisfactory empirical models can be found. A crucial issue, of course, is what is meant by "satisfactory." In Section 2 of her paper, it is shown that early econometricians had clear ideas about this. First of all, there were requirements for the individual model equations in terms of coefficients, their signs and stability and statistical significance. These requirements can be called "statistical requirements." Secondly, there were requirements resulting from the purpose of the model. A forecasting model must yield satisfactory forecasts; a policy model should give satisfactory information on alternative policy options; and so on.

These latter two sorts of requirements relate to macro-models. It seems to me that we need little discussion on the statistical criteria; they are well understood. It's also not difficult to decide on what a satisfactory forecast is. But much more discussion is possible – and maybe needed – on whether a model is satisfactory from an economic-analytical point of view. What are satisfactory effects of alternative policy simulations? Since these effects, by definition, are only dependent on the structure of the model, the question becomes, What is a satisfactory structure? The answer clearly is *not* that structure which fits the data best. It is, in principle, possible that more than one model fits the data very well, so it is not possible to prove in that way which model is to be preferred.

I conclude, therefore, that a satisfactory model structure is one considered most plausible by its designer, using "plausible" in Klant's sense. So there is not one, but many, "satisfactory" model structures. This situation is, as we know, considered disappointing by journalists, politicians, and others who accuse macroeconomists of quarreling all the time, but it seems inevitable.

From a scientific point of view, what is important is that researchers follow the rules of the game; that is, that they make clear *what* data they use, *how* they estimate, *why* they choose what they choose, so that they can constantly check each other's work. For me this is the enduring message of Klant's book.

Nooteboom: I have a problem. It ties in with the problem of a background theory that is not tested. The empirical phenomenon, that when you regress labor productivity on relative wages it yields a significant coefficient, can be interpreted in at least four ways. One can be that it indicates substitution. And that has the immediate policy implication that when the wage rate rises, capital is substituted for labor, so we should be careful not to let that happen. Another interpretation might be: Labor is not homogeneous; there are quality differences in labor, and high-quality labor is awarded a higher wage rate, and that accounts for the empirical relationship. This may lead to different policy conclusions. Thirdly, wages may be actually determined on the basis of productivity. A fourth interpretation: If you have markup pricing, this will also lead to a significant coefficient.

Thus, because here we are *not* testing the basic theory of optimization, of production functions with substitution, etc., we must a priori select one interpretation. Now econometricians are modest. They say, "Well, look, I haven't invented the background theory; all I am doing is fitting it, and this is what emerges." This opens the way to arbitrary or ideological influences in the selection among interpretations, and if we are not careful, we miss this and the discussion about interpretations which should occur does not.

Morgan: Very disturbing, that. The point is to compare alternative theories. For any econometrician, the process of doing econometrics means that he or she is usually concerned with just one empirical model. The problem of comparing different empirical models which might incorporate different economic theories is a problem which is hardly addressed in Tinbergen and is only now being confronted. There is no easy answer, but clearly econometricians too must carry part of the discussion.

Fase: A few comments, and a question. I enjoyed the paper, but I had some problems. I've always had problems in *doing* econometrics. I think that the *only* thing you can do in econometrics—this, anyway, is my belief—is to measure or estimate but not test. I agree with Mary Morgan that the first thing in building an empirical model is trying to make the thing work. But this implies that you are on a fishing expedition—you throw away all those things that you believe are threats to the working of the model. This is a kind of testing, is it not?

Now the Neyman–Pearson framework of testing has two requirements. Firstly, you need a null hypothesis. That's no problem; but you also need to state the alternative. My question is: Is economic theory able to produce enough alternatives to make for real tests in the Neyman–Pearson sense? A negative example is the monetarists' claim to test. All they are doing is trying to prove that their opinions are right. They do not chance their opinions against real alternatives.

Morgan: This throwing-away business . . . the ad hoc manipulations that econometricians do. Econometrics seems to me not so much an art as a craft skill. It requires lots of judgment, as well as some artistic skills and luck. A good econometrician, like a good historian, will take account of all the problems and will not throw away any of the inconvenient things encountered.

On Neyman–Pearson. Yes, I think that when econometricians talk about testing, they are not really testing in the sense of comparing serious alternative theories. Even in Neyman–Pearson one has only a straw alternative. They are "testing" in order to get a better and better version of what they have, *assuming* that the underlying theory is right.

Blaug: It may be helpful to say that the problem of econometrics is, as Samuelson puts it, to turn a qualitative calculus into a quantitative calculus. If you throw away econometrics you are left with the qualitative calculus and you deprive economic theory of any useful contribution to economic policy.

Pen: Even more: We need econometrics for understanding the world, which is more fundamental than policy needs. Economics is all about numbers; hence econometrics cannot be divorced from economics.

Cramer: Bravo!

Weintraub paper

Summary remarks

My paper is an adumbration of a theme implicit in Professor Pen's last comment: In the future, only econometricians will have the right to be intelligent! My job is to begin where Popper might have taken us, but did not. The argument follows very naturally on Neil de Marchi's paper and on Mary Morgan's paper.

On the other hand, I disagree entirely with the view that Mark Blaug just expressed, that there is a division between theory and testing or empirical work; that there are theorists here and empirical workers there, and that it is somebody's task to bring them together. I'd argue that there is only one task, and that is to make sense of what's in the middle. The paper tries to do something like that.

I take a series of three studies and try to show how theory and evidence intertwine, in ways that are associated in a Lakatosian research program and are associated with Lakatosian progress. I used a Lakatosian framework because it limited me to asking only a certain number of questions, questions which interested me.

The sequence I examine is a series of papers in microeconomics. These embody three theories in the Lakatosian belt of what I call the "neo-Walrasian program." M_T is a neoclassical theory of household behavior; M_{T+1} is Becker's theory of the household; and M_{T+2} is a Nash-bargained theory of the household.

What is this Nash-bargained theory about? You can set up utility functions for a man and a woman – marriage partners. Each utility function has as arguments some that are geared to the individual, to the person, and some that are held in common. There are constraints for each individual: income that is common and income that is specific. These functions can be set up and one can work out an interdependent optimization problem – a bargaining problem, in the sense of John Nash. Using the Nash solution to the special bargaining problem, which involves the choice of a status quo point, one can come up with a solution which is a division of utilities, and come up with a generalized demand system which involves, in an intrinsic way, the interrelationship of two individuals who happen to be married to one another and who in that relationship hold certain kinds of income in common.

That's a theorist's problem. But what happens when you ask, exactly how does this theory work? What data would be used to support it? How could the theory be developed further? I describe in the paper how the move from M_{T+1} to M_{T+2} was accomplished. The creators of M_{T+2} concluded that the Nash model provided, for the first time, an analytical framework for examining the effect of the marriage tax on the joint labor supply of husbands and wives. Her current married after-tax marginal wage rate is an argument in the full family income constraint, whereas her hypothetical unmarried after-tax marginal wage rate is an argument of her threat point. This is just one of a whole class of applications where, due to taxes and transfers, the prices and nonwage incomes faced by an individual differ according to his or her marital status.

Thus we have a specific implication associated with the Nash model which was not present either in the Becker household model or the standard neoclassical model of two individual decision makers. In the second paper, a data set was painstakingly developed to appraise the excess content of the Nash demand system. This was a nontrivial part of the overall task. It required much time (two years) and a great deal of ingenious analysis. It is not sufficient to state, as some falsificationists do, that in good science facts falsify theories and that since economists don't look for falsifying facts, they are not doing good science. Getting the "facts" is not trivial.

In the third paper, the bargaining model is applied to an entirely new problem, that of household membership. Specifically, where some earlier work treated household membership as an exogenous dummy variable in studies of youth earnings, the third paper examines joint decisions on wages, consumption, and household membership.

What does all this mean? Whatever one believes about the value of research programs, the methodological literature leaves one with the impression that empirical economics is unimportant to the economics enterprise. Yet most of Kuhnian normal economic science is incoherent without a view of the role of empirical work. My own suggestion, that such work fits naturally into the Lakatosian research program idea, is simply an attempt to locate applied economics and its concerns in some kind of context.

The idea that facts can falsify theories and that the role of applied work is to produce the facts is to simultaneously misunderstand facts, theories, testing, and falsification. The activity of applied economic analysis is appropriately characterized, in my view, as *developing evidence to appraise excess content,* a view which the paper undergirds.

Discussion

Birner: If this series of papers that Professor Weintraub discusses is part of *the same* (neo-Walrasian) research program, and *if* they are indeed empirically progressive, they provide *one instance* of an application of general equilibrium theory's [GET] being progressive. I agree with Weintraub that many more case studies of empirical work are needed in order to appraise GET as a whole. But preliminary to this is an examination of the nature of the neo-Walrasian program and the manner in which it is supposed to operate. In my comment I shall concentrate on two items:

1. Are the different studies discussed by Weintraub indeed part of the same Lakatosian research program?
2. Is it true that, as Weintraub emphatically asserts, the progress could *only* have been made in the framework of the neo-Walrasian program?

My comments will be in part requests for clarification, and in part criticisms.

In the sequence of papers for which Weintraub claims both theoretical and empirical progress, there is a clean break. Before the work published by McElroy and Horney, agents, whether interpreted as persons or as households, were modeled as making *independent* choices, subject to a budget constraint. In the later work, agents were modeled as *mutually dependent* decision makers in a Nash-bargaining framework. For this sequence Weintraub claims three things:

1. It is a sequence of theoretically and empirically progressive theories *that belong to the same research program.*
2. The development was generated by an "interpretive shift" in HC3 ("agents choose independently of one another").
3. The progressive development "could have been made *only* by a neo-Walrasian."

These are strong claims. I shall argue that all three claims cannot be maintained consistently.

If one maintains that a program develops (progressively) by interpretative shifts in the hard-core propositions, the question naturally arises of whether the resulting theories are still part of the same program. Lakatos would deny this, condemning the reinterpretation as being ad hoc; the program would lack continuity, as it does not stick to its hard core. But perhaps we may be less strict than Lakatos. In Becker's case, where "agent" was redefined from "person" to "household," my intuition would still allow me to say that the resulting theory was part of the same research program. But replacing HC3, *in*dependent choice, by HC3′, *inter*dependent choice, and calling this a "reinterpretation" surely stretches the meaning of that word. If in the development of a research program a hard-core proposition is replaced by its denial, we must conclude that we have left the original program behind and are dealing with a new one.

Weintraub's very strong claim that the progressive shift (or, more neutrally, the development) he describes could only have been made by a neo-Walrasian general equilibrium theorist, and not by someone using a Marshallian partial equilibrium approach, presupposes that the neo-Walrasian program exerts a very strong directing influence. (At the very least, it presupposes that it provides constraints.) And this is indeed what he claims for it; the positive heuristic of the program "forces attention to the *interdependent* optimizing that occurs in households, and predisposes the analyst to consider adopting a game theoretic model" (p. 223–4; *italics added*). But it does so by altering the content of HC3. This raises severe problems.

Firstly, if the positive heuristic is derived from the hard-core propositions, as Weintraub's examples suggest, how can it give directions for altering the hard-core propositions themselves?

Secondly, I do not see the difference between taking the leap toward an interpretative shift in one of the hard-core propositions and "a judicious use of the ceteris paribus clause" (p. 224). Indeed, there is nothing in a partial equilibrium framework that prevents one from coming up with an M_{T+2}-type bargaining model.

Thirdly, lacking any rules guiding interpretative shifts, I think Weintraub's use of the idea that hard-core propositions are partially interpreted makes him vulnerable to Alexander Rosenberg's criticism: "If the partial interpretation claim is correct, any set of non-self-contradictory propositions can become a perfectly adequate theory about any sort of phenomenon antecedently described. All that is required is the appropriate correspondence [= interpretation] rules" [1984].

To sum up, I do not think that Professor Weintraub has proved his case that this particular application of general equilibrium theory is an episode in a Lakatosian research program. It may be a research program, and a progressive one at that, if one sees a research program as defined by a *problem* such as labor force participation of household members, and by attempts to come up with ever better solutions to the original problem and to subsequent problems that arise. But this seems to put the development Weintraub describes squarely back in a Popperian framework.

Weintraub: When I talked about hardening of the hard core, I was talking about taking a "fixed" term like "economic agent" and extending the range or scope implicit in that term over time, e.g., adding futures markets to the concept of commodity or allowing a capital good to be a commodity so that an interest rate could be a price in a later version. There are interpretative shifts in hard-core notions and, by analogy, propositions. In the heuristics something else is going on. There we are talking about models and theories which are specifications – restrictions on the hard-core propositions and their instantiation in models. Take "agents." We mean men and women at a point in time. This is fleshed out in various models. So the modifications in the moves from M_T to M_{T+1} to M_{T+2} are occurring in the protective belt – in the theory or modeling changes – and are not associated with shifts in the hard core.

My evidence for the view that the sequence I describe is associated with the neo-Walrasian program and could not have been produced by Chicago economists is quite direct. McElroy spent a year at the University of Chicago trying to persuade Gary Becker and Jim Heckman that this was a worthwhile approach. They rejected it entirely as being too general equilibrium in character: There are too many parameters, and one needs a much tighter kind of framework. Moreover, the Horney contribution – the idea of the Nash-bargaining solution – came out of a seminar I taught, and she was being trained as a neo-Walrasian.

Blaug: Does Professor Weintraub believe that game theory is part of general equilibrium theory?

Weintraub: Game theory is a calculus of interdependent optimization. If optimization theory is associated with neoclassical economics, then game theory is associated with – provides a model of – microeconomics. The two – game theory and microeconomics – grew up together. The first existence proof of competitive equilibrium used the basic tools of game theory, and the culminating theorem of Arrow–Debreu used the theories of Nash – they treated the issue as an n-person game.

Birner: The fact that Chicago economists did not in fact agree with the McElroy approach shows only that they did not act along those lines. It does not show that they *could* not have developed their theory in that direction.

Hands: I would like to talk about the possibility of violating some hard-core proposition in negotiating the transition from M_T to M_{T+1} to M_{T+2}. My question is not about interdependency – I think that's an unhelpful pursuit – but about independent agents in the Becker model. There you have a household production function and utility function. I find the idea of *household* maximizing to be quite *non*-neo-Walrasian. You might argue therefore that the second stage of theory development here was not in the neo-Walrasian hard core. I'd answer my own question by saying that consistency with the hard core is perhaps a matter of degree – there are degrees of ad hocness. A way to think about Becker's contribution, therefore, might be to think of it as a gain in *empirical* content at the cost of heuristic progress. The third stage, however – the game theoretic approach – seems to involve both empirical and heuristic content. There may be trade-offs of this sort.

Weintraub: I don't disagree with this. The Becker move involves a re-interpretation of "agent" as "household." I'm not wholly comfortable with appraising this move within the neo-Walrasian tradition, though the next move can, I think, be appraised within that tradition. It could not have been made, however, by Becker for very specific reasons.

Klamer: It is once more clear that there is a difference between a spoken and a written presentation of an argument. The argument as written [by Weintraub] is not entirely convincing. It depends critically on the McElroy shift being within the neo-Walrasian program. In his informal comments, however, Weintraub *adds* factual information about how Chicago economists preferred to operate.

Nooteboom: Does not the whole debate turn on whether the word "independent" belongs to the core? If so, this merely tells us that cases and programs are not sharp-edged.

Weintraub: I like that. I have found, in trying to write down what I mean by the hard core of the neo-Walrasian program, that the same general propositions have satisfied me over some years and through several attempts. But words like "independent" and "interdependent" – I don't want these to be fixed. I don't regard my reconstruction in this paper as fixed and definitive. As to the heuristics, these are capable of variation and extension almost indefinitely. They are meant to make the conversation more productive.

Birner: I don't think we are having a quarrel about words only. The claim is that the neo-Walrasian program exerts a strong, definite influence on further research. The whole point of the hard core in a Lakatosian program is that certain propositions have a privileged status; but now we hear that they don't. So what's the point of using the Lakatosian framework?

Weintraub: There's a marked difference between the hard core and what's in the belt. The core is regulative; nonetheless, if one of our axioms involves, say, something like the concept of a line, then in different geometries that will have different interpretations. There are some things that a neo-Walrasian will not give up; that's a way to get at the hard-core propositions.

Birner: But if we have the freedom to reinterpret hard-core propositions, what really drives the program? It would be nice if you could make a prediction as to what the next move would be in the program.

Weintraub: I would make the next move if I could make the prediction!

Caldwell paper

Summary remarks

My paper is concerned with the problem, How should we do methodology?

What is the purpose of methodological work? Answers I've run across include the following:

1. Methodology tells us the difference between science and nonscience.
2. Methodology tells us how to choose among competing theories.
3. Methodology tells us how to proceed, how to actually do economic science.

I have long felt that the philosophical literature did not argue for any of these three alternatives very adequately. Indeed, I've come to be more interested in problems that I've run into in looking at economic methodology than in philosophical questions as such. Let me mention four such problems.

1. There seems to be little connection between economic methodology and learning how to be an economist.
2. Some of the best-known economists talk about methodology, but it is not a subject held in high repute.
3. Groups outside of the mainstream are the only ones who appear really interested in talking about methodology, but they frequently do not get beyond this.
4. The mainstream, on the other hand, disparages methodology yet uses methodological arguments constantly, both in attacking various outside groups and in defending themselves.

Now both Blaug and Klant have a certain coherence in their positions, imparted by their acceptance of some sophisticated variant of falsificationism. I have gone a different route – a pluralistic route.

To come back to the question of how and why we should do methodology, one purpose is to better understand economic science (and, it is to be hoped, improve it). We should also be evaluating research programs to identify their strengths and weaknesses. Then, too, it seems appropriate to emphasize novelty.

This may not sound like a very tight set of goals. It is not. But it contrasts sharply with some alternatives that I think we need to be rid of. Firstly, there are no a priori grounds for excluding anything. I make no attempt to solve the demarcation problem. Science is too rich and varied to separate it from nonscience very successfully. We have *not* succeeded up to this point. [Secondly,] but worse, trying to solve this problem has created many other problems in methodology today. For the attempt sets methodologists up as experts, arbiters. It is one reason for the gap between scientists and methodologists – a gap that emerges clearly in Mary Morgan's paper. Thirdly, demarcation criteria often seem to be used dogmatically to exclude unwanted approaches.

Now an obvious response is, "Well, doesn't your position lead to anarchy?" I defend myself with three arguments. Firstly, this fear of anarchy misunderstands science as it is currently practiced. Science tends more toward conservatism and dogmatism than toward anarchy. Secondly, it misunderstands the role of methodology. It is not the role of the methodologist to keep science "free." Citizens in general must oppose restrictions on discourse. Thirdly, it ignores that criticism is very important in my own position. Only via criticism are the strengths and weaknesses of research programs brought to light. And the criticism may be from a multiplicity of standpoints. I give more detail in the paper.

But I suspect the more deep-seated objection is this: Can I, by mere criticism, be confident that I will be led to true theories? No. I can't establish that being open but critical will guarantee truth. I do claim, however, that it promises to yield a richer understanding of economics than less inclusionary alternatives.

Discussion

Hamminga: Dr. Caldwell defends his pluralism in a pluralistic way. As an economic methodologist, I do not think there is a professional reaction to pluralism.

Let me, then, try to supply an economist's reaction to pluralism. The pluralist seems to be considerably more tolerant toward what I am doing than the referees of journals and reviews whom I want to accept my drafts (and he seems to be so on purpose). To me, as an economist, reviews and journals are like huge dragons, and I want them to swallow the food I prepare for them. Consequently, I would accept the assistance of anyone who has clear-cut *empirical* information concerning the chemical structure of the food the dragons refuse and of the chemical structure of the food the dragons swallow. That is, I would certainly be willing to listen to the results of those descriptive studies about science that are welcomed by the pluralist.

The pluralist, however, calls these studies "nonmethodological." That means, I conjecture, that he does not consider them to be his own specific affair. What, then, is the specific affair of the pluralist, apart from *welcoming* all the different ideas and all the different ways to criticize them? All in all, as an economist, I would not disagree with the pluralist, but I do not see how the assistance of a pluralist expert in argumentation could improve my performance in making these dragons swallow my food. And that is what I want.

Now I could have done wrong in dressing as an economist. Pluralism could be meant as assistance not to the individual economist, but to the dragons: what they *ought* to refuse and what they *ought* to swallow. Pluralism may be a recommendation for more variety in the dragons' menu. Dressed as a dragon, I would answer pluralism as follows: My stomach is of limited size. If I start accepting some kinds of papers that I used to refuse, this implies that I have to refuse papers that I used to accept. If I would follow the pluralist's recommendation to enlarge my bouquet of standards for criticism, I thereby stop revealing *stable and predictable digestion behavior* to those who present food to me. As a result, submitting economists will soon start to look for other dragons to feed. Whimsical evaluation behavior repels economists, especially those who make the kind of food that they know to be desired by many dragons. I would become ill-fed.

As you see, it is as if an invisible hand makes dragons and economists, both simply acting in accordance with their own interests, cooperate to make that stable and predictable system of evaluation that we empirically observe, causing Dr. Caldwell's worries about "dogmatic demarcation." Both dragons and economists depend upon this "dogmatism." They depend upon it for their survival. In other words, *this dogmatism is rational,* and pluralism means either no assistance or bad assistance.

There is, however, a third possibility for pluralism. It may be considered to be a position that is "methodological" in the very specific sense of being not about the contingent interactions of economists and their dragons that we can observe in the imperfect world around us. In this specific sense, methodology is meant to be about "knowledge," the real thing. My view on this is that if pluralism wants to form *its own* opinion of "strengths and weaknesses," instead of restricting itself *exclusively* to empirical study of the economists' opinions, it distracts methodologists from their *only* meaningful task: that of making corroborated empirical theories about real – that is, really existing, observable – economics.

Hausman: Does Bert Hamminga mean to say that there is no point to the evaluation of any human practice? In other words, if we discover economists behaving imperfectly in some regard, that just shows we've made a mistake in our theory.

Hamminga: If you study science you study ideals and frustrations, but you study them empirically.

Nooteboom: A varied diet is healthy for dragons. What Caldwell is saying is like a plea for a varied diet. I support such a plea. Nor is the epistemological basis for pluralism entirely lacking. I see it in Rorty, Goodman, and Putnam . . . the coherence view of truth. Putnam put it this way. He said: In between the swamps of metaphysics – that's the correspondence theory of truth – and, on the other side, the quicksands of relativism, we should find a path. The epistemological basis of pluralism is that path, and it's in the making.

Caldwell: I choose to remain agnostic at the moment about truth, because I see the problems that McCloskey and Klamer are running into. They are having to learn a lot of philosophy – how Rorty and others can get them around the problem of truth. And this is taking them off the subject, which, in their case, is rhetoric; in my case, it's trying to give a role to the economic methodologist. I don't think I'll find it in philosophical discussions of truth. These discussions have not in the past helped us to understand what economists are about, and that is my concern.

Klamer: I would like to suggest that rather than talk about pluralism, we talk about argumentative strategies – theoretical, empirical, historical. This does not imply any particular epistemological position.

Hutchison: About fifty years ago, I wanted a distinction between science and nonscience. I wouldn't use these words now, but *distinction* is vital – as to how far a particular theory has been tested, and so on, as I have said before. We don't necessarily want those who "fail" in some sense to be cast into outer darkness, but we want the distinction.

Again, Bruce Caldwell went on about criticism, criticism, and Daniel Hausman has urged empirical testing. But that's just a kind of falsificationism; without some such principle, criticism is merely a matter of likes and dislikes. Otherwise talk of criticism is empty.

Blaug: If you really take methodological pluralism seriously – that there are no meta-methodological principles on the basis of which one might compare different programs – then programs can only be criticized from within. But if you take this position, why should logical consistency be a desirable attribute? Such consistency is restricting; it creates anomalies in the light of empirical evidence. Such a criticism must come from some higher-order standard. Methodological pluralism is just a copout.

Birner: I've always considered pluralism to be harmless and uninteresting. If you want a true theory, you look for falsifiable statements. If you want to be able to apply a theory, you may be happy to apply instrumentalism. Typically, however, we look for theories which are true, applicable, and perhaps satisfy other criteria as well. How could Caldwell make the trade-off?

Klant: I have the feeling that by "pluralism" Caldwell has in mind a uniform theory, in the using of which, however, various methods can be brought to bear. That is not methodology, but method.

As to the demarcation line, I would argue that economics is on both sides of Popper's line. I am not interested in where economics falls along this particular line. He does not describe economics. I claim that in economics we are trying to follow plausibility strategies. And I agree with Hamminga that we should find out exactly what strategies *are* being followed.

I agree with Caldwell insofar as I think that there are many strategies, some more, some less empirical. The only thing methodological about this is the recognition that there are various plausibility strategies.

Caldwell: We should criticize in many different ways. Where do our criteria come from? Popper's don't seem to be very useful in economics. Why elevate his criteria to some special status?

McCloskey paper

Summary remarks

I think I should start by reminding you of George Stigler's conference handbook, and in particular his comment that in assessing the work under discussion it is always good form to say, "I can be very sympathetic with the young author; up until a few years ago, I was thinking along similar lines" [1977, p. 442]. Up until a few years ago, I was a logical empiricist. You don't see any former methodological anarchists who have converted to logical empiricism, but you do see a great number of the other kind. This is an argument for a move away from logical empiricism. I claim that philosophical criticism of science looks thin beside what actually happens in scientific conversation. Philosophy might have proven to have been helpful in understanding science, but it hasn't worked out that way. As Roy Weintraub says in his recent *General Equilibrium Analysis: Studies in Appraisal,* a use of the Lakatosian framework raises problems that rest uneasily on a Lakatosian bed. But even if, with certain trimming of the feet, a piece of economics could be made to fit easily in the bed, I ask, "So what?" What have we gained by forcing science into a Popperian or Lakatosian mold?

I see evidence that philosophy, which has urged economists to impoverish the economic argument, has not been of much help. We might use philosophy to judge progress in economics, but I don't think Lakatos claims that his framework is an accurate guide to history. Again, one might think that economic theory leads to truth. But I don't think this works either. If the philosophical criticism of science is not about what we know, what is it about?

I think it is about morality. An ethical conversation cannot be taken seriously, however, when the conversationalists themselves don't know that they are dealing with ethical questions. To the extent that they understand but are not prepared to defend their conversations as ethical, the same holds. They are unprofessional conversations. We are invited to believe that certain conversations have political effects – the barbarians again – but these effects are undemonstrated.

If the philosophers of science will reason together with us, they will find that the values they want to protect are the same as those Klamer and I want to protect. The *sprachethik* is the same for us all: Don't shout; pay attention; don't lie; don't use violence. A good scientific society is the ideal speech situation. The logical empiricists and the rhetoricians both have in mind the preservation of the same values, and these are the values of good conversation. It is a conversational model of science.

This raises the question of standards. But we know when the conversation in our own field is going well. Conversations overlap and the *sprachethik* is transmitted through the scientific society in this way. A value in a good conversation, for example, is that we are careful to read what has gone before. Not only would the ideal methodology have this character of studying conversations, but that is what historians of economic thought already actually do.

The close study of conversation is a natural – indeed, empirically progressive – research program in methodology and history of thought. The only close competitor is a fine program in the sociology of science – the Edinburgh or Strong Program. What is unique about that program, and what is interesting about history of science generally, is its rhetorical dimension. The sociology of science in fact reduces to a rhetorical study: how arguments of all kinds are actually made. But with an explicit use of the long tradition of rhetoric, you can go much further than conventional sociology of science or history of thought. You can analyze the audience for economics, for example, and show how the texts of economics make appeals to certain audiences. You can show how genres such as the scientific paper developed. You can show how metaphors, theorems, and statistical appeals to authority are employed. In other words, the conversational approach to economics has virtue for both the positive and the normative parts of methodology and for the history of economic thought.

Discussion

Pen: The organizers of this conference thought of me, apparently, as one who would be able to characterize . . . shall we call it the "thick" school [laughter] . . . and discuss it in an objective way. Until recently, that would have been correct. I am a structuralist *and* an economic journalist, but I've always tried to keep the two separate. But this clear distinction started to crumble some years ago, a critical point being my reading of Don McCloskey's article in the *Journal of Economic Literature*. I'm still not a certified member . . .

McCloskey: Certifiable, perhaps [laughter]

Pen: . . . of the McCloskey–Klamer school, but the profession should be grateful to the man who held up to us the mirror – not the mirror of nature – and showed us what we are doing: We are practicing story-telling, we are using metaphors and rhetoric, whether we like it or not. It is a problem to me that the general reaction in the profession to this article is one of irritation.

I have been under the spell of metaphors for a long time. Economists use optical metaphors – woods, ships, water supplies, battlefields – and some of them are very powerful. Perhaps we should remember that it is not only the optical but the auditory metaphor which is important. In the legal subculture, speaking and listening [are] taken much more seriously than in economics. One reason is that the legal profession has a strong normative role: You tell people what to do, you promise, you threaten. Therefore, in normative fields like law and theology, the auditory meta-phor is more readily accepted. Is McCloskey perhaps leaning towards a normative view of economics? If so, that may explain some of the resis-tance to his viewpoint.

Another question that troubles me is this: Isn't McCloskey afraid that under the new "thick" culture economists might slip away from the core of economic science, which is quantitative? Our task – I speak as a structuralist – is to find out what is constant in a changing world.

Klamer paper

Summary remarks

My paper presents a philosophical argument in favor of a practice differ-ent from the one normally adopted with respect to understanding what economists do.

I am interested in the problems experienced by novices in economics.

I maintain four things. Firstly, it is by paying attention to the problem of communication, and not to the problem of knowledge, that we will make economic conversations once more interesting. The problem of knowledge is concerned with how we manage the relationship between our thoughts and objects. This is the relationship between Popper's first and third worlds. We don't get very far by proceeding this way. Proceed-ing analytically, we ignore the sender, the audience, and most of the signals, and concentrate on a series of statements. That is how we sim-plify the communication process. Form and the structure of statements is all we see handled by methodologists. Thereby we ignore the ethos of the speaker – can we trust him? What is his reputation? – and the *interpre-tation* of signals at the other end. Economists get their message across by means that go far beyond mere statements. I submit that we will learn much more about what is going on if we pay attention to discursive practice.

Point number two. If this is true, we must become like anthropologists, studying and interpreting economists as they communicate.

Thirdly, to think of economics as discourse is better than thinking of it as rhetoric. It helps us to think beyond an individual facing others and trying to persuade them. Speech communities, as distinct from the I–them model, are more complex and richer.

Fourthly, a focus on problems of communication makes sense only if we recognize differences. The prevalent emphasis on form, structure, criteria of justification stresses identity, consensus, and the basis of agreement. But there are many conversations, different ways of world making. We can reach an understanding of similarities when we have recognized differences. But seeking identity will not help us.

Discussion

Weintraub: I would have liked to open up an additional line of communication by dancing. I can't dance. What I want to do, then, is to describe a ballet – one of my own invention. The prima ballerina, *l'economie,* is fought over by the black prince, Le Poppér, and the white prince, Le Rorty, or their armies, Les Positivistes et Les Pragmatistes. The dances of the former are heavy and plodding, martial in step. The latter's dances are opportunistic, free. In the end, Les Positivistes die of self-inflicted exhaustion, and sprightly Rorty carries off *l'economie.*

Short of being able to dance this – all parts – myself, I'd like to extend an invitation to Don McCloskey and Arjo Klamer to have a conversation, and not just to *talk* about conversations [applause]. My recent book on general equilibrium theory is an extended conversation with Mark Blaug (the reader over my shoulder). I used many styles and contexts to come at points in different ways. We need more studies, of the sort that Klamer gave us of the New Classical discourse, in his unpublished dissertation [1980], and of the sort that McCloskey gives us of Fogel and of Purchasing Power Parity, in his new book [1985, chs. 7, 9]. We can do with less talk. As Eliza Doolittle said:

Words, words, words;
I'm so sick of words.
I hear words all day through
first from him now from you.
Is that all you blighters can do?
      [Laughter. Hear, hear.]

General discussion (McCloskey and Klamer papers together)

Birner: Where's the substance of economics in all this? If you want to focus on the *metaphors* economists use, why not analyze the *explanations* they put forward? This has all the advantages and none of the drawbacks of speaking in the rather vague terms of metaphors.

McCloskey: I have an example that speaks to this, the Cambridge controversy in the theory of capital. The two sides spoke at each other and past each other. Why? Both sides played the game by mathematical rules, treating the aggregability of the capital stock as a mathematical question. In a formal sense, Cambridge, England, won. Yet neoclassical economists go on talking about the marginal productivity of capital. What has happened is this: The debate was really about a metaphor. To attack the metaphor with mathematics is to attack Shakespeare for saying that a woman (or perhaps a man; we don't know) is like a summer's day. A capital stock is a metaphorical idea. The debate about its physical or value characteristics is therefore beside the point. One can only do this kind of analysis of a conversation if one recognizes that economic arguments are not "thin"–they are not *just* mathematical or statistical, but involve analogies, stories, appeals to authorities. We will get better arguments in economics if we know what we are talking about.

Birner: How far would you get trying to understand the success of a book like *The Open Society* or Hayek's *Road to Serfdom* without viewing it as a criticism of *ideas?*

Nooteboom: There is an important bit of unfinished, or rather unstarted, business. On demarcation, Hutchison has said that we need some demarcation, some language rules, or order–some way of distinguishing good from bad. I believe in demarcation, but I don't think that there is a demarcation *line.* Gaston Bachelard talked about epistemological obstacles, and I think that we have this obstacle that something is either "in" or "out." Now there is a demarcation *area,* but it is fuzzy. As Wade Hands has maintained, there are many sorts of ad hocness. In some respects, things may be acceptable and in some they may not, but it is not sharp and fixed. There is this fundamental idea, which I call "Feyerabend's fallacy," that there is either a strict, logical, context-independent order or there is chaos. Things are not in fact like this. If you talk about moving from semantics to pragmatics, you are talking about moving from in-and-outness, extension, truth or untruth to context-dependent answers. Can we not seek for an order of the latter sort, gaining demarcation order yet not being able to define a demarcation line?

Blaug: Of all the different ways one can analyze what economists do, why should one choose to invest exclusively in rhetorical analysis? I think there are many more interesting ways to look at what is going on in the history of economics. I'm not unsympathetic, however.

McCloskey: I understand that you are not unsympathetic, and I have no answer in the abstract. It would be absurd for me to stand up here and say that I have a philosophical theory that rhetorical analysis is *the* way to do history of economic thought. That would be self-contradictory. So I accept that I have to show you. I have analyzed particular papers, constructed partial grammars of economics, made this an empirical question.

Caldwell: Both novelty and criticism are important to me. I welcome your program because it is novel, and when it has a bit more content, I'll be happy to criticize it.

McCloskey: That's fair comment.

Klamer: In reaction to Mark Blaug, I am working on discourse analysis, and part of that deals with what he would call the "sociology of economics." That's essential if you want to understand the audience. If the economics audience prefers formal over historical arguments, this can be understood in part by looking at how the discipline is organized. I do not exclude that.

References

Archibald, G.C. (1965). "The Qualitative Content of Maximizing Models," *Journal of Political Economy;* reprinted in M. Morishima et al. (1973), *Theory of Demand.* Oxford: Oxford University Press.
Hamminga, B. (1982). "Neoclassical Theory Structure and Theory Development," in W. Stegmüller, W. Balzer, and W. Spohn, eds. *Philosophy of Economics.* Berlin: Springer-Verlag.
Hicks, J. (1969). *A Theory of Economic History.* Oxford: Clarendon Press.
(1979). *Causality in Economics.* Oxford: Basil Blackwell.
(1983). "A Discipline not a Science," in Hicks, *Classics and Moderns. Collected Essays on Economic Theory,* Vol. III. Oxford: Basil Blackwell.
Klamer, A. (1980). "A Methodological Appraisal of Rational Expectations Economics." Ph.D. dissertation, Duke University. Mimeo.
(1984). *Conversations with Economists.* Totowa, N.J.: Rowman and Allenheld.

Klant, J.J. (1984). *The Rules of the Game. The Logical Structure of Economic Theories.* Cambridge: Cambridge University Press.

Levinson, P., ed. (1982). *In Pursuit of Truth. Essays on the Philosophy of Karl Popper on the Occasion of his 80th Birthday.* Atlantic Highlands, N.J.: Humanities Press.

Lipsey, R.G. (1981). "The Understanding and Control of Inflation: Is There a Crisis in Macro-Economics?" *Canadian Journal of Economics* 14:, 545–76.

McCloskey, D.N. (1985). *The Rhetoric of Economics.* Madison: University of Wisconsin Press.

Popper, K. (1957). *The Poverty of Historicism.* London: Routledge & Kegan Paul.

Rosenberg, A. (1984). "Partial Interpretation in Microeconomics," in W. Leinfellner and E. Köhler, eds., *Developments in the Methodology of Social Science.* Dordrecht: Reidel.

Stigler, G.J. (1977). "The Conference Handbook," *Journal of Political Economy* 85:441–43.

PART I

Popper as a philosopher of science

CHAPTER 1

An appraisal of Popperian methodology

DANIEL M. HAUSMAN

Professor Klant, in his masterful overview of economic methodology, *The Rules of the Game*, relies heavily on Karl Popper's writings on the philosophy of science. For, like Popper, Professor Klant is concerned about whether theories are genuinely testable and whether they are truly supported by empirical evidence. I respect these concerns and share them, yet I have serious objections to Popper's philosophy of science. Indeed, I shall argue in this chapter that nontrivial questions about the testability of economics cannot be asked within the confines of Popper's falsificationism. A reasoned concern with falsifiability demands the repudiation of Popper's philosophy of science. Moreover, there is no way to amend his views without eviscerating them and making Popper's central theses little more than truisms accepted no less by anti-Popperians than by Popperians.[1]

Much of the appeal of Popper's philosophy of science depends upon ambiguities and equivocations concerning the notion of falsifiability. I shall argue that the notion of falsification as a purely logical relation between theories and basic statements or observation reports, which Popper has stressed again and again throughout his long career, is irrelevant to any important questions concerning science. On the other hand, Popper's relevant views concerning falsificationism as a methodology or a policy are unfounded and unacceptable.

---

[1] Many of the points made in this chapter are not new. The critique of Popper's views on induction follows, to a considerable extent, criticisms made by Levison (1974), Lieberson (1982a, 1982b), Putnam (1974), Grunbaum (1976), and Salmon (1981), although only Lieberson was a major influence. Isaac Levi's work (1967, 1980) has also influenced me, and in my argument for the possibility of verifications, I was assisted by Nisbett and Thagard's (1982) discussion of induction. Lakatos's critique and his plea for a "whiff of inductivism" is much weaker, since his own treatment of induction differs so little from Popper's (Lakatos, 1974, pp. 241–73). David Miller's defense of Popper's account of induction (1982) does not touch the simple and, in my view, decisive arguments given in this chapter. I would like to thank Ernie Alleva, Clark Glymour, Wade Hands, Kevin Kelly, Jonathan Lieberson, Michael McPherson, Jonathan Pressler, Teddy Seidenfeld, and Wilfrid Sieg for comments on earlier versions of this chapter.

1.   Logical falsifiability

Popper argues that what distinguishes scientific theories, such as Newton's or Einstein's, from unscientific theories, such as Freud's or those endorsed by astrologers, is that scientific theories are *falsifiable*. Intuitively speaking, a theory is falsifiable if it is not guaranteed that it will pass all tests. There must be some possible tests or observations that, if the results are unfavorable, would be evidence that the theory is false. "All swans are white" is the sort of statement that is appropriate in science, because the observation of a nonwhite swan would establish its falsity (Popper's own example, 1968, p. 27).

Popper refines this intuitive notion as follows: First, he distinguishes a class of "basic statements" upon whose truth agreement is easily obtained. Basic statements are true or false reports of observations that are of an "*unquestioned empirical character*" (1963, p. 386; see also 1968, sect. 28, 29). Accepted basic statements are not certain, infallible, or incorrigible. We are not *forced* by the facts to accept them. But we do (albeit tentatively) *decide* to do so, and we rather easily reach lasting agreement on which basic statements to accept. Basic statements have a special importance because of this agreement, since they are particularly easy to test, and since, as empiricists, we take test reports to be particularly important in the acceptance or rejection of scientific theories.[2]

Given the notion of a basic statement, Popper can then give a precise construal of falsifiability. A theory is falsifiable if and only if it is logically inconsistent with some finite set of basic statements. A theory that is, in fact, true would not, of course, be inconsistent with any set of *true* basic statements, but the definition does not say that the basic statements whose negation is entailed by a scientific theory are true.

It is, unfortunately, impossible to tell how important logical falsifiability is to Popper, since he contradicts himself on the question.[3] In an introduction to the *Postscript to the Logic of Scientific Discovery* written in the early 1980s, he states:

> It is of great importance to current discussion to notice that falsifiability in the sense of my demarcation criterion is a purely logical affair. It has to do only with the logical structure of statements and of classes of statements. . . .

---

[2] Although Popper takes basic statements in *The Logic of Scientific Discovery* to be existential statements, I shall cautiously simplify, as Popper also does (1972, p. 7), and take them to be singular statements.

[3] Partly as the result of reading Lakatos's "Falsification and the Methodology of Scientific Research Programmes" (1970), I had been inclined, out of what I took to be charity, to ignore logical falsificationism. Although Popper (1983, pp. xxii–xxiii) is correct to distinguish it from what Lakatos calls "dogmatic falsificationism" (pp. 95–103), its vices are, as I shall argue subsequently, just as serious.

A statement or theory is, according to my criterion, falsifiable if and only if there exists at least one potential falsifier – at least one possible basic statement that conflicts with it logically. (1983, p. xx)

Yet in *The Logic of Scientific Discovery* itself, Popper writes:

Indeed, it is impossible to decide, by analysing its logical form, whether a system of statements is a conventional system of irrefutable implicit definitions, or whether it is a system which is empirical in my sense; that is, a refutable system. . . . *Only with reference to the methods applied* to a theoretical system is it at all possible to ask whether we are dealing with a conventionalist or an empirical theory. (1968, p. 82)

If we take the first quotation as representing Popper's current views, then logical falsifiability is supposed to be the criterion that demarcates science from everything else. But throughout his career, Popper has stressed the importance of methodological decisions in distinguishing science from other activities.

As a corollary of the precise notion of logical falsifiability, Popper repeatedly emphasizes a trivial "*asymmetry* between verifiability and falsifiability; an asymmetry which results from the logical form of universal statements" (1968, p. 41; see also 1983, pp. 181–9). A universal statement concerning an infinite or unbounded domain may be falsifiable – that is, it may be inconsistent with some basic statements. But it will not be verifiable – it will not be deducible from any finite set of basic statements (its negation will not be inconsistent with any finite set of basic statements). For example, "This swan is black" falsifies "All swans are white." It is not possible to verify any truly universal statement, but we can, of course, verify its negation.

Popper argues that this asymmetry between falsifiability and verifiability leads to a solution to the problem of induction. In more or less the formulation Popper prefers (1972, p. 7), Hume's problem of induction is the problem of finding a good argument with only basic statements as premises and some universal statement as a conclusion.[4] If by "good

---

[4] But, as is obvious from the subsequent argument, I do not concur in Popper's sharp separation of what he calls the "logical" from the "pragmatic" problem of induction. Although I do not know precisely what the identity criteria for problems are, it seems to me that there is basically only one problem here. Thus Popper manages to be extremely misleading when he makes the entirely correct (within his set of definitions) claim, "For anybody who adopts an instrumentalist view, *the* [logical] *problem of induction* [as formulated by Popper] *disappears*" (1983, p. 117). But, as Popper himself notes (1983, p. 120), the point is an entirely trivial one, since the instrumentalist faces an entirely analogous problem of deciding which statements to rely on. The point would hardly be worth making but for the fact that Popper's formulation has perhaps misled Lawrence Boland, who argues mistakenly that instrumentalism is a response to the problem of induction (1979, p. 508).

argument" one means "valid deductive argument" (and I shall not discuss any alternative interpretations here), than there are no good arguments with only basic statements as premises and universal statements as conclusions. But one can provide valid deductive arguments *against* universal statements. One can thus (albeit fallibly, since basic statements are not themselves infallible) find out that theories are wrong. By the elimination of error our knowledge can, in this Pickwickian sense, grow.

Notice that even if Popper's insistence that scientific theories be logically falsifiable were not plagued by the difficulties to be discussed soon, this so-called solution to the problem of induction would be profoundly unsatisfactory. Only the fallacy of elimination enables one to find theory T meritorious merely because an alternative theory, T′, has been refuted. The logical conclusion, although clothed in soothing words about how rational the procedure is (for example, 1972, pp. 22, 27, 58, 81, 95), is a skepticism that is as extreme as Hume's, for Popper explicitly denies that there is any room for argument in support of any theory or law. He writes, for example, "that in spite of the 'rationality' of choosing the best-tested theory as a basis of action, this choice is *not* 'rational' in the sense that it is based upon *good reasons* for expecting that it will in practice be a successful choice; *there can be no good reasons* in this sense, and this is precisely Hume's result," (1972, p. 22). We have no better reason to expect that the predictions of well-tested theories will be correct than to expect that completely untested theories will predict correctly.

But this purported solution to the problem of induction falsely presupposes that individual scientific statements, or at least individual scientific *theories,* are falsifiable. Statistical and probabilistic claims are obviously not logically falsifiable. Even flipping a million heads in a row does not logically falsify the claim that a particular coin is unbiased. Even more seriously, all claims that cannot be tested *individually* are not logically falsifiable. For if a sentence is not, *by itself,* inconsistent with some finite set of basic statements, then it is not logically falsifiable. And the fact is that virtually no scientific claims of any interest are *by themselves* inconsistent with basic statements. To falsify even an utterly simple scientific claim, such as Galileo's law of falling bodies, requires not only basic statements, but also some nonbasic statements concerning whether nongravitational forces are present. If individual statements can be regarded as scientific only if they are logically falsifiable, it will turn out that almost all interesting science is not science after all.

Although Popper talks constantly of the falsifiability of scientific theories, he nevertheless knows all this; and he has discussed at length not only the role of background knowledge in testing, but also the sort of "conventionalist stratagems" one might employ to shield theories from falsification. Sometimes he seems to forget what he knows, as, for example, when he mistakenly argues against Lakatos that the observation of a dancing tea cup would, by itself, falsify Newton's theory of motion and gravitation (1974, p. 1005).[5] But he does have an answer to this criticism. His answer is that *logical falsifiability is not a criterion that scientific statements or even whole scientific theories have to satisfy individually*. What distinguishes scientific theories from nonscientific theories is that the whole systems of scientific theories, auxiliary assumptions, and statements of initial conditions created to derive predictions are falsifiable (1983, p. 187). Logical falsifiability enters when one concludes that the experimental results conflict with what was predicted on the basis of a conglomerate, including the particular theory under test. Let us call such conglomerates, which will often be mammoth, "test systems." Galileo's law of falling bodies is not itself logically falsifiable, but conjoined with claims about resistance and friction, it forms a falsifiable test system.

Although there is no mistake in demanding logical falsifiability of test systems, there are nevertheless three things wrong with the proposal that to be scientific, a theory need only be incorporated or incorporable into logically falsifiable test systems. First, logical falsifiability turns out to play only a minute role in the actual process of theory rejection or revision.[6] The fact that a theory is part of a logically falsifiable test system enables the further methodological rules that guide the scientist to get some grip, but logical falsifiability itself becomes merely an uninteresting necessary condition. Furthermore, although this necessary condition that theories be part of logically falsifiable test systems may have escaped the crude, early attempts of the logical positivists to capture the logic of science, it is an undisputed truism.

The second thing wrong with Popper's restriction of the requirement of logical falsifiability to test systems is that it no longer functions as a plausible criterion of demarcation. Freud's psychological theories are

---

[5] Watkins (1984, p. 326) also notices Popper's blunder here. Popper says that the observation report would falsify the theory if we ignore the possibility of immunizing stratagems. But it is not just the observation report that falsifies the theory. We also need the knowledge that the other explanations of the predictive failure are in fact merely immunizing stratagems.

[6] Zahar's proposed phenomenological reconstrual of basic statements (1983, pp. 156–61) and of logical falsifiability would only underscore how small a role logical falsification plays in the process of theory revision. Popper disputes this claim, which was emphasized by Duhem (1954, p. 187), by arguing that H2 might entail $\sim P$, whereas H1 entails P when H1 and H2 are conjoined to a common set of additional premises, S. But even in such a case, $\sim H2$ does not, of course, follow deductively from our acceptance of P as a true basic statement. We still need to decide (for whatever reasons) to regard the members of S as true. See Grunbaum (1976, pp. 248–50) and footnote 15.

not unfalsifiable in this sense. On the contrary, analysts and amateurs alike are constantly deriving predictions about how people will talk and act from Freudian theory and a wealth of other assumptions. The problem is not that these predictions (and thus the test systems from which they are derived) are never inconsistent with sets of basic statements. The problem with Freud's theories (if there is one) is rather (as Popper himself notes[7]) that the logical falsifications are not taken by analysts as evidence against the theories. The mistake is always taken to lie elsewhere. Astrologers, similarly, constantly make predictions that can conflict with basic statements. Since astrological theory is best interpreted as a statistical theory, these predictions are not deductive consequences of astrological theory and the various other premises. But, as Popper himself points out (1968, pp. 198–205), by adding methodological rules specifying the permissible range of disagreement between measured values and probabilistic predictions, one can deduce predictions that can be inconsistent with sets of basic statements. The problem, once again, is not that there are no logically falsifiable astrological test systems. The problem is rather that astrologers refuse to take failures of their predictions as casting doubt on astrology. As a criterion of demarcation, logical falsifiability applied to whole systems of theories is far too weak; little, if anything, will fail to count as science.

The third difficulty with the claim that only whole conglomerates need be logically falsifiable is that its negation is presupposed by Popper's purported solution to the problem of induction. Since individual scientific theories need not be falsifiable, Popper must concede that there is no logical asymmetry between the verifiability and falsifiability of particular scientific *theories:* They are *neither* (logically) verifiable *nor* (logically) falsifiable. And thus, there is no longer any semblance of a solution to the problem of induction. Accepted basic statements and deductive logic can get one to the falsity of whole test systems and no further. There is never a shred of evidence for *or against* any particular statements or theories. As we shall see later, Popper explicitly allows that we can also make use of what he calls "background knowledge" to achieve falsifications, but in this section I have been concerned exclusively with logical falsifiability.

Whether taken as a condition on individual scientific claims or as a condition that applies only to test systems, logical falsifiability and the logical asymmetry between falsification and verification should be of little interest to philosophers of science or economic methodologists. Few theoretical claims in economics are, by themselves, logically falsifiable, but

---

[7] "But what kind of clinical responses would refute to the satisfaction of the analyst not merely a particular analytic diagnosis but psycho-analysis itself?" (1963, p. 38n)

the same goes for science as a whole. And I know of no economic theories that cannot enter into logically falsifiable test systems (which would, of course, include specifications of statistical techniques and *ceteris paribus* clauses in addition to theories from economics and from other domains). Popper's claims about the asymmetry of logical falsifiability and logical verifiability (of whole test systems) are as correct as they are irrelevant. They provide no solution to the problem of induction.

2. Falsificationism as a methodology – a set of norms that should govern the behavior of scientists

So, let us move on to a notion of falsification that is of interest and importance to philosophers of science and economic methodologists. Popper has always recognized and stressed that methodology is concerned with rules, not simply with logic. Indeed, as previously documented, he sometimes maintains that what distinguishes sciences from nonsciences is not logical falsifiability, but the norms and behavior of scientists.

Conceived of as a methodology, Popper's falsificationism consists in outline of three simple rules addressed to the scientist: (1) Propose and consider only testable or falsifiable theories; (2) seek only to falsify scientific theories; (3) accept theories that withstand attempts to falsify them as worthy of further critical discussion, never as certain or even as probably true or close to the truth.

In somewhat more detail these rules can be restated as follows:

1. Although untestable theories may be suggestive and useful for theory generation, consider as candidates for scientific knowledge only theories that may be subjected to hard tests. A hard test is a test that a theory not only could fail but, moreover, a test that, given background knowledge or the alternatives, one should expect the theory to fail. Prefer theories with much content and many possibilities for falsification.

2. Scientists should, at least collectively, have a critical attitude; they should try to falsify existing theories, not to support or confirm them. This attitude requires, in particular, three things: First, scientists must look for harsh tests of existing scientific theories. In order to do so, they must, second, accept both some basic and nonbasic statements as true, at least for the purposes of testing. Otherwise there would be no way to falsify anything apart from whole test systems. In other inquiries, they can (and should) test their presuppositions, although these further tests will have their own further presuppositions. Finally, when a theory fails a test and scientists cannot find a reasonable excuse, they must reject the theory and look for an alternative. A reasonable excuse is at least an

excuse that can itself be readily tested. A scientist might, for example, question whether a particular instrument was operating properly. There is no simple algorithm stating when it is unreasonable to make further reasonable excuses, but provided that one is seeking to falsify rather than to hold on to theories, no algorithm is needed.[8]

3. If a theory has not yet been falsified, scientists should accept it tentatively. Theories that have survived harsh testing are not better supported or more worthy of belief than are theories that have not been tested at all. They are merely particularly difficult to falsify and worth testing further. "The theoretician's choice," in Popper's view, "is the hypothesis most worthy of *further critical discussion* (rather than *acceptance*)" (1963, p. 218n). Although Popper argues that there may be evidence that one theory has more true and fewer false consequences than another (1972, pp. 58, 81–2; 265), there is never, in his view, any good evidence that a law or a theory is correct or even close to correct.

> What we do – or should do – is to *hold on, for the time being, to the most improbable of the surviving theories* or, more precisely, to the one that can be most severely tested. We tentatively *"accept"* this theory – but only in the sense that we select it as worthy to be subjected to further criticism, and to the severest tests we can design.[9] (1968, p. 419)

Are these good rules of procedure for scientists to follow? The answer presumably depends on what the objectives of scientists should be. And therein lies a long and tangled story, which we had better avoid here. In order to keep this chapter short and focused on Popper's views, I shall not argue that these are in fact bad rules. Instead I shall merely show that Popper has not provided any good arguments in their defense. Given their implausibility, this demonstration of their lack of justification should be a sufficient criticism.

One can, at least in outline, grant the first rule, that proposed scien-

---

[8] This requirement, like the last, is not so much a requirement of each individual scientist as it is of the institution of science as a whole (1969, p. 112; but see 1972, p. 266). Provided that there is open and free communication, the institution as a whole may be critical, even though each individual scientist attempts to protect his on her own theory from criticism.

[9] Popper chides Lakatos (1974, p. 1003) for, in effect, ignoring the sentence that follows: "On the positive side, we may be entitled to add that the surviving theory is the best theory – and the best tested theory – of which we know." But this last sentence changes nothing concerning what Popper takes corroboration and "acceptance" of scientific theories to be. Popper has, of course, a theory of verisimilitude that met with an unfortunate formal demise (Tichy, 1974). But regardless of formal vicissitudes, Popper has insisted that corroboration is no evidence of verisimilitude. In very special and limited circumstances we can justifiably maintain that one theory has greater verisimilitude than another, but there is never any justification for maintaining that a theory has high verisimilitude (1972, pp. 47ff).

tific theories be testable, that science seeks theories with much content and theories that can be tested harshly and in many ways. But apart from the important insistence on content, there is no news in any of these methodological rules. Inductivists have been saying these things since at least the seventeenth century (Grunbaum, 1976, pp. 217ff).

The second and third rules are less plausible. To claim that scientists should seek only to falsify theories, never to support them, and that they should never regard theories as anything more than conjectures that may be worthy of criticism is to make two apparently outrageous suggestions.[10] Why should anyone accept them? Popper offers four reasons. First, he maintains that confirming evidence is worthless, since "it is easy to obtain confirmations, or verifications, for nearly every theory – if we look for confirmations" (1963, p. 36). So it is a mistake to look for confirmations or to regard what one finds as really supporting or establishing any theory. But Popper is mistaken. Cheap confirmation is readily available; merely locating another instance of a generalization may be as easy as it is worthless. Good supporting evidence is, on the other hand, hard to obtain. Much of it comes from just the sort of harsh testing that Popper insists on (see Grunbaum, 1976, pp. 215–29).

Second, Popper argues that to seek confirmation or to believe that one has found quite a lot is to show a dogmatic attitude rather than the sort of open and critical attitude shown by those who seek falsifications (1963, pp. 49ff). But this is just name calling. Even someone devoted to giving evidence in support of a favorite theory need not be credulous, closed-minded, or dogmatic in doing so. And it is certainly not the case that a person seeking the solution to a problem, who is thus concerned *both* with confirming *and* with disconfirming evidence, automatically qualifies as a dogmatic, unscientific sort.

Third, Popper suggests that to seek supporting evidence or to regard scientific theories as sometimes well established rests on a view of scientific knowledge as infallible. Popper argues that the overthrow of Newtonian physics renders such a view completely untenable. But one can, of course, concede that human knowledge is fallible without denying that particular knowledge claims may be well supported.[11]

Popper's fourth argument for the injunction to seek to falsify theories and never to seek to support them rests on the thesis that it is impossible

[10] And indeed, Popper is unable to follow his own advice consistently, for he writes:
What we believe (rightly or wrongly) is not that Newton's theory of Einstein's theory is true, but that they are *good approximations* to the truth, though capable of being superseded by a better one.
But this belief, I assert, *is* rational. (1983, p. 57).
[11] And Isaac Levi (1980) has even argued that one can regard one's knowledge as *in*fallible, without regarding it as as incorrigible.

for evidence to support scientific theories. Scientific theories simply *cannot* be confirmed, so it is obviously a mistake to attempt to do so. Popper says bluntly, "there *are* no such things as good positive reasons; nor do we need such things" (1974, p. 1043). There is no such thing as supporting evidence.[12] This argument may appear to be inconsistent with the claim that supporting evidence is easy to obtain. But there is no real contradiction here. In Popper's view, evidence that *truly provides* a positive reason for accepting a scientific claim cannot be had, whereas evidence that inductivists *mistakenly take to support* scientific theories is easy to obtain.

It would be foolish to attempt to find evidence in support of scientific theories if such evidence were completely unattainable. But why believe that one *never* has good reason to accept any scientific claims or that one *never* has good reason to believe that some claims are more likely to pass future tests than others? Popper makes just these assertions.

What convinces Popper that we can never have evidence in support of scientific claims is the problem of induction. There are no good arguments with only basic statements as premises and scientific laws and theories as conclusions. So there is no supporting evidence, no sense in seeking it, and no sense in believing that one has found it. In Popper's view, it remains rational to seek to falsify and to criticize scientific theories, because such theories are falsifiable: There are good arguments against them.

But this argument restates Popper's solution to the problem of induction, which in turn depends on the mistaken view, explicitly denied by Popper, that individual laws and theories in science are falsifiable. So this argument derives its specious plausibility from Popper playing fast and loose with what it is that is supposed to be falsifiable. If the problem of induction gave one good reason not to seek confirming evidence, it would also give one good reason not to seek falsifying evidence.

But Popper introduces a complication that needs to be examined with care. For he stresses that for the purpose of testing, it is entirely legitimate to make further decisions to take nonbasic statements as unproblematic background knowledge. Given these further decisions, it becomes possible to falsify specific scientific theories.

To avoid possible confusion let us call falsifications that not only

---

[12] There are, however, some verbal difficulties here, since Popper offers an explicit analysis of what it is for evidence to support a theory (see esp. 1983, pp. 236ff). This is not a contradiction, however, for in the Popperian sense in which evidence "supports" or "corroborates" theories, it gives one no reason to believe that the theory is true or close to the truth and no reason to believe that the theory will pass any future tests. Evidence that supports or corroborates theories in Popper's sense does not support theories.

depend on basic statements and deductive logic but that require decisions to regard portions of a test system as background knowledge "conventional falsifications," as opposed to logical falsifications that depend only on logic and basic statements.[13] Perhaps Popper's solution to the problem of induction (and the methodological injunctions that depend on this purported solution) can be saved if we interpret Popper as arguing that there is an asymmetry of conventional falsification that enables us to provide good arguments against scientific theories even though no good arguments can be provided for them. The premises in such arguments would not, of course, be restricted to basic statements. Background knowledge must be allowed in as well.

But there is no asymmetry of *conventional* falsification and verification. There are two ways to establish this claim. Others have argued that if we cannot verify statements, we do not have enough premises to get beyond mere logical falsification of whole test system conglomerates – if we can get even that far (Lieberson, 1982b). In answer to this criticism, Popperians maintain that decisions will do in place of verifications (Watkins, 1984). In response, one can point out (correctly, in my view) that arbitrary decisions will not do. We need to consider how well confirmed different statements are. Popperians implausibly (in my view) dispute this claim.[14] But I shall not pursue this line of argument. Regardless of

[13] These labels may be somewhat misleading. Remember that our tentative acceptance of some basic statements as true is just as conventional as our decision to regard nonbasic statements as background knowledge.

[14] In actual scientific practice, the bulk of the premises needed to derive the refuted implication are regarded as well established and either true or good approximations to the truth. This judgment may change, of course, but it is crucial to the interpretation of experimental failures. If, for example, someone reports experimental results showing that particular objects fell toward the earth with decreasing acceleration, physicists would, of course, conclude that there was some experimental error or that other forces besides gravity were involved. This conclusion, obviously (unless one is a Popperian), is based on the judgment that Galileo's law of falling bodies is a good approximation to the truth. If this judgment is unsupportable, as Popper alleges, science proceeds irrationally and should be replaced by a rational Popperian science.

It is, perhaps, possible to describe a completely noninductive enterprise (see Watkins 1984). In deciding what to do in light of the failure of a prediction of a whole theoretical system, one might be guided entirely by consideration of which revisions are maximally content increasing, least ad hoc, etc. Questions about how well supported the various constituents of the system are might conceivably play no role. But such an enterprise is radically unlike science, and, indeed, Popper is hesitant in presenting it. Zahar (1983, p. 168) quotes the following passages from Popper (1979) (written in 1930–31), which illustrate vividly Popper's early hesitance.

We unquestionably believe in the probability of hypotheses. And what is more significant: our belief that many a hypothesis is more probable than others is motivated by reasons which undeniably possess an objective character (*Grunde, denen ein objecktiver Zug nicht abgesprochen werden kann*). (1979, p. 145)

The subjective belief in the probability [of hypotheses] can be based on their corroboration, but it goes beyond what corroboration can effectively do. This belief

the basis upon which the decisions are made, only decisions to take other statements as premises in refuting arguments make it possible to falsify particular scientific theories and claims.[15]

What I shall argue instead is that if it is permissible to enlarge the set of permissible premises to include background knowledge in order to make conventional falsifications possible, one also makes conventional verifications possible. Given the background knowledge that scientists employ, there may be no more difficulty in verifying universal statements than there is in falsifying them.

Consider, for example, a scientist attempting to determine the spectrum of a newly discovered metallic element (Nisbett and Thagard, 1982). The scientist already knows that the spectrum of an element is invariant in particular ways from pure sample to sample. Given (1) this background knowledge, (2) the report of a particular Bunsen burner's flame turning orange, and (3) the claim that the particular sample was pure, the scientist can *deduce* that all pure samples of the element will turn a Bunsen burner's flame orange. So conventional verifications are no more impossible than are conventional falsifications. Straightforward probabilistic arguments can, of course, also be made. Given background knowledge in addition to basic statements, one can thus provide good

assumes that a corroborated hypothesis will be corroborated again. It is clear that without this belief we could not act and hence that we could not live either. There is in this belief nothing further which should intrigue us. Its objective motives are clarified by the notion of corroboration to such an extent that this belief should not give rise to the deployment of any further epistemological questions. (Ibid., p. 155)

In his better-known discussions in English, Popper states that in the course of testing, scientists do and should take various propositions to be unproblematic background knowledge, although this background knowledge may itself be regarded as problematic in other inquiries. "There is first the layered structure of our theories – the layers of depth, of universality, and of precision. This structure allows us to distinguish between more risky or exposed parts of our theory, and other parts which we may – *comparatively speaking* – take for granted in testing an exposed hypothesis" (1983, p. 188). There is perhaps no formal contradiction here, since Popper could maintain that decisions to take propositions as part of background knowledge are unaffected by any judgment of how well supported the propositions are. But without an illegitimate whiff of inductivism, this is an odd way to talk.

[15] Popper (1957, p. 132) and some of his followers (e.g., Zahar, 1983, pp. 155ff) suggest a method for making such decisions, which might appear to do away with the need for such decisions after all. Suppose the conjunction (S and U) has been logically falsified. The problem is to determine which is the culprit. If (S and U'), (S and U''), (S and U'''), etc., are all not logically falsified, whereas at least one of (S' and U), (S'' and U), (S''' and U), etc., is, we may conclude that U is the culprit, not S. As Glymour (1980, pp. 34–5) has pointed out, this suggestion faces serious formal difficulties. But the crucial point for my purposes is that this suggestion in no way obviates the need to rely on background knowledge. Indeed, what is happening here is that the failure to falsify (S and U'), (S and U''), (S and U'''), etc., is being used to provide an unacknowledged inductive justification for S, so that we can take the logical falsification of (S and U) as a falsification of U.

arguments for as well as against universal statements. There is, of course, no claim to incorrigibility in pointing to such possibilities of verification, and one need be no more dogmatic in offering such arguments than one is when one relies on basic statements and background knowledge to falsify scientific claims. Notice that the possibility of providing such arguments is entirely independent of the question of whether there exists any sort of inductive logic, in the sense of a rational procedure according to which the acceptance of basic statements might justify the acceptance of nonbasic statements.

So Popper has provided no good arguments for his implausible second and third methodological rules. He has not shown that one should not seek evidence in support of scientific theories, and he has not shown that one should never regard scientific theories as well established. And, indeed, there are no good arguments for these injunctions, for they are mistaken. It is sensible to regard theories that have been extremely well tested and have passed those tests as close to the truth, and as admissible into the background knowledge that we rely upon in developing and testing new theories – just as it is sensible to regard such theories as a reliable basis for engineering purposes. In learning more, we are stuck on Neurath's boat, and as it becomes more seaworthy, we can repair it better.

3.   Further comments on induction, falsification, and verification

Popper believes he had solved the problem of induction almost sixty years ago, and he is not reticent about saying so (1963, p. 55; 1972, pp. 1–2). In a 1980 Addendum to the *Postscript to the Logic of Scientific Discovery* he writes:

> When I first wrote this section, I did not lay much stress upon the refutation of the historical myth that Newton's theory is the result of induction, because I thought that I had destroyed the theory of induction twenty years earlier; and I was enough of an optimist to believe that all the resistance still emanating from the defenders of induction would soon disappear. . . .

> Since then, inductivists have taken some heart; partly because I have no longer replied to their arguments, which were all clearly refuted in various parts of my earlier writings. I no longer replied to them because I thought, and still think, that the issue was long settled and therefore boring. (1983, p. 147)

At the risk of boring Popper further, let me return to the problem of induction. For the issues are central not only in Popper's philosophy of science but in most accounts of the nature of science.

Hume's problem of induction follows from the combination of (1) his *empiricism,* which limits the evidence that can support or disconfirm statements to reports of sensory experiences and which treats reports of sensory experiences as self-justified, justified somehow by the experiences themselves, or as not needing justification and of (2) his *foundationalism,* which stipulates that a statement is justified only if it is self-justified or follows from self-justified statements by means of a good argument. It seems to me that, put together, empiricism and foundationalism create an insoluble problem of induction. But the proper reaction is not to conclude that all generalizations are equally unsupported. The proper reaction, rather, is to recognize that the piecemeal, nonfoundational justification of generalizations relative to what one regards as unproblematic background knowledge differs drastically from generalization to generalization and that this piecemeal "internal" justification is what matters in both science and practice. As Isaac Levi has rightly stressed, justification plays its part in responding to specific challenges to parts of our body of knowledge and in changing our body of knowledge (1980; compare Williams, 1977, and Popper, 1963, p. 228).

Popper almost grants the point. For he recognizes and stresses that human knowledge does not rest on any epistemically privileged foundations. Even basic statements are not certain. We decide to accept them, even though such decisions may lead us astray. And our decisions do not stop there. The way that we advance beyond the uninformative logical falsification of a whole test system is to *decide* to take a large portion of the system as background knowledge and to attribute the failure or error to the remaining part. In doing so, one may err, but without doing so, one cannot learn anything.

We must go beyond merely logical falsification, and if we want science to grow rationally, we need a rational basis for deciding what statements to take to be true in order to test others. Popper denies that the extent to which a hypothesis is "corroborated" by the data ever provides such a basis. We may take various claims to be part of background knowledge, but we never have any good reason to believe that they are true. But as we have seen, either this claim is part of a complete skepticism about empirical knowledge, or it is unjustifiable.

This question of whether we can rely on what we think we have established in learning more about the world goes to the heart of traditional discussions of economic methodology, which have been dominated by what Professor Klant calls "empirical a priorism." Nassau Senior, John Stuart Mill, John Neville Keynes, and Lionel Robbins all emphasize that basic axioms of economic theory–claims such as "Agents prefer more commodities to fewer"[16]–are well established by everyday experience, including introspection. In using them in economic theorizing, one employs what Mill called the "deductive method" (see

---

[16] The example would, of course, have to be changed for the classical economists.

Hausman 1981b). The economist takes the axioms as already well established and explores their implications deductively. In doing so, he or she provides positive reasons to accept the derived conclusions. Testing the deductive conclusions is important to determine whether one has left out some relevant factor, not to determine whether the axioms or their deductive implications are correct.

So, for example, the strongest argument for the hypothesis of rational expectations is surely not that it survives hard tests, but that it seems to follow from the axioms of neoclassical theory, once one accepts the claim that knowledge is, from an economic perspective, a commodity like any other. Consider the famous argument that John Muth offered:

> . . . I should like to suggest that expectations, since they are informed predictions of future events, are essentially the same as the predictions of the relevant economic theory. . . .
> If the prediction of the theory were substantially better than the expectations of the firms, then there would be opportunities for the "insider" to profit from the knowledge – by inventory speculation if possible, by operating a firm, or by selling a price forecasting service to the firms. The profit opportunities would no longer exist if the aggregate expectation of the firms is the same as the prediction of the theory. (1961, pp. 316, 318)

This argument can be reformulated as deductively valid – that is, as an argument whose conclusion must be true if its premises all are true (see Hausman, 1988). The conclusion here is the generalization that, *ceteris paribus*, the expectations of firms "are essentially the same as the predictions of the relevant economic theory." Some of the largely implicit premises, such as that few firms run by economists make extraordinary profits or that the expectations of some firms are informed by and coincide with the predictions of economic theory, are roughly reports of observations. But also involved in the argument are premises concerning the advantages of accurate expectations and the accuracy of the predictions of economic theory, which are very far from being reports of observations. Some of these premises are questionable and have been questioned; and I do not maintain that the premises are all true and that the argument is thus sound. But whether or not the argument is sound, it is still valid, and the premises are largely contained within the background knowledge of a neoclassical economist. If one permits scientists to make use of background knowledge – as one must if there is to be any science at all – then there are some valid arguments with acceptable premises for the truth of general scientific conclusions.[17]

---

[17] McCloskey's (1986) interesting discussion of the sense in which it is metaphorical to claim that knowledge is a commodity may thus contribute little to understanding why many economists accept the hypothesis of rational expectations without waiting for experimental confirmation.

If one surrenders foundationalism and regards conventional falsifications and verifications as acceptable arguments, one has immediately a partial non-Popperian solution to the problem of induction. Note that this solution turns crucially on its reformulation and on changing what one takes justification to be, as well as what one expects of a justification. For Hume would not, of course, permit us to help ourselves to the premises in the preceding argument that are not reports of perceptions. But without a foundationalist epistemology, there is no good reason even for an empiricist to insist that the premises can only be basic statements or, more stringently still, reports of sensory experiences. Popper correctly notes that epistemology should be concerned with *changes* in our body of knowledge. But his proposed solution to the problem of induction is a step backward toward the foundationalism that he rejects. Falsifications in the significant conventional sense depend not only on results of observations, but on many other statements that scientists take to be true. And the same expanded set of premises permits verifications as well.

4.   Conclusion and applications to economic methodology

Even if Popper's rules for scientific procedure were free of the difficulties discussed previously, they would be of little or no value to economists. For within Popper's philosophy of science, there are no interesting questions to be asked concerning the falsifiability of economic theory (or of any other theory). Are economic theories logically falsifiable by themselves? No, of course not, but neither are any interesting theories in science. Can economic theories be incorporated into logically falsifiable test systems? Yes, of course they can, but the same goes for theories of practically all disciplines, no matter how patently unscientific they may appear to be. Can one take the other statements in such test systems to be background knowledge and regard economic theories as conventionally falsifiable? It all depends on whether the other statements have been falsified and thus, ultimately, on whether one can decide to take still other statements to be background knowledge. Such decisions are, in Popper's view, more or less arbitrary. If one wants to, there is little difficulty in taking any statement to be conventionally falsifiable.

So, if one is concerned about whether economic theory is falsifiable, as many economists have been, what question is one asking? Once one leaves Popper's frame of reference, the answer is simple. Economists have wanted to know whether one could come, as the result of experiment or observation, to have *good reason* to believe that economic theories are false and mistaken. A necessary condition is that it be possible to incorporate such theories into logically falsifiable test systems. What is needed, in addition, is that one have good reason to believe that the other statements in such test statements are true or close to the truth. But, according to Popper, one never has such good reason. One can never justify the decision to regard a claim as a part of background knowledge on the grounds of its confirmation or corroboration (Lieberson, 1982b). Consequently, within Popper's philosophy of science, there is no way to capture the questions economists ask concerning the falsifiability of their theories.

I should note parenthetically that although it might be reasonable to demand such a non-Popperian falsifiability of scientific theories, it is still not reasonable to seek falsifications only and unflinchingly to discard falsified theories. As I have argued before (Hausman, 1985), virtually all of the fundamental "laws" and theories of economics have been falsified. For, as commonly stated, claims such as "All firms attempt to maximize profits" or "The preferences of individuals are transitive" are false (Hausman, 1981a, chs. 6, 7). If one insisted that science consists only of falsifiable but unfalsified claims, either one would have to regard economic theory as a simple empirical failure or one could give it a conventionalist twist and regard it as an unfalsifiable metaphysical theory that might be of use in the development of empirical theories.[18] Although Popper does not explicitly say so, in his discussion of "the logic of the situation" he seems inclined to the latter view (Hands, 1985). Even though one might still find economics of value as useful metaphysics, the costs of such an interpretation are considerable. For on such a view, there are no empirical discriminations to be drawn between neoclassical economics and other approaches (unless, unlike neoclassical economics, some of the other approaches actually qualify as scientific), nor can one discriminate among propositions of neoclassical theory in terms of the extent to which they are supported by the evidence.

The most prominent economic methodologists who have defended parts of the Popperian gospel – and these are major figures such as Klant, Blaug (1980), and Hutchison (1977, 1978) – have been unwilling to draw such drastic conclusions, for they are too sensible and too knowledgeable about economics. Rather than defending extreme and indefensible views, they have simply argued for the importance of criticism and of empirical testing. In doing so, they have certainly not done the profes-

---

[18] It might be suggested that economic theory remains of normative importance even though of no positive merit. But norms concerning what one ought to do must be based in part on positive theories of what will happen if . . .

sion harm. Indeed, in their emphasis on the importance of testing in science, they may have done some significant good.

But to base one's advice on a mistaken philosophical doctrine, even when that doctrine has some true and uplifting things to say, is a dangerous practice that should stop. Some of Popper's general slogans can be retained, for they are consistent with the reasoned consensus within the philosophy of science. Empirical criticism is important to science, and scientific theories must, however indirectly, be open to criticism that uses the results of observations and experiments. The most important evidence in support of scientific theories comes from hard tests and analogous remarkable explanatory achievements, not from adding up unimportant favorable instances. Scientific knowledge is corrigible, and we may be led to surrender even the most important and best established theories. All of these Popperian (and equally, non-Popperian) theses may be retained and used to criticize quacks and irresponsible proponents of ill-founded and unsupported theories. But once nonphilosophers tie themselves to a philosophical system such as Popper's, they will be trapped with the unhelpful and even absurd consequences of such a system. A greater measure of philosophical agnosticism among economic methodologists would be more sensible.

If one takes Popper's methodology for science seriously, its flaws both from the perspective of knowledge acquisition and from the perspective of error avoidance are dramatic. Decisions about what to regard as unproblematic background knowledge must depend on the evidence. Just as we want theories to be well supported when we rely on them to build bridges or to manage inflation, so we want the theories we use to test other theories to be well supported. Without knowledge of the degree to which various claims about the world are supported by the evidence, scientists are as unable to engage in intelligent testing as engineers are unable to make practical use of the results of science. We need confirmations in order to decide which theories to use in practice and to decide which theories to rely on when testing others. And, as I have shown, we can have confirmations, too, although I do not pretend to understand all their complexities.

But one might object that this critique of Popper is really just semantics. It all comes down to the same thing. Are not the decisions Popper would have us make to take some things as true in order to test others motivated in fact by just the considerations of confirmation, whose necessity I have been stressing? Popper prefers his language because he wants to stress the absence of foundations and the consequent necessity of choice, with its complexities and uncertainties. But perhaps the disagreement is only one of language. He writes, for example, "the decision to ascribe the refutation of a theory to any particular part of it amounts, indeed, to the adoption of a hypothesis; and the risk involved is precisely the same" (1983, p. 189). Perhaps Popper is only denying that we can have foundational justifications for our claims.

I wish there were such an easy reconciliation, but there is not. We not only cannot have foundational justifications; we cannot have foundational falsifications either, both because basic statements are not foundational and because they do not suffice to falsify significant individual claims in science. The relevant notion of falsification is conventional falsification, and at this level there is no sharp asymmetry between verification and falsification. To make his philosophy of science acceptable, Popper would have to start by conceding that both in theory and in practice we need to consider how well supported theories are by the evidence. But to make such a concession, Popper would have to surrender most of his characteristic theses. He would have to consider what induction is and how it is justified, rather than denying that it exists. He would have to reject falsificationism as an apt label for his views, for science would sensibly be devoted to seeking verifications as well as falsifications, although, of course, neither is incorrigible. Essential to Popper's life's work has been not just the bland message that scientists should be critical and should seek and take seriously disconfirming evidence, but the striking and mistaken message that there is nothing to scientific rationality except conjecture, evidentially unsupportable methodological decision making, and consequent refutation. I doubt that an enterprise that functioned according to Popper's methodology could exist. It would be a poor tool for acquiring knowledge and of no use in practice. I should also note that despite Lakatos's plea for a "whiff of inductivism," his so-called methodology of scientific research program is also vulnerable to the criticisms presented in the preceding discussion of induction.

References

Adorno, T., ed. (1969). *Der Positivismussstreit in der Deutschen Soziologie.* Darmstadt: Hermann Luchterhand Verlag.
Alchian, A. (1950). "Uncertainty, Evolution and Economic Theory." *Journal of Political Economy* 57:211–21.
Bar Hillel, Y. (1974). "Popper's Theory of Corroboration," in Schilpp (1974), pp. 332–48.
Blaug, M. (1980). *The Methodology of Economics; or How Economists Explain.* Cambridge: Cambridge University Press.
Boland, L. (1979). "A Critique of Friedman's Critics." *Journal of Economic Literature* 17:503–22.

Duhem, P. (1954). *The Aim and Structure of Physical Theory*. Princeton, N.J.: Princeton University Press.

Friedman, M. (1953). "The Methodology of Positive Economics" in *Essays in Positive Economics*. Chicago: University of Chicago Press, pp. 3–43.

Glymour, C. (1980). *Theory and Evidence*. Princeton N.J.: Princeton University Press.

Grunbaum, A. (1976). "Is Falsifiability the Touchstone of Scientific Rationality? Karl Popper versus Inductivism" in R. Cohen et al., eds., *Essays in Memory of Imre Lakatos*. Dordrecht: Reidel, pp. 213–52.

Hands, D. (1985). "Karl Popper and Economic Methodology." *Economics and Philosophy* 1:83–100.

Hausman, D. (1981a). *Capital, Profits and Prices: An Essay in the Philosophy of Economics*. New York: Columbia University Press.

(1981b). "John Stuart Mill's Philosophy of Economics." *Philosophy of Science* 48:363–85.

(1985). "Is Falsificationism Unpractised or Unpractisable?" *Philosophy of the Social Sciences* 15:313–19.

(1988). "Arbitrage Arguments." *Erkenntnis*.

Hutchison, T. (1977). *Knowledge and Ignorance in Economics*. Chicago: University of Chicago Press.

(1978). *On Revolutions and Progress and Economic Knowledge*. Cambridge: Cambridge University Press.

Klant, J. (1984). *The Rules of the Game*. Cambridge: Cambridge University Press.

Kuhn, T. (1970). *The Structure of Scientific Revolutions*, 2nd ed. Chicago: University of Chicago Press.

Lakatos, I. (1970). "Falsification and the Methodology of Scientific Research Programmes" in I. Lakatos and A. Musgrave, eds., *Criticism and the Growth of Knowledge*. Cambridge: Cambridge University Press, pp. 91–96.

(1974). "Popper on Demarcation and Induction," in Schilpp (1974), pp. 241–73.

Laudan, L. (1976). *Progress and Its Problems*. Berkeley: University of California Press.

Levi, I. (1967). *Gambling with Truth*. Cambridge, Mass.: MIT Press.

(1980). *The Enterprise of Knowledge*. Cambridge, Mass.: MIT Press.

Levison, A. (1974). "Popper, Hume, and the Traditional Problem of Induction," in Schilpp (1974), pp. 322–31.

Lieberson, J. (1982a). "Karl Popper," *Social Research* 49:68–115.

(1982b) "The Romantic Rationalist," *New York Review of Books* 29 (December 2, 1982).

McCloskey, D. (1986). *The Rhetoric of Economics*. Madison: University of Wisconsin Press.

Miller, D. (1982). "Conjectural Knowledge: Popper's Solution to the Problem of Induction," in P. Levinson, ed., *In Pursuit of Truth: Essays on the Philosophy of Karl Popper on the Occasion of his 80th Birthday*. Atlantic Highlands, NJ.: Humanities Press, pp. 17–49.

Muth, J. (1961). "Rational Expectations and the Theory of Price Movements." *Econometrica* 29:315–35.

Nisbett, R., and Thagard, P. (1982). "Variability and Confirmation," *Philosophical Studies* 42:379–94.

Popper, K. (1957). *The Poverty of Historicism.* New York: Harper & Row.

(1963). *Conjectures and Refutations; The Growth of Scientific Knowledge.* London: Routledge & Kegan Paul.

(1968). *The Logic of Scientific Discovery,* rev. ed. London: Hutchinson & Co.

(1969). "Die Logik der Sozialwissenschaften," in Adorno (1969), pp. 103–23.

(1972). *Objective Knowledge; An Evolutionary Approach.* Oxford: Clarendon Press.

(1974). "Replies to My Critics," in Schilpp (1974), pp. 961–1200.

(1979). *Die Beiden Grundprobleme der Erkenntnistheorie.* Tubingen: Mohr-Siebeck.

(1983). *Realism and the Aim of Science; From the Postscript to the Logic of Scientific Discovery,* ed. W. Bartley III. Totowa, N.J.: Rowman and Littlefield.

Putnam, H. (1974). "The 'Corroboration' of Theories," in Schilpp (1974), pp. 221–40.

Salmon, W. (1981). "Rational Prediction." *British Journal for the Philosophy of Science* 32:115–25.

Settle, T. (1974). "Induction and Probability Unfused," in Schilpp (1974), pp. 697–749.

Tichy, P. (1974) "On Popper's Definition of Verisimilitude," *British Journal for the Philosophy of Science* 25:155–60.

Watkins, J. (1984). *Science and Scepticism.* Princeton, N.J.: Princeton University Press.

Williams, M. (1977). *Groundless Belief.* New Haven, Conn.: Yale University Press.

Zahar, E. (1983). "The Popper–Lakatos Controversy in the Light of 'Die Beiden Grundprobleme der Erkenntnistheorie.' " *British Journal for the Philosophy of Science* 34:149–74.

CHAPTER 2

The natural order

J.J. KLANT

Science and art

Do economic theories propound laws that describe how events occur, or do they contain rules showing how we must behave? It is an old question. In the nineteenth century, when economics was still called "political economy," the practitioners compromised by that name asked themselves: Are we occupied with a *science* teaching us how we do it or with an *art* teaching us how we must do it? In the introductory chapter of the book devoted to the principles of political economy, they often represented themselves as research scientists, curious about the way the world is made up. But anyone who read on could also discover how they designed a blueprint for changing the world.

Adam Smith had left no doubt about the latter. He too had come under the spell of the idea proclaimed by John Locke: The laws of nature do not really differ from the moral laws by which man should behave and society must be ordered. They both relate to the *natural order* desired by God. Smith, impressed by Descartes and Newton, regarded society expressly as one large mechanism, the operation of which can be explained by reasoning and observing with the aid of a small number of principles, but in line with ideas of Shaftesbury and his teacher Hutcheson, he also devoted attention to the world's beauty.

Smith devoted considerable attention not only to what happens in the world, but also to what has to be changed in that world for the sake of natural beauty. The principle of laisser-faire, which according to *philosophes* and physiocrats was part of the natural order, but had been incompletely realized in the positive order, was for Smith too a determinant of his "obvious and simple system of natural liberty," which at the same time was a *just* system (1976b, pp. 606, 687). And yet his natural liberty was not a fact, but a desideratum. Nature in the language of the moral philosophers is something quite different from the inescapable and immutable nature that was described for them so impressively in the laws of the experimental natural philosophers. It is an *ideal*.

This is a revised version of a contribution published previously in Dutch (Klant 1982). The author wishes to thank Trevor S. Preston for the translation.

However it might be presented, there is no escaping the fact that the ideal relates to *possible* human behavior. It is within the grasp of all who are prepared to heed its call, but it can also be neglected by them. There are not only ideals that we, as if motivated by an inner voice, try to live up to, but also *potential ideals,* in which fine results of behavior are held up to us that after careful consideration, we can decide to accept or not. Natural laws *describe* in the form of contingent statements, which are true or not true. They are logically subject to refutation by empirical research. Moral laws, on the other hand, *prescribe* in the form of pro-nouncements without truth value. They can be neither confirmed nor refuted by empirical research (Wright, 1963, p. 2).

Today we class the "natural" principles – prescriptions in accordance with which life is or may be lived – as *values.* They are something like *slogans* "capable of providing for the rationalization of action by encap-sulating a positive attitude towards a purportedly beneficial state of affairs" (Rescher, 1969, p. 9). The rules of art are dependent on values, for instance, on the slogan "long live natural liberty!" The natural order of the physiocrats and that of Smith are apparently what Karl Mannheim has called "orientations transcending reality." In his view they may be a *utopia,* namely, orientations "which, when they pass over into conduct, tend to shatter, either partially or wholly, the order of things prevailing at the time." They may also be free from such shattering tendencies. In that case they are an *ideology,* whether or not "congruent with reality" (1979, p. 173). However, in both cases an image is designed that func-tions as an ideal and thus comprises norms for action.

A natural order evident to thinking persons, utopian or ideological, is to be found in every classical economist. Jean-Baptiste Say, for exam-ple, proved desirous of expressly following the procedures of experimen-tal science, but nevertheless already gave himself away in his introduc-tion. Exactly like laws of nature, the general laws of the political and moral sciences proceed, according to Say, from the *nature of things.* We do not devise them, but find them. They rule those people who rule others and they are never violated with impunity. Like the philosophers of the natural order, Say is a victim of his own imagery. Laws of nature cannot be broken. It is possible that someone who ignores them breaks his neck, but anyone who, convinced of the immovable order of nature, proclaims how we must behave therein, is occupied with art. The rules described are not laws of nature. They relate to recommended behavior and are dependent – if you like, by virtue of divine inspiration and ra-tional insight – on what is considered desirable.

The law of gravitation cannot be violated by a single particle; rules of the road *can* be violated by people. Say warns that anyone who does not adhere to these rules may be run over. His advice in that case belongs to art, but the theory he applies regarding the rules that are followed also proves not to be free of the a priorism that gives shape to an order of which the evident naturalness must be recognized rationally. Despite his sincere endeavor to base his theory on facts, it proves to be derived from a number of *principles that require no proof* because everyone knows them (1972, p. 16).

Malthus too was not lacking in meddlesomeness, the basis of art. In the introduction to his *Principles of Political Economy* he states:

One of the specific objects of the present work is to prepare some of the most important *rules of political economy for practical application* [my emphasis], by a frequent reference to experience, and by endeavouring to take a comprehensive view of all the causes that concur in the production of particular phenomena. (1951, p. 16)

Incidentally, I gave the title of his book in abbreviated form. It reads further: *considered with a view to their practical application.*

David Ricardo, convinced as he was of the exemplariness of *his* natural order, was no less in his love of interference. He put into practice the twofold plan of his promoter, James Mill: publication of an economic work and – "following up the written into the spoken message" – proclamation of a new doctrine of political economy in Parliament (Hutchison, 1978, p. 27). He designed a highly abstract model of production and distribution that, in the absence of specific information, had little to do with reality. Nevertheless, it proved in that barren state to give him sufficient assurance to declare in the House of Commons, with reference to a petition by weavers who had become unemployed through mechanization:

Gentlemen ought . . . to inculcate this truth on the minds of the working classes – that the value of labour, like the value of other things, depended on the relative proportions of supply and demand. If the supply of labour were greater than could be employed, then the people must be miserable. But the people had the remedy in their own hands. A little forethought, a little prudence (which probably they would exert, if they were not made such machines of by the poor-laws), a little of that caution which the better educated felt necessary to use, would enable them to improve their situation. (1971, p. 303)

Ricardo described the laws of wages, rent, and profits by the logical analysis of a number of principles and did not require his theory to be tested. After all – as he wrote to John McCulloch when the latter had queried the truth of his revised theory regarding unemployment as a result of mechanization – that theory was "as demonstrable as any of the truths of geometry" (1973, p. 390). However, the result of his treatise resembled, in its form, a science of inescapable nature. Taking the laws into account, some things can be changed in the world, for instance by abolition of the corn laws and the poor laws, and by modification of farming methods in Ireland, but the poverty of today could have been prevented only by the poor of yesterday, namely, by their not reproducing themselves. The distressed weavers could draw the conclusion that, given the immovable order in which they lived, they might improve their personal fate, and thus that of the nation, only by hanging themselves. The rule of art that damned them apparently accorded with the values of the gentlemen who dined to the accompaniment of pleasant conversation at the King of Clubs, the Political Economy Club, and Holland House, and who liked to see account being taken of laws accepted by them, devised and "geometrically" demonstrated by an evidently sagacious, universally respected, well-to-do, and amiable man. Political economy was a science.

That science had been constructed by Ricardo in a very striking way from *idealizations*. However, that was not what was wrong with it. For no science at all can manage without "neglective fictions" (Cohen and Nagel, 1963, p. 371). "Analysis," as economists call their theoretical research, is based on considering matters in abstraction. In physics such abstractions are used by combining them with each other in order to establish resultants that describe concrete situations with sufficient accuracy. Tests and applications taking into account the complexity of reality, "disturbances," and the inaccuracy of observations are thus made possible. The method of decreasing abstraction is a first step in this direction. Here, however, Ricardo by no means led the way.

The real deficiency of Ricardo's method did not consist in the voids in which he let imaginary events occur, but in the fact that he did so little about adequately reconstructing the concrete events by subsequently filling the voids. Whereas Adam Smith, though rejecting political arithmetic, still makes an extensive call on historical experience, Ricardo seems to regard his theory as a means to prescription instead of description. On the basis of observations, Ricardo is more inclined to conclude that the facts are wrong than that his "science" is. For him idealization serves an ideal. It is not the means for ultimately arriving at reality – the positive order – but for constructing a natural order and vesting it with "scientific" authority.

John Stuart Mill made allowance for the abstract character of economic theories and therefore called them "hypothetical." In one of the essays he wrote in 1829–30 and published for the first time in 1844, he called political economy "the science which traces the laws of such of the phenomena of society as arise from the combined operations of mankind for the production of wealth, in so far as those phenomena are not modified by the pursuit of any other object" (1974, p. 140). The restriction contained in his definition even gave the unemployed a second chance, for evidently other goals might be pursued in society than were permitted in Ricardo's dismal science. According to Mill, distribution is open to change by structural interventions. The laws of production are inescapable, but those of distribution can be amended. In his opinion, science describes a world in which change must occur in accordance with ideals that are not expressed in the theory itself.

Incidentally, Mill seems to confront us with a paradox. In his *Logic* he makes a distinction between science and art:

The relation in which rules of art stand to doctrines of science may be thus characterized: The art proposes to itself an end to be attained, defines the end, and hands it over to science. The science receives it, considers it as a phenomenon or effect to be studied, and having investigated its causes and conditions, sends it back to art with a theorem of the combinations of circumstances by which it could be produced. Art then examines these combinations of circumstances and according as any of them are or are not in human power pronounces the end attainable or not. (1843, *Bk*. VI, ch. 12, sect. 2)

In its dealings with science art keeps a respectful distance, but in his definition of the science of political economy, Mill nevertheless reintroduces art.

For the "operations of mankind" spoken of in the definition relate to a "pursuit of objects." Economists postulate laws of behavior by assuming that individuals act in accordance with rules as they pursue their objectives. But this paradox too can be solved, like other ones, by making a distinction between object language and metalanguage. According to Mill, political economy is not an art but an investigation of the (possible) consequences of behavior in accordance with a certain art. In economics the agent acts as someone who aims at maximum net returns in order to satisfy wants, as a homo economicus, a protector of personal interests, and a hunter of profit. Since 1871 the agent has been a rational decider who weighs utility or neatly ranks preferences. Economics is not an art but examines art and, like every empirical science, yields pronouncements from which those who wish to practice art may learn how the objectives set by them can – or cannot – be attained.

The natural order, the ideal that inspires deeds, was, however, not yet banished therewith. Schumpeter has called the fundamental assumption on which neoclassical theory bases the description of the behavior of deciders, as sociologists also do, "*methodological individualism*" (1908, pp. 88–98). The explanation of economic events is based on the decisions and corresponding actions of separate individuals. It has nothing to do with democracy and suffrage, and the slogan laissez-faire is not implied in it either. Nevertheless, it demonstrates a similarity to the ancient natural order. It is a different view of the importance of every human being in society from that which proceeds from a holistic philosophy, which has its adherents among Marxists, historicists, and institutionalists. It can, of course, be presented, as Schumpeter in fact did, as a fundamental hypothesis that is justified by logical analysis and the outcome of empirical tests. But if testing is deficient – and that is the case in economics as a rule – the opposite may also apply: Methodological individualism will then contribute to justification of the theory, just as natural liberty once did.

The believer in the theory can try to advocate the *plausibility* of the fundamental assumption by, for instance, recalling that it is a fact that all individuals act and thus decide, but by doing so one does not demonstrate that this proposition contributes to a better explanation of events than, for example, the premise that individuals usually act without really deciding and that their behavior is in fact determined by institutions. If acceptance of that hypothesis cannot be decided on by intersubjective testing either, we are left with a choice that is partly dependent on extrascientific values, our view of humanity and society, and thus of what can be made of the world.

If empirical argumentation proves inadequate, it will, for that matter, not remain at such a simple choice. The decision to accept or reject a theory will then depend on a complex of properties thereof.

If a choice has to be made between theories on the basis of preferences and prejudices, the strict separation between science and art desired by Mill has little chance. A view of humanity taking action implies norms. The natural order, the preferred picture of society, is then not easy to eliminate, even by those who are all in favor of the practice of economic science. Science that examines the consequences of art does then, in any case, yield potential ideals.

The new natural order

That Locke's natural order did not disappear from economics with either the physiocrats or the classical economists is shown by the work of Léon Walras, who laid the foundations of contemporary neoclassical general equilibrium theory. He distinguishes between three forms of political economy. The first is that of pure political economy. To him this consists of a static theory in which transactions are assumed to be subject to an unspecified process of *tâtonnement* that leads to a general equilibrium, as represented by a number of equations relating to demand, production, and supply of goods and services. Prices are formed through perfect competition on interdependent markets of finished goods, productive services of labor, land, and capital, and of financial assets. The participants are fully informed about the prices that have come about and act in accordance with utility functions that are invariant during the process of tâtonnement.

Walras was aware that economic equilibrium does not occur in reality and that in the latter the conditions of his model are insufficiently satisfied: "the Walrasian attempt to explain the market system takes place in a *cognitive, motivational and institutional vacuum*" (Albert, 1979, p. 119). His proof of existence – at least the attempt to do so – is purely mathematical, namely, of a unique solution of his system of equations. But, like Quesnay and Smith, he wanted to reform the world in terms of his ideal. He investigated not out of pure curiosity, but in order to be able to use science (Boson, 1950, p. 106). In applied political economy he endeavored to examine how the ideal could be realized as much as possible. Disturbances of his desired system ought to be avoided and countered: "*la science étant definie l'idéalisation de la réalité; et l'art étant definie la réalisation de l'idéal*" (1936, p. 21; my emphasis). Science brings about an idealization, and art realizes the ideal. Idealization functions in Walras too as ideal.

To that end, the necessary inroads had to be made into the principle of laisser-faire. Walras advocated government intervention, such as control of money creation, protection of consumers and supervision of advertising, nationalization of businesses with increasing returns to scale, supervision of railways and freight rates, a ban on speculation on the stock exchange by other than well-informed specialists, and international labor legislation. He believed that it was not possible to leave all enterprises free. On the other hand, he considered it quite feasible to expropriate them all, for that would not be at variance with liberty, equality, order, and justice, if only the free market mechanism were to continue to exist. The operation thereof thus proves, in his opinion, to conform to the values of the French Revolution and his natural order allows of variants. Market socialism is a form of Walrasian nature. No wonder, therefore, that his general equilibrium theory could be applied in the theory of planned production and that Oskar Lange managed to combine Marxism with neoclassical microeconomics.

The reason Walras wanted to see the world organized in accordance with his pure theory was that, he believed, thanks to the perfect market mechanism, a maximum of utility is produced within certain limits, or, as he could have put it today, that, given the circumstances, an optimum situation is realized for each individual participant in the system. Everyone aims at maximum satisfaction of wants and achieves the best position compatible with that of the others. Because of some obiter dicta of Vilfredo Pareto on maximum collective ophelimity, we today call that imaginary state of affairs "Pareto-optimal" and a system of making its achievement possible "Pareto-efficient." The welfare of no single individual can be increased without at least one other individual suffering a setback as a result.

Walras was convinced that by demonstrating the efficiency of his potential ideal, he had supplied no proof of its justness. The Pareto-optimum defines an ideal called "efficiency," which is worth pursuing, but for the rest, it has no ethical effect. It depends on a number of boundary conditions, such as the distribution of property, that are open to change and then result in a different income distribution. Each distribution has a different optimum.

Walras wished to see the question of a just distribution posed in "social economics." His own contribution to this consisted principally in a plea for nationalization of land; in emulation of his father, Auguste Walras, and of Hermann Heinrich Gossen and John Stuart Mill (1926, pp. 267–80); and in agreement with the demands of the Communist Manifesto. He was an advocate of consumer and producer cooperatives, by which everyone would be a capitalist and a worker at the same time, firms would be democratized, and democracy would be activated. He called himself a "scientific socialist" in contradistinction to the Marxists, who took no account of the laws of supply and demand (1936, pp. 229–33). Perhaps for that reason he will one day be given a statue in Yugoslavia, Hungary, or China. His socialism was responsible for the rules he devised, taking into account the laws of the market mechanism, for realization of the ideals of efficiency and justice.

According to William Jaffé, Walras had much more drastic moralistic intentions with his pure theory (1977). Donald A. Walker has rightly disputed this interpretation (1984), but Walras's statement on the relation between science and reality is not affected by his criticism. Walker is of the opinion that Walras used the word *idéal* for "idealization" (1984, p. 452). However, that opinion is not supported in the cited statement. Walras considered art necessary to realize the ideal, and he therefore gave the word a normative connotation. As Jaffé mentions, Pareto was in any case not very taken with Walras's idealism. With reference to it, he wrote to Pantaleoni that he did not agree that pure theory demonstrates what the facts ought to be. He considered it inadmissible to study what ought to be instead of what is. In his publications too he evinced such empirical scientific intentions. In his opinion, pure science describes but does not prescribe.

However, our problem is not solved by uttering such good intentions. The thinkers may mean well, but the question of whether economics *is* science or art is not concerned with what the economists want, but with what they do and can do. Walras's example shows, in any case, that pure theory can be used to reform the world. It is a potential ideal, for economics is research into the consequences of art. The question remains of whether the theory that is then used is an *ideal* to live by, which may be embraced or rejected because it is regarded as attractive or not, can at the same time – as Pareto desired – be an indirectly tested *idealization,* such as Galileo's law describing free fall in a vacuum. And what is the art of which, it seems, both the applied and the social economics of Walras form part? Does it contain a description of economic policy, for which the politicians supply the objectives and the economists a description of the means and measures? Or is the art an "instrumental theory" based on further research because pure theory yields too little information?

The latter interpretation was proclaimed by Nassau William Senior. Upon assuming his chair at Oxford on 6 December 1826, he said that the science of political economy may be divided into two great branches, the theoretic and the practical (1966a, p. 7). A quarter of a century later, he came to speak again of his division into two branches in four lectures on the development and the nature of political economy, and he called practical political economy an art: "the art which points out the production and accumulation of wealth," or, more broadly: "most conducive to that production, accumulation, and distribution of wealth, which is most favourable to the happiness of mankind" (1966b, p. 36).

Senior's Ricardo-inspired a priorism, which leads to a Cartesian structure of the theory, is characteristic of the methodology of the classical and many neoclassical economists (Klant 1984, pp. 47–84). Senior's description of the theoretical branch of political economy thus recalls the natural order, which is assumed to be evident to anyone who reflects for a moment and examines himself and his surroundings. The practical branch, which he later calls "art," cannot manage without inductions with dubious conclusions. Is that not empirical science par excellence? Apparently the practical branch is science and art at the same time.

In political economy art and science seem to merge, despite Senior's attempt to separate them. Moreover, it seems very much as if pure theory, which describes the "natural state," functions not only as an idealization for explaining reality, but, as was to find unconcealed expression in Walras, also as an ideal for changing it. The rules of art, which can be made subservient to values other than those solely of efficiency, cannot, in Senior's view, be drawn up without further empirical research. Despite the geometric proofs of Ricardo, he believed, for instance, that it ought to be investigated whether the poor laws caused the population of England to increase or decrease (1966a, p. 9).

John Neville Keynes advocated a different division of work. He was in favor of an independent science, in which Senior's pure theory and the empirical part of his practical theory would be combined. However, in his view science was practiced for the sake of art, *la science pour l'art* (1963, p. 47). He made a distinction between positive science, normative science (ethics), and art (politics). The art that is the last aim of economists depends on the normative and the positive science. The division of work was for him a matter of expediency. The question of whether economics, in which it is assumed that people act in accordance with certain rules, *can* be practiced as a positive science without implying normative science – that is, without the conception of a natural order that represents the conditions that the world should satisfy – did not occur to him.

Nor was the question put in the article that Lujo Brentano published in 1896. He drew attention to the disunity among economists, which had increased in his day; they were governed by differing sociopolitical ideals and accused one another of servitude to pressure groups. The definition of a professor by Lorentz von Stein – "someone who is of a different opinion" – seemed to him precisely applicable to those occupying chairs of economics (1911, p. 45). In his opinion, the true science teaches firstly "what was and why it was so," secondly "what is," and thirdly affords clues for the future (1911, pp. 709–10). Not for nothing was he a member of the historical school.

Interpretation of history opens the possibility of a natural order that – as in Karl Marx – proceeds in time. However, Brentano is convinced that research necessarily leads to objective results if only the researcher is unbiased. He therewith describes a symptom of what I call the "St. Anthony syndrome." This occurs among industrious social researchers who, convinced of their virtuousness, believe that they can resist all temptations. In Brentano's opinion, they must be on their guard above all against themselves, for national circumstances, membership in a social class, family circumstances in which they grew up, and special individual interests and traditions summon up for every problem associations of ideas among the researchers that threaten to divert them from their purpose (1911, p. 699).

In so warning, Brentano is demanding something inhuman that is not even necessary for the attainment of scientific objectivity. The St. Anthony syndrome is curable. Without preferences and prejudices – if there is in fact a difference between the two – in other words, without ideals, no researcher can exist before, during, and after his or her work. The researcher's view of the world cannot be an empty one. *Der Mann ohne Eigenschaften* does not exist. "Do your research without bias" is therefore a piece of advice that will not lightly be given to natural scientists unless the intention is that, if they are to be able to maintain their theory successfully, they must make allowance for criticism. "To attain objectivity we cannot rely on the empty mind," writes Karl Popper; "objectivity rests on criticism, on critical discussion, and on the critical examination of experiments" (1975, p. 79). The objectivity of theories consists in the fact that they can be tested intersubjectively (1959, pp. 37–44). As a result, the suspicion arises that Brentano's requirement could proceed from the belief that it is possible for research scientists to resist all criticism if they stick to their ideals. The disputes between professors would then be impossible to resolve.

The value judgment conflict

Lujo Brentano was an adherent of German socialism of the chair. These academic socialists expressly rejected laissez-faire and had combined in 1872, under the leadership of Gustav Schmoller, to form the Verein für Sozialpolitik, whose aim was to disseminate the idea of social reform and state intervention so as to restrain the class struggle and avert the danger of revolution that had been summoned up by the advent of the Social Democrats.

According to Schmoller, it was wrong to derive economic laws of nature from human rules of behavior and to speak of a natural economic order (1873, p. 52). Nevertheless, the natural order in the sense of a social ideal was not alien to him, as evidenced by what he wrote about the association's points of departure. They set themselves the aim, he stated, to go into not only the natural technical causes but also the psychological ones. They assumed that an ethical process of development was going on. They believed in progress (1873, p. 65).

Progress manifested itself to Schmoller as the gradual realization of the principle of distributive justice. The ideal of a just income distribution is for him the leading idea of social reform (Gehrig, 1914, p. 197). *Otherwise than in the case of Walras*, however, his social economics is not based on the ideal of justice in combination with a pure theory, but with historical description in which, as befits the country of Hegel, the idea of justice being gradually realized is reflected.

The mix of ethics and science advocated by academic socialists like Gustav Schmoller, Adolph Wagner, and Georg Friedrich Knapp was opposed by a younger generation in the association, to which Max Weber, Werner Sombart, and Franz Eulenburg belonged. Weber, in an article published in 1904 on the objectivity of socioscientific and sociopolitical knowledge, in which a declaration of principle was made on behalf of the new editorial board of the Archiv für Sozialwissenschaft und Sozialpolitik, consisting of Weber, Sombart, and Edgar Jaffé, argued in favor of a positive science (1951, pp. 146–214). Five years later the value judgment conflict broke out in Vienna. Eugen von Philippovich, an adherent of the Austrian school and of *verstehende* historical research, described by his pupil Ludwig von Mises as a "Viennese Fabian" and by his pupil Joseph Schumpeter as "one of the greatest teachers of the period," had submitted to the annual congress of the association a lengthy paper. A contribution by Friedrich von Wieser was also discussed on that same afternoon.

To judge by the verbatim report, in which frequent mention is made of emotional utterances, the discussing company must have evinced convictions firmly rooted in an opposite sense of values. The influence of German philosophers was clear to see – as it indeed already had been in Weber's article. Those philosophers had since the end of the nineteenth century, through the intermediary of Hermann Lotze, come to recognize concepts such as "justice," "virtue," and "beauty" not only by their own nature but also by the intension of the set of "values." Risieri Frondizi, in his introduction to axiology, calls this a real discovery. Henceforth a fundamental distinction was made between *being* and *value* (1971, p. 3).

The influence of the philosophers was reflected in the fact that the ancient methodological problem was no longer discussed in terms of "science" and "art" but of "is" (*Sein*) and "ought" (*Sollen*). The latter term relates to norms, that is to say, to values, subdivided into "ought to be" (*Seinsollen*) and "ought to do" (*Tunsollen*). The assertion, expressible par excellence in an evaluative sentence in the indicative, that a value is being satisfied or not, or being satisfied more or less, is a *value judgment* or *statement of value*. The statement, expressible par excellence in the optative, by which a norm – that is, a *value* – is set, is not a judgment (a statement) but a *prescription,* wish, or injunction. Like a value judgment, it can be justified by having recourse to values. It is then a *hypothetical* prescription, that is, one based on values. If it is justified in itself, in other words with recourse to *intrinsic* value, it is a *categorical* prescription (Taylor, 1961, pp. 223–39). Prescriptions and value judgments are often wrongly identified with each other.

Werner Sombart, who had opened the attack on Philippovich, posed the problem and in doing so adopted, in his innocence, a positivistic point of view by declaring himself in favor of the exclusion of value judgments because they are not susceptible of proof and, in his opinion, are therefore not open to discussion. As long as scientific proof cannot be given that blondes or brunettes are prettier, he said, value judgments cannot be discussed (Verh., 1910, p. 572).

The most well-thought-out criticism came from Max Weber. He allied himself with Sombart. An empirical science, he said, is concerned with *Sein* and not with *Sollen*. He did not deny that formulations of problems depend on what we consider worth knowing, but that has nothing to do with the scientific discussion thereof. The question of whether such a scientific treatment exists or is capable of existence in economic research did not occur to him, however.

The fact that in an association for social economics (in the sense of Walras) *Seinsollen* was argued against was not without irony, but there was still more reason for surprise. After all, theoretical explanations in which value freedom is advocated cannot themselves manage without values. Both Sombart and Weber reasoned on the basis of hypothetical prescriptions that do not allow the mixing of science and art. Value freedom itself is a value. By adhering to it, they *demanded* research without value judgments. By arguing about the use of that desideratum based on value judgments, they showed that it is definitely possible to discuss blondes and brunettes in a reasonable manner, even if no empirical proof can be supplied.

However, it would testify to a misunderstanding of their intentions if it were thought that Sombart and Weber wished to abstain from political statements. If we may paraphrase their point of view, they merely declared that they were opposed to the decision to accept or reject theories – and when all is said and done, these are necessary for practicing art – being taken on the strength of value judgments. They were also against a theory containing prescriptions. Theories must be objective and positive.

In Sombart's opinion, a theory has to be proved "scientifically." In the opinion of Weber, this implies that values and value judgments may in fact be the subject of research and may determine the choice of problem and the formation of concepts, but that the theory itself does not set norms. There are no scientifically provable ideals (1951, p. 585). An empirical science cannot teach anyone what he must do, but only what can be done and sometimes what he or she wants to do (1951, p. 151).

In Weber's opposition to "ethical science" he thus emphasized an implication of the objectivity that he desired. In the final analysis, prescriptions can be justified only by having recourse to values. However, a theory must be proved "scientifically," that is, objectively on the strength of facts. An objective theory is therefore, of necessity, nonnormative, that is, positive. It contains no prescriptions. Nor does it contain value judgments. "The thesis of 'value-freedom'," as W. G. Runciman summarizes Weber's view, "is . . . about the irrelevance to the validity of scientific hypothesis of the standards by which the social scientist himself judges human conduct" (1972, p. 59). English authors such as Robbins (1946, p. 90), Hutchison (1964, p. 55), and Blaug (1980, p. 134) rightly identify *Wertfreiheit* with objectivity. Empirical science pursues an objective description of what is happening.

Weber was aware that objectivity is itself a value that is propounded by a methodological prescription. It is an ideal that inspires theories, but it is not always attained. On behalf of the editors of the *Archiv* he even acknowledged that personal philosophies of life always tend to play a part in the social sciences. They obscure the discussion. They influence the assessment of causal relations. Even the editors of the journal, he affirmed, were only human. Nevertheless, he was of the opinion that there was a considerable distance between this confession of human frailty and belief in an "ethical" economic science that must produce norms (1951, pp. 151–2).

Apparently he also was of the opinion that "scientific" or "objective" research is the same as research without prejudices. According to Popper that is impossible, because an "empty mind" cannot exist. In Weber's view, however, it is simply a question of a human frailty that can be overcome. He too suffers from the St. Anthony syndrome. According to Popper, an empty mind is not necessary at all. Objective research is based on intersubjective testing in accordance with methodological conventions that leads to a consensus. Weber seems to adopt a phenomenological point of view. Apparently, to him, the empty mind is a methodological ideal.

The way to ethical science might in that case, however, be shorter than he presumed. A theory that, as a result of human frailty, is based on a philosophy of life gives anyone desirous of applying it to achieve his objectives answers colored by that philosophy of life. The theory may then seem positive, just like the theory according to which the eyes of the all-seeing Argus were transformed into markings on peacock tails, but as a result of the way in which it has been assessed and accepted, it conveys a message that could also be expressed in the form of an explicitly normative theory. The indicative in which it is framed is a disguised optative.

The sensitivity of economic theory to the human frailty pointed to by Weber indicates that evidently putting economic theories to the proof by intersubjective testing fails. Sombart and Weber therefore realized that there is something special about the provability of theories of the social sciences compared to those of the natural sciences. If both categories could be objectively demonstrated in the same way, there would never have been a value judgment conflict. Sombart and Weber saw a fundamental difference. They complicated their metatheory considerably by the distinction they made in the style of Wilhelm Dilthey, Heinrich Rickert, and Wilhelm Windelband between the natural sciences and the cultural sciences and between nomographic and idiographic science. They postulated the ideal of the value freedom of all science, but saw a difference in the knowledge furnished by theories of the natural sciences and those of the cultural sciences. For, according to Sombart, the cultural sciences, of which economics is one, furnish essential knowledge (*Wesenserkenntnis*), an insight into the "necessity" that is not derived from experience and that, thanks to *Verstehen,* causes us to see the significance of the phenomena. This makes it difficult for us to understand what he must have meant in Vienna by "scientific proof."

Max Weber, however, was somewhat less receptive to the hermeneutic philosophy. To him *Verstehen* is a necessary but insufficient condition for accepting a socioscientific theory. Identification with the acting persons and their culture strengthens the plausibility or what he calls the "qualitative certainty (*qualitative Evidenz*)" of a social theory, but this must be checked by the usual methods of "causal imputation" (1951, p. 428). If we assume that the customs in the social sciences are the same on this point as in the natural sciences, the value freedom of all science would then be explicable.

But Weber proceeds from premises that undermine his own thesis of general value freedom. He quite incorrectly assumes that only in the social sciences is use made of idealizations. He derived the term *Idealtypus* from Georg Jellinek, the legal philosopher, and attached to it the meaning that, according to Runciman (1972, p. 9), he must have found in Georg Simmel, who in his *Philosophie des Geldes* tried to reproduce an ideal construction (1907, p. VIII). Ideal constructions, according to Weber, indicate how a certain form of human action would end if it were directed solely at one economic target (1951, p. 50). Neither this definition nor its variants to be found in his writings are startling to a natural scientist. According to Ernst Mach, all universal physical concepts and laws are in the form of idealizations (1906, pp. 192–3).

However, Weber distances himself from the natural sciences. In Mach's view, facts, however complicated, are reconstructed by a synthetic combination of idealizations. In Weber, on the other hand, an idealization has only a heuristic function. It has been brought about by abstraction and is not a hypothesis but a guideline for the formation of hypotheses to explain concrete events (1951, p. 190). In my opinion,

Weber thus correctly characterizes general economic theories. Basic theories are heuristic systems with which specific models can be designed to explain concrete events (Klant, 1984, pp. 158–87).

Yet Weber's metatheory of ideal types has a poor foundation. Not only does he fail to see that idealizations also occur in the natural sciences; he also ignores the fact that concrete events can be explained precisely by laws in the form of idealizations. Weber is of the opinion that only the social sciences are faced with the problem of the reconstruction of unique, nonrepeatable happenings. However, the facts that Mach was talking about also include historical ones. Today we even have an explanation of what happened in the first nonrepeatable ten seconds of the creation of the universe. Of course, a synthesis of idealizations does not represent the *complete* reality, any more than does the explanation of the selected aspects of events that Weber calls "unique concrete social phenomena." Indeed, that is impossible, but there is no reason for assuming, as Weber does, that economic theories cannot describe laws purely and simply because they do not explain concrete events. If no laws can be found in economics, that must be due to something else.

Walras's pure theory, for instance, is to Weber an idealization that provides indications for the interpretation of concrete events. His requirement of "checking by causal imputation" – dare I say testing? – is then applicable to a specific interpretation of this kind. But then the question arises: Is the idealization not being tested at the same time? That could in fact be the case if ideal types contain sufficient restrictions with regard to admissible interpretations to make them falsifiable. But then they would describe a general behavioral structure that quite definitely may be called regular. They would describe laws. If, on the other hand, they are not falsifiable, it is possible that they are so formulated that they do in fact answer to Weber's characterization and function as heuristic theories for forming specific testable models. Since in that case the ideal types cannot be put to the proof by stringent testing, the speculative decision to accept them nevertheless as guidelines can be taken on the basis of extrascientific value judgments. Weber's thesis of value freedom is therefore at variance with his view on ideal types.

Weber's philosophy implies that pure theories cannot be objective. Since, as he acknowledges, philosophies of life happen to play a part, they cannot really be value free. True, they can be taken for positive, because norms are not explicitly set in them, but, like myths, they are accepted on the strength of an assessment in accordance with extrascientific values. By utilizing Weber's misplaced apology on account of human frailty, one may continue improperly to call them "value free," because the theories that have come about in that way do not contain any explicit prescriptions. If, however, as Mill wanted, "art hands its end over to science," it receives in return a nonobjective theorem that is dependent on value judgments that, in Weber's view, are irrelevant in science to the decision of whether to accept or reject.

In accordance with Hume's law, "*is* judgments" cannot imply prescriptions. *Ought* does not follow from *is*. Prescriptions in which norms are set are justified by recourse to values. They can, it is true, be derived from a conjunction of prescriptions and *is* judgments. However, nonobjective ideological pronouncements, as meant by Weber, are not pure *is* judgments. They are based in part on value judgments. The facts are examined in the light of ideas about a natural, that is, attractive order. If a nonobjective theory of this kind is to be called "value free," Schmoller's ethical theory of just distribution will have to be taken as value free. After all, that theory too can be reproduced without explicit prescriptions. "A value judgment may be found without being uttered in an evaluation sentence" (Taylor, 1961, p. 3). It is possible to describe evaluatively and to evaluate descriptively. According to R. M. Hare, the distinction between *is* judgments and value judgments is not exclusive (1952, pp. 111–26; 1972, pp. 55–75). If art makes an appeal to Schmoller's "positive" science, it promptly receives an ethical reply, but not from Schmoller alone.

Just as *ought* does not follow from *is, is* does not follow from *ought*. What should be objective or value free, in accordance with the methodological norm, is not so if it is not satisfied because of whatever weakness. For clarity's sake, it would also be better if we never spoke again of *value freedom* but simply of *objectivity,* for, as Weber himself clearly realized in his 1904 article, that norm forms the problem proper.

If philosophies of life always interfere with research, it will not be possible anyway to keep them away in the case of testable idealizations either. For, because we require a set of abstract laws to explain a concrete situation and to interpret our observations of that situation, hypotheses cannot be independently tested. According to Pierre Duhem, critical experiments therefore do not exist, and Willard Van Orman Quine has rightly established that "our statements about the external world face the tribunal of sense experience not individually but only as a corporate body" (1964, p. xii). The one theory depends on the other.

However, Duhem-Quine's holistic thesis does not exclude the possibility that researchers, by making alternating attempts with different combinations of hypotheses, may arrive by testing at a decision as to what they will choose and what they will reject. But the conditions of the static metatheory of naive falsificationism (Klant, 1984, pp. 40–6), which completely excludes arbitrariness and speculation, are never satisfied. They apply a *partial equilibrium analysis*. Corroborations are based on guesses. Research is always on the go. It is, as Otto Neurath said, a ship that, although already sailing, is built with means available at sea. It is hampered by unsolved problems, contradictions, hiatuses, faulty constructions, errors, and failures. It is never in a state of general equilibrium that offers an opportunity for a unique solution and forges Quine's "corporate body" into a perfect unity.

In recent years Thomas Kuhn, Imre Lakatos, Paul Feyerabend, et al. have made us aware that every branch of science has its traditions, paradigms, and systems of concepts that may be interpreted as so many "prejudices" that for a long time are not made the subject of discussion. It is possible to evade the falsification of certain hypotheses and to follow strategies by which hard cores of theories are spared. As a result, even the natural sciences are partly dependent on preconceived views and habits of thought. The way in which we wish to see the world has an effect on how it looks. The belief in hypotheses is not determined solely by the recent results of research, but also by the faith one has – rightly or wrongly – in future results.

According to Stephen Toulmin, we proceed in physics too from a preconceived natural order that remains unaffected in critical discussion. In his opinion, Newton's law of inertia is part of the ideal of the natural order that cannot be demonstrated empirically. According to him, real laws describe deviations from the natural order. Snell's law of the refraction of light depends on the unprovable natural-order principle that light travels in a straight line (1960, pp. 57–104). Hypotheses cannot be falsified without assuming that the principles of the natural order are true.

As Karl Popper has argued, the empirical basis of science therefore has nothing "absolute" about it. Theories are built in a swamp on piles that can be lengthened but that will never reach hard ground (1959, p. 111). Nevertheless, we assiduously devote ourselves in empirical science to testing theories by means of experiments, systematic observations, and practical applications. We thus scan possibilities by the assessment of alternative hypotheses in varying combinations that are falsifiable by *choice* if, for that purpose, we regard the remaining supplementary and auxiliary hypotheses each time as true. For in testing, we decide on logical grounds: If the statements that we make with reference to observations are contradictory to the propositions that we are testing, these are in principle falsified, which may qualify them for rejection and in any case makes a reorganization of Quine's "corporate body" necessary. Our predictive successes and the staggering triumphs of technical application show what imposing structures can be erected right in the swamp of nature.

In the natural sciences, central ideas can be used to continue to *see* the world in a certain way. In the social sciences, in which the consequences of art are investigated, they are, however, also used to *change* the world. The ideas then become ideals, that is to say, values. For the social world is a changing system that we make ourselves. It is inevitable that the view of the structure or of the process is at the same time an idea about what can be done with it. Every social theory is a train that is ready to be boarded to take us to a–somewhat–better country. In his faith in the possibility of "causal imputation" without speculation, Weber has not shown us how the mix of idealization, idea, and ideal desired by Othmar Spann can be avoided in order to realize the ideal of a rightly value-free social science.

The value judgment conflict yielded a large number of publications, especially in Germany, by both the *Wertiker* and the *Wertfreien* (Weber, 1952). The former succeeded in involving in the conflict the philosophy of the day, such as that of Edmund Husserl. However, they made little impression on the mainstream economists. Political economy had in the meantime become economics or, better still, *economic science*. The principles of value freedom that had been proclaimed by the *verstehende* sociologist Max Weber were well received by the neoclassical economists. However, his related philosophy of the heuristic ideal types did not take root. The metatheory of value freedom, purged of hermeneutics, was taken for granted, the problems of provability, which were sensed but not solved by Weber, being overlooked. In probably the most widespread view among economists, the objectivity of research is guaranteed by the "analysis," which takes place without value judgments and values (except the methodological ones) being involved.

According to Schumpeter, analysis consists of taking note of facts, forming concepts, positing hypotheses, and applying logic. However, he distinguished two phases. One starts with a prescientific *vision* of presumptive relations that can be ideologically influenced. Unlike Brentano, he believed that prejudice can be a condition for inspiration. However, next *analysis* takes place, through which the vision, if it does not prove tenable, is discarded or converted into a theory from which the ideological element has been eliminated (1949, pp. 345–59).

Schumpeter acknowledges that "in economics, and still more in other social sciences, [the] sphere of the strictly provable is limited in that there are always fringe ends of things, that are matters of personal experience and impression from which it is practically impossible to drive ideology, or for that matter conscious dishonesty, completely"

(1954, p. 43). Prejudice proves to be not entirely harmless after all, because conviction blinds and, as Schumpeter notes: "The first thing a man will do for his ideals, is lie" (1954, p.43n). Not everyone is a St. Anthony. Ideological remnants thus are almost inevitably lodged in every theory on account of a form of Weberian human frailty, namely, the stubborn belief of the researchers. However, Schumpeter proves to be of the opinion that a theory is nevertheless demonstrably true or not true. He believes that the truth or untruth is seen by anyone who is completely open to scientific criticism. Evidently he assumes that there are only two possible answers to the question of whether a statement is true: "yes" or "no." He forgets a third possibility: "The question is not decidable." In the last case, the way remains free for the convinced to maintain their theses fearlessly and without lying.

The positivism conflict

The life expectancy of a metatheory of the heuristic ideal types was not great in an environment in which economists increasingly felt that they had to behave like natural scientists. They concentrated on making formalized theories and testing them by statistical analysis. Their pretensions are often called "positivistic," which is not of benefit to the clarity of the philosophical discussion. In 1944–5 they had already received critical-rationalistic recognition by Karl Popper, when he published what became *The Poverty of Historicism* as a series of articles in *Economica*.

In Popper's view the method of the social sciences ought to be a "technological approach," imposing "a discipline on our speculative inclinations" and forcing us "to submit our theories to definite standards, such as standards of clarity and practical testability." Perhaps we owe it to the intercession of Friedrich von Hayek, but Popper showed great respect for economics. He recommended social scientists not to look further than their Galileo or their Pasteur, but added in a footnote: "It must be admitted, however, that mathematical economics shows that one social science at least has gone through its Newtonian revolution" (1957, pp. 59–60). The *pretensions* of the economists were indeed Newtonian, but were their deeds too? Popper did not go into that question.

In the same work he drew attention to what he regarded as "a really fundamental similarity between the natural and the social sciences" by pointing to "the existence of sociological laws or hypotheses which are analogous to the laws or hypotheses of the natural sciences" (1957, p. 62). Strangely enough, in so doing he brought forward only the similar formulation of hypotheses that, in both cases, render possible logical transformations into corresponding "technological corollaries": $p \rightarrow q$ is equivalent to $\neg(p$ and $\neg q)$. He devoted no attention to the question of whether, for instance, the universal statement in technological form "You cannot have full employment without inflation" is also falsifiable. Apparently he assumed that the hypotheses of the social sciences satisfy the same conditions of his logical demarcation criterion as those of the natural sciences.

Popper believed that he could also demonstrate the unity of methods with an example from Hayek in which the latter represents an economist as a physicist who, through direct observation, knows the inside of atoms but has only a limited knowledge of the complex outside situation, and therefore is rarely capable of predicting the precise outcomes of particular situations, "although they might be *disproved* by the ob servation of events which according to his theory are impossible" (Hayek, 1964, pp. 41–2; Popper, 1957, pp. 136–7). However, Popper concluded his concurring argument by acknowledging that economists have fundamental difficulties connected with the application of methods of measurement:

In physics . . . the parameters of our equations can, in principle, be reduced to a small number of natural constants – a reduction which has been successfully carried out in many important cases. This is not so in economics; here our parameters are themselves in the most important cases quickly changing variables. This clearly reduces the significance, interpretability and testability of measurements. (1957, p. 143)

Parameters that are variable? Popper refers in a footnote to Lionel Robbins (1957, p. 143n). He too failed to see that parameters that are variables of which the changes cannot be predicted turn the relations into definitions. The testability is in that case indeed reduced, namely, to nil. The outcome then cannot be disproved.

In 1961 Popper presented a paper – "Die Logik der Sozialwissenschaften" – in Tübingen at a meeting of the Gesellschaft für Soziologie, where it came to an open clash of opinions of dialecticians and critical rationalists. In that paper too he dealt rather carelessly with the requirement which he had clearly stated for the first time in 1935 in his *Logik der Forschung:* the statements of empirical science must be "conclusively decidable," that is, refutable by experience (1959, pp. 40–1). In Tübingen, in the den of the sociocritical lion, he calls his own point of view "criticistic." Criticism should consist in attempts at refutation (1972, p. 106), but he makes no mention of the requirement that the social theories to be criticized must also be empirically refutable. The words "falsify" and "test" do not appear in the paper.

"Criticism" consists, in Popper, in "attempted refutations" (1983, p.

20). Philosophical theories, although irrefutable, are also subjected to it, for "every *rational* theory, no matter whether scientific or philosophical, is rational in so far as it tries to *solve certain problems*. . . . Now if we look upon a theory as a proposed solution to a set of problems, the theory immediately lends itself to critical discussion" (1965, p. 199).

I call a critical discussion on such theories, which can be confirmed but cannot be refuted by experience (i.e., which are not testable), a rational discussion on their *plausibility* (1984, p. 36), meaning the same as what Popper calls "to assess an irrefutable theory rationally" (1965, p. 198). The assessment serves to justify acceptance or rejection of such a theory, that is, of a choice that cannot be based exclusively on empirical scientific values. If the logical conditions of falsifiability, about which Popper is silent in his paper, should not be satisfied, economics must be regarded as a form of philosophy, with the then inevitable differing schools of thought. Their adherents try to convince others of the plausibility of their point of view.

According to Popper, "the main task of the social sciences . . . is to trace the unintended social repercussions of intentional human actions" (1965, p. 342). It is also "the task of social theory . . . to construct and to analyse . . . models carefully in descriptive or nominalist terms, that is to say, *in terms of individuals,* of their attitudes, expectations, relations etc. – a postulate which may be called "methodological individualism" (1957, 136).[1] Here the method of *situational logic* is applied, which Popper presents in *The Poverty of Historicism* as a method for historians (1957, pp. 147–52) and in his Tübingen paper as the result of logical examination of economic methods that is applicable to all the social sciences (1972, p. 120). With this he has the same in mind as Max Weber, to whom sociological knowledge is acquired by application of the ideal type of *Zweckrationalität*. It is a method that excludes nontestable psychological explanations and thus is called by Popper "objective Verstehen." The assumptions concerning homo economicus or the decision theories that well-balanced individuals equipped with preference schemes and considerable knowledge are assumed to apply are in the service of that objective understanding.

However, Weber-Popper's objective understanding cannot guarantee objectivity of the theory. If, as a result of the parameter paradox, theories are not testable and thus susceptible only to a rational discussion of their plausibility, it is conceivable that a situational analysis is extended by other means, equally lacking in real objectivity, or even replaced by

---

[1] Methodological individualism had already been explicitly defended by Joseph Schumpeter and Max Weber.

them. In that case application of situational logic is not a methodological but a theoretical problem, as in Spiro Latsis, who regards situational determinism as characteristic of a separate research program, namely, that of the neoclassical theory of the firm (1976, pp. 16–18).

Methodological individualism, situational logic, and the task of detecting unintended social repercussions of individual action seem to be based on a choice that is bound up with a view of humanity, society, and history. As regards Popper, he did not leave us in doubt about that. He also proclaimed a normative social theory. His natural order of the Open Society, which, in his opinion, has been most realized in the existing "Society of the Atlantic Community" (1965, p. 369), is a problem-solving organization in which, in accordance with Popper's neo-Darwinian interpretation of evolution, piecemeal moderate social engineering and planning are utilized for the gradual lessening of misery by trial and error, on condition of a liberal democracy, in which tolerance and freedom exist, reason is preferred to violence, and the State is a necessary evil. That world must be made and maintained.

However, his view of objectivity is less easy to reconcile with his choice of the most attractive society. Just as over half a century before in Vienna, where the *Werturteilstreit* broke out, in Tübingen, where the *Positivismusstreit* was waged, value freedom came up for discussion. Popper again emphasized that the objectivity of science does not consist in the objectivity of the scientist but in that of the method. Objectivity is not an individual matter for the researchers but a social matter with mutual criticism, with a friendly inimical division of work and with cooperation and opposition at the same time (1972, p. 112). The objective and value-free scientist, said Popper, is not the ideal scientist. Passion is essential, certainly in pure science (1972, p. 114). However, he thus immediately states the conditions of dependence on values. Friendship and passions guarantee that extrascientific values are respected if the scientific values cannot be sufficiently complied with.

Once again Popper makes no mention of falsifiability as a condition that results in there also sounding in the debate the voice that, as Kant puts it, makes nature's answer heard (1956, p. 23). If only logic and not, at the same time, empirical testing forces mutual criticism in the direction of a consensus, a gap is left for extrascientific values that may lead in various directions. Objectivity is a property of the empirical scientific method and not of its users, indeed. Objectivity is not a property of a nonempirical scientific method like that of philosophy. Precisely because the objectivity of science does not depend on the objectivity of the scientist, the social sciences are not value free.

In the Tübingen paper Popper incidentally makes a statement that betrays the fact that he too sees objectivity threatened by extrascientific values. He regards it as a task of criticism to purge the truth problems from extrascientific values. According to him, that does not always prove successful, but remains a constant task. The purity of pure science is an ideal, he says, that is presumably unattainable, but for which criticism persistently struggles and must struggle (1972, p. 114). So the St. Anthony syndrome after all? It is a somewhat disconcerting conclusion after he had promised his audience to solve the so-called problem of value freedom in a freer way than usually happens (1972, p. 113). In fact, we are concerned here with the same solution as that of Weber and Schumpeter, which had caused the mainstream economists to be satisfied with themselves. Criticism, Popper believed, must expose the mixing of values (1972, p. 115). But *awareness of values,* also advocated by Gunnar Myrdal (1970, pp. 55–6), however greatly it is worth pursuing, does not eliminate any values, but converts the plausibility discussion into a critical discussion of the implicit ideals. Dependence on values is clarified by it.

However, Popper's formulation, even more clearly than that of Weber and Schumpeter, can preserve us from illusions about value freedom. Objectivity is a presumably unattainable ideal, Popper says. Evidently he considers it unattained so far. Therefore, the social sciences *are not* value free. The scientist in the social sciences, however virtuous he or she might be, could on account of the absence of testability, and driven by personal passions, attend to a considerable deviation from the ideal pursued. The difference between physics and the social sciences seems to be only one of degree, namely, very large.

Political economy

The idealizations that are applied in economic research fail to reconstruct concrete events by synthetic combination in accordance with Mach's wish. That is clear to see when we are concerned with a formalized general theory that describes a set of relations, that is, a structure, by means of a number of equations. In these equations no universal numerical constants occur. They do not represent unique structures, but sets of structures. An exact imputation by the forming of cross sections or of differences to explain complex events or to determine the operation of fictitiously isolated relations is impossible.

In economic theories it is usually assumed that the structural parameters vary with place and time, that is to say, are connected in an indeterminate way with changes in incompletely defined social spaces. With regard to the possible changes, restrictions may have been postulated.

But then too, as a rule, even a qualitative prediction (namely, of the direction of changes) is not possible. If, for instance, the marginal propensity to consume dC/dY is assumed to be always positive, but less than unity, the theory nevertheless permits an actual change that is greater than unity, if it is assumed at the same time that the propensity to consume $C(Y)$ can change unpredictably. The hypotheses about the properties and inconstancy of the propensity to consume yield a tautological conclusion regarding changes: "With a rise (fall) in income, consumption rises (falls) or consumption does not rise (fall)."

Even if stability of the structural parameters is assumed, for example, by supposing that they vary with place but, within a certain period, hardly if at all with time – that is to say, very slowly – exact imputation is not possible. The theory is too general for that. Moreover, it is static and, if it is dynamic, it is too strongly stylized. It then allows of so many dynamic interpretations that acknowledgment of the failure of empirical applications does not logically compel amendment or rejection of the general theory.

Today's practitioners of economic science, having returned to the ideal of William Petty, try to measure more accurately than those of nineteenth-century political economy, who were satisfied with the "tendencies" that could always be recognized by the willing. Econometric models that have been estimated for social spaces characterized by time and place are, however, nothing more than dynamic interpretations. The hypotheses that are interpreted in one model may have been derived from different theories. They do have numerical parameters; they do explain complex events; they can be tested and, if they fail empirically, they must logically be amended or rejected. However, the assertion that a specific model is untrue does not tend to contradict the set of universal hypotheses that have been interpreted in the model by a choice of operational definitions and mathematical form, by dynamization, by specification, and by augmentation by hypotheses that have not been posited in the basic theory. In that theory, inadequate restrictions tend to be made with regard to admissible interpretations. The basic theory can then be maintained after rejection of a specific model, and a different interpretation can be sought. It is true that by statistical analysis singular statements on historical developments can be tested. That is then an establishment of facts. However, it is not possible to test theories for *explaining* those facts if the theoreticians cannot be contradicted by statements on what is observed.

Economists cannot be blamed for the fact that so far they have not succeeded in making theories that are just as strong as many of those in the natural sciences. They will probably never be able to do so. The world with which they are confronted, if they try to solve economic problems couched in causal terms, happens to be subject to much more rapid historical change than nature. Humans, who learn and create, change their world constantly and evoke unforeseeable situations one after the other. The verbal interpretations, which can be much more subtle but less exact than the econometric ones, also fail in the process of give-and-take converging toward the truth that Schumpeter thought he saw happening.

The cultural sciences are indeed different from the natural sciences. The absence of universal numerical constants, as a result of which synthetic combination and fictitious isolation do not yield testable results, means that the world of the economists appears much more complex than that of the physicists. Their basic hypotheses are not "conclusively decidable." They are heuristic systems, decided on in a rational critical discussion to which the inconclusive recourse to experience also belongs. Economics is philosophy, science, and art. John Maynard Keynes was rightly of the opinion that economics is a moral science that cannot be practiced in the same way as the natural sciences (Klant, 1985).

Economists who were to decide on acceptance or rejection of their theories in accordance with the system of values of their colleagues in the natural sciences would have to be desperate and, in any case, undecided and highly uncertain researchers. However, the opposite is the case. In economics it is almost only metatheoreticians and historians, who write not about the world but about theories, who permit themselves skepticism and neutrality. The real theoreticians, when they present their speculative solutions, are as a rule very sure of themselves. Even the word "probably" does not pass their lips. They have more about them of prophets or mathematicians than of careful, empirical, scientific researchers. Even if they remain much further removed from the realization of the empirical scientific ideal than physicists, they are usually more firmly convinced of the correctness of their theory.

However much economists may evoke their purity, they want to change the world. They want to contribute to the solution of urgent *practical* problems. The theories of Quesnay, Smith, Ricardo, Mill, Marx, Walras, Marshall, Pareto, Wicksell, Veblen, Keynes, Schumpeter, Hayek, Tinbergen, Hicks, Friedman, and Samuelson contain messages. Perhaps the tame cattle, peacefully grazing in the manner of Kuhn's normal scientists in an area enclosed by definitions of Robbins, will succeed in simply enjoying their own digestion. The creative economists – and they are much more numerous than the "extraordinary" ones, according to Kuhn, and the seventeen I have listed – entertain more or less veiled but recognizable ideas about a natural order and a "meaning" of history, ideas that are not scientifically provable but do help to determine the content of their theories. They try to make the latter acceptable by invoking plausibility.

Of course, they also pursue the consistency of the theories they make, for he who contradicts himself proves nothing. However, it testifies to excessive indolence in furnishing proof to do as Walter Eucken did, and take consistent theories for true ones (1947, p. 269). It equally testifies to dogmatic blindness, and thus also to indolence, to regard a consistent theory that one considers plausible as having been conclusively demonstrated. Discussions in economics often lead to strengthening of both opposite points of view and not to "objective" knowledge, that is, established in accordance with the rules of the game, but provisional and uncertain.

If we look at things from the aspect of the logical structure of their theories, it can hardly be otherwise. Whatever Popper may have thought of economics, it can be demonstrated with his own means: A door is open to extrascientific values because basic economic theories are not falsifiable. Even if they were, ideals are given an opportunity to penetrate the hard core of ideas that is maintained as long as possible. The fact is that ideas about a world that is lived in easily become ideals if they relate to action. Welfare theory, for example, which is the result of a formal analysis of rational action, shows us the properties of an idealized, timeless system in which the attainment of joint ends is in equilibrium. Of course, the implications can be shown without the introduction of value judgments other than those already contained in the premises, but because it is an idealized social decision system, it is a potential ideal. If welfare theory is applied, it functions as an ideal.

Sometimes the values of the economists are professed in a wide circle, such as laissez-faire in the nineteenth century or methodological individualism or Pareto efficiency today. Sometimes too the supporters of differing values are irreconcilably opposed, such as the Keynesian interventionists and the monetarist neoliberals, or the "bourgeois" and Marxist economists. However, there is little reason to regard the one ideal as legitimate, formal, indifferent, or neutral and the other as a sign of lack of respect for value freedom and objectivity. Economic theories cannot be objective. What matters is to explicate the values by self-examination and by unmasking others; to continue the discussion on each relevant aspect, without paying attention to what connoisseurs of the subject matter of economics forbid; to extend empirical research and the study of history; and to abandon the hypocrisy of the so-called value freedom, about which Weber said untenable things more than seventy years ago.

This does not mean to say that in economic research we can waive the

114   **Klant**

ideal of objectivity and give free play to what our desires suggest to us. The empirical scientific ideal cannot be abandoned by any serious participant in the joint discussion on problems in terms of cause and effect. "All science, and all philosophy, are enlightened common sense" (Popper, 1983, p. 34). In our attempts to convince one another, we are again and again confronted with decisions that cannot be postponed, because it is not only a matter of acquiring knowledge of what there is, but also of what has to be done. In that case, our methodological value judgments are mingled with other value judgments if we are lacking in proof. In our attempts to refute the empirically irrefutable, we seek consistent and plausible solutions to problems and an association of minds on the basis of common value, not only – with due respect to Marx – to understand our world, but also to change it. Economics *is* political economy.

References

Albert, H. (1979). "The Economic Tradition," in K. Brunner, ed., *Economics and Social Institutions.* Boston: Martinus Nijhoff.
Blaug, M. (1980). *The Methodology of Economics,* Cambridge: Cambridge University Press.
Boson, M. (1950). *Léon Walras, fondateur de la politique économique scientific.* Rennes: Imprimeries Réunies.
Brentano, L. (1911). "Uber Werturteile in der Volkswirtschaftslehre," *Archiv für Sozialwissenschaft und Sozialpolitik* 33:695–714.
Cohen, M.R., and Nagel, E. (1963). *An Introduction to Logic and Scientific Method* (1934). London: Routledge & Kegan Paul.
Entrèves, A. P. d' (1970). *Natural Law* (1951). London: Hutchison.
Eucken, W. (1947). *Die Grundlagen der Nationalökonomie* (1939). Godesberg: Küpper.
Frondizi, R. (1971). *What Is Value?* La Salle, Ill.: Open Court.
Gehrig, H. (1914). *Die Begründung des Prinzips der Sozialreform.* Jena: Fischer.
Hare, R. M. (1952). *The Language of Morals.* Oxford: Oxford University Press. (1972). *Essays on the Moral Concepts.* London: Macmillan.
Hayek, F.A. (1964 [1955]). *The Counter-Revolution of Science.* London: Free Press.
Helvetius, C.A. (1973 [1758]). *De l'esprit,* ed. F. Chatelet. Verviers: Gérard.
Hutchison, T.W. (1964). *"Positive" Economics and Policy Objectives,* London: Allen & Unwin. (1978). *On Revolutions and Progress in Economic Knowledge.* Cambridge: Cambridge University Press.
Jaffé, W. (1977). "The Normative Bias of the Walrasian Model," *Quarterly Journal of Economics* 91:371–87.
Kant, I. [1781] *Kritik der reinen Vernunft,* Werke, III. Wiesbaden: Suhrkamp.

Keynes, J.M. (1972 [1933]). *Essays in Biography, The Collected Writings of J.M. Keynes,* Vol. X. London: Macmillan.

Keynes, J.N. (1963 [1880]). *The Scope and Method of Political Economy.* New York: August M. Kelley.

Klant, J.J. (1982). "Idealisatie: idee en ideaal," in B. de Gaay Fortman, ed., *Economie en waarde.* Alphen aan de Rijn: Samson.

(1984). *The Rules of the Game.* Cambridge: Cambridge University Press.

(1985). "The Slippery Transition," in T. Lawson and H. Pesaran, eds., *Keynes' Economics.* London: Croom Helm.

Latsis, S.J. (1976a). "A Research Programme in Economics," in S.J. Latsis, ed., *Method and Appraisal in Economics.* Cambridge: Cambridge University Press, pp. 1–41.

(1976b). "Situational Determination in Economics," *British Journal for the Philosophy of Science* 27:207–45.

Laudan, L. (1981). *Science and Hypothesis.* Dordrecht: D. Reidel.

Losee, J. (1980 [1972]). *A Historical Introduction to the Philosophy of Science.* Oxford: Oxford University Press.

Mach, E. (1906 [1905]). *Erkenntnis und Irrtum.* Leipzig: Barth.

Machlup, F. (1969). "Positive and Normative Economics," in R.L. Heilbronner, ed., *Economic Means and Social Ends.* Englewood Cliffs, N.J.: Prentice-Hall.

Malthus, T.R. (1951 [1823]). *Principles of Political Economy.* Oxford: Blackwell.

Mannheim, K. (1979 [1928]). *Ideology and Utopia.* London: Routledge & Kegan Paul.

Mill, J.S. (1843). *A System of Logic,* various editions.

(1974 [1844]). *Essays on Some Unsettled Questions of Political Economy.* Clifton: August M. Kelley.

Myrdal, G. (1970). *Objectivity in Social Research.* London: Dackworth.

North, D. (1954 [1691]). *Discourse upon Trade,* in J.R. McCulloch, *Early English Tracts* (1856). Cambridge: Cambridge University Press.

Papandreou, A.G. (1958). *Economics as a Science.* Chicago: Lippincott.

Plato, 1976. *Protagoras.* Trans. C.C.W. Taylor. Oxford: Clarendon.

Pope, A. (1924). *Collected Poems,* ed. B. Oobrée. London: Dent.

Popper, K.R. (1956 [1945]). *The Open Society and Its Enemies.* London: Routledge & Kegan Paul.

(1957). *The Poverty of Historicism.* London: Routledge & Kegan Paul.

(1959). *The Logic of Scientific Discovery.* London: Hutchison.

(1965 [1963]). *Conjectures and Refutations.* London: Routledge & Kegan Paul.

(1983 [1972]). *Objective Knowledge.* Oxford: Clarendon.

(1972). "Die Logik der Sozialwissenschaften," in T.W. Adorno, ed., *Der Positivismusstreit in der deutschen Soziologie.* Darmstadt: Luchterand.

(1975). "The Rationality of Scientific Revolutions," in R. Harré, ed., *Problems of Scientific Revolution.* Oxford: Oxford University Press.

116   **Klant**

Quine, W.V.O. (1964 [1950]). *Methods of Logic.* New York: Holt, Rinehart & Winston.

Reisman, D. (1976). *Adam Smith's Sociological Economics.* London: Croom Helm.

Rescher, N. (1969). *Introduction to Value Theory.* Englewood Cliffs, N.J.: Prentice-Hall.

Ricardo, D. (1971). *Speeches and Evidences,* in *Works,* Vol. V. Cambridge: Cambridge University Press.

(1973). *Letters 1819–June 1821, Works,* Vol. VIII. Cambridge: Cambridge University Press.

Robbins, L. (1938). "Live and Dead Issues in the Methodology of Economics," *Economica* n.s. 5:342–52.

(1946 [1932]). *An Essay on the Nature and Significance of Economic Science.* London: Macmillan.

Runciman, W.G. (1972). *A Critique of Max Weber's Philosophy of Social Science.* Cambridge: Cambridge University Press.

Say, J.B. (1972 [1803]). *Traité d'économie politique.* Paris: Calman-Lévy.

Schmoller, G. (1873). "Sendschreiben," *Jahrbücher für Nationalökonomie und Statistik* 20:47–70.

(1911). "Volkswirtschaft, Volkswirtschaftslehre und methode," *Handwörterbuch der Staatswissenschaft,* Vol. VIII. Jena: Fischer.

Schumpeter, J.A. (1908). *Das Wesen und der Hauptinhalt der theoretischen Nationalökonomie,* Leipzig: Dancker & Humblot.

(1949). "Science and Ideology," *American Economic Review* 39:349–59.

(1954). *History of Economic Analysis.* London: Allen & Unwin.

Senior, N.W. (1966a [1826]). *An Introductory Lecture on Political Economy,* in N.W. Senior, ed., *Selected Writings on Economics.* New York: August M. Kelley.

(1966b [1852]). *Four Introductory Lectures on Political Economy,* in N.W. Senior, ed., *Selected Writings on Economics.* New York: August M. Kelley.

Simmel, G. (1907 [1900]). *Die Philosophie des Geldes.* Leipzig: Duncker & Humblot.

Smith, A. (1976a [1750]). *The Theory of Moral Sentiments,* ed. D. D. Raphael and A.L. Macfie. Oxford: Clarendon.

(1976b [1776]). *An Inquiry into the Nature and Causes of the Wealth of Nations,* ed. R.H. Campbell, A.S. Skinner, and W.B. Toell. Oxford: Clarendon.

(1980 [1795]). *Essays on Philosophical Subjects,* ed. W.P.D. Wrightman and J.C. Pryce. Oxford: Clarendon.

Stegmüller, W. (1979). *The Structuralist View of Theories.* Berlin: Springer-Verlag.

Taylor, P.W. (1961). *Normative Discourse.* Englewood Cliffs, N.J.: Prentice-Hall.

Toulmin, S. (1960 [1953]). *The Philosophy of Science.* New York: Harper & Row.

Verhandlungen der Generalversammlung in Wien, 27, 28, und 29. September 1909, *Schriften des Vereins für Sozialpolitik,* Leipzig, 1910.

Walker, D.A. (1984). "Is Walras's Theory of General Equilibrium a Normative Scheme?" *History of Political Economy* 16:445–69.

Walras, L. (1926 [1874–7]). *Eléments d'économie politique pure.* Paris: Pichon.

(1936 [1898]). *Etudes d'économie politique appliquée.* Lausanne: Rouge.

Weber, M. (1951). *Gesammelte Aufsätze zur Wissenschaftslehre,* ed. J. Winckelmann. Tübingen: J.C.B. Mohr.

and Topitsch, E. (1952). "Das Wertfreiheitsproblem seit Max Weber," *Zeitschrift für Nationalökonomie* 13:158–201.

Wright, G.H. von (1963). *Norm and Action.* London: Routledge & Kegan Paul.

PART II

Popper among the economists

CHAPTER 3

Ad hocness in economics and the Popperian tradition

D. WADE HANDS

This chapter discusses the literature on ad hoc theory adjustment both within economics and within the Popperian philosophical tradition. It will be shown that there are two fundamentally different concepts of ad hocness[1] within the Popperian tradition, one associated with Popper himself and one with Lakatos, and that these two different concepts are mirrored in the way the term is used by economic methodologists and economic theorists, respectively. In Section I, Popper's use of the term "ad hoc" and its fundamental importance to the Popperian program will be discussed. In Section II, Lakatos's three different notions of ad hocness will be reduced to two (one the same as Popper's and one uniquely Lakatosian), and the importance of each of these to the methodology of scientific research programs will be examined. These first two sections, although simply surveys, are necessary because this particular aspect of both the Popperian and Lakatosian philosophy of science has been badly neglected in the recent literature on economic methodology. Section III discusses the use of "ad hoc" by both economic methodologists and economic theorists, and compares these uses with those in the philosophical literature. In the conclusion (Section IV) the methodological implications of the discussion in the first three sections will be examined. It will be argued that proper emphasis on the different notions of ad hocness, and the different groups who tend to emphasize each use, have significant implications for economic methodology, particularly Lakatosian economic methodology.

I. Ad hocness: Popper

There is a long tradition, within both scientific philosophy and scientific practice, that argues that a new theory is less than satisfactory if it is *designed solely to deal with a previously anomalous observation.* Such theories do not go beyond their predecessors and are considered to be

Helpful comments on earlier drafts were received from Bruce Caldwell, Daniel Hausman, Bart Nooteboom, and Alexander Rosenberg.
[1] In the interest of clarity, the convention of italicizing or underlining ad hoc and its derivatives will be abandoned throughout (except where it occurs in quotations).

ad hoc. Although the term "ad hoc" has no universally accepted definition within the philosophy of science, it is usually reserved for a particular type of face-saving/falsification-avoiding theoretical adjustment. For
instance, Laudan's (1977, p. 115) popular definition states, "a theory is
ad hoc if it is believed to figure essentially in the solution of all and only
those empirical problems which were solved by, or refuting instances
for, an earlier theory."

As an example of the ad hocness problem, consider the following
(hypothetical) case from economic theory. Suppose a macroeconomic
theory T1 predicts that for any country whose money supply changes by
the amount m, the price level in the following period will change by the
amount p. Suppose further that after this result has been successfully
corroborated for several countries, a contrary result is obtained for country A, that is, T1 is refuted by the evidence from country A. How can T1
be saved? How can T1 be adjusted so that the potential refutation is
avoided? One approach is to simply modify T1 in an ad hoc way to avoid
the refutation. For instance, we could modify T1 so that it now says, "for
all countries except country A, m implies p." This new theory – call it
T2 – is confirmed by all the countries that confirmed T1, and in addition,
it is confirmed in country A, where T1 failed. Thus, it could be argued
that since T1 was refuted and T2 is more confirmed (or, in Popper's
terms, more "corroborated"), the move from T1 and T2 constituted
scientific progress.

It seems obvious that this type of theory modification should not
count as progress. T1 was refuted, but T2 is not really any better. The
change from T1 to T2 was patently ad hoc; it was contrived solely to
protect the theory from an observed anomaly, and served no other
purpose. Not only does this amount to "cheap success" (Worrall, 1978,
p. 49), it also makes "progress" trivially easy.[2] By this technique a
successful theory can always be constructed out of one with a dismal
track record. The history of human speculation abounds with such (ultimately unsuccessful) face-saving moves.[3,4]

Within the Popperian tradition, the ad hocness problem is even more

---

[2] For this reason, Watkins (1984, p. 166) refers to the non-ad hocness requirement as an
"antitrivialisation principle." The principle states that "any philosophical account of
scientific progress must be inadequate if it has the (no doubt unintended) implication
that it is always *trivially easy* to make theoretical progress in science."

[3] Grunbaum (1976, pp. 329–30) cites historical examples.

[4] It should be noted that although the undesirability of ad hoc theories is being presented
as obvious, not all philosophers of science would agree. Laudan (1977, pp. 114–18), for
instance, finds no difficulty with this type of ad hoc modification, claiming that to
condemn such adjustments puts "an epistemic premium on theories which work the first
time around" (p. 117). Grunbaum (1976, pp. 358–61) advocates a similar position.

important than in other philosophies of science. As a matter of intellectual history, Popper's reaction to precisely this type of ad hoc defensive stratagem contributed to his initial interest in the demarcation problem.[5] Philosophically, the entire Popperian approach to science is characterized by *bold* conjecture and *severe* tests – precisely the opposite of such ad hoc/defensive behavior. For Popper "the aim of science is to get explanatory theories which are as little *ad hoc* as possible: a 'good' theory is not *ad hoc,* while a 'bad' theory is" (1963, p. 16).

Now although ad hoc adjustments are undesirable in general, one should not be too reckless in eliminating ways that a theory can be adjusted in response to contrary evidence. As Popper explained in his autobiography, he "also realized that we must not exclude all immunizations, not even all which introduced *ad hoc* auxiliary hypotheses" (1976, p. 42). Popper cites the modification of Newton's theory in response to the observed motion of Uranus as an example of an ad hoc adjustment that eventually contributed to the development of the Newtonian program. What is needed is a methodological rule that is strict, but not too strict, in the way it bars ad hoc adjustments. Popper's solution is the requirement of *independent testability*.

By "independent testability" Popper simply means that a new theory should make testable predictions independently of the predictions made by its predecessor.[6] Or to put it more in the Popperian vernacular, the new theory should have *excess empirical* content; in addition to inheriting and correcting the potential falsifiers of the early theory, the new theory must have additional falsifiers of its own.[7] A new theory that meets this requirement will be more bold and "better testable than the previous theory: the fact that it explains all the explicanda of the previous theory, and that, in addition, it gives rise to new tests, suffices to ensure this" (Popper, 1963, p. 242). An independently testable theory cannot be ad hoc in the way discussed previously.[8]

[5] Popper (1963, pp. 33–7; 1976, pp. 41–44).

[6] Popper (1963, pp. 217–20, 240–8; 1972, pp. 191–205).

[7] Recall that Popper defines the *empirical content* of a statement as the set of all its potential falsifiers (1963, pp. 332, 385; 1965, pp. 113, 119–211; 1976, p. 26; and Lakatos 1970, p. 111).

Although Popper's definition of empirical content is sufficient for present purposes, it should be noted that some neo-Popperians find it to be problematic. Watkins (1984, pp. 167–83) discusses the difficulties of the Popperian definition (actually, definitions) and offers his own modification called the "comparative testability" criterion.

[8] Although independent testability is sufficient to rule out cases like T2 in the preceding economic example, it is not sufficient to rule out every type of ad hoc adjustment. To really guarantee that the new theory is non-ad hoc, Popper also requires that some of the excess content actually *be confirmed.* As he says, "This becomes clear if we consider that it is always possible, by a trivial stratagem, to made an *ad hoc* theory independently testable, *if we do not also require that it should pass the independent tests in question:* we

Let us see how the independent testability requirement might be applied to the previous economic example. Suppose that further examination of the anomalous country A reveals that the government of this country was running an extremely large deficit during the years when theory T1 failed to predict inflation accurately. Suppose further that a reexamination of the countries where T1 had been successful reveals that the governments of these countries had budgets close to balanced for the years in question. These observations might suggest a new, much bolder theory, T'2. T'2 would predict the initial result (same as T1) for countries with budgets close to balanced and a different result, the one obtained in country A, for countries with large deficits. Notice that T'2 predicts the same results as T1 where T1 was successful, corrects T1 for the case of country A, and provides independently testable predictions. For example, T'2 tells us that for any as yet unexamined country, we should find different results during years when the country was at war (and thus running a large deficit) than during years when the country was at peace. T'2 has excess empirical content; it leads to "new testable consequences, suggested by the new theory and never thought of before" (Popper, 1963, p. 243).

The last few words of the preceding quotation reveal another aspect of the Popperian response to the ad hocness question, that is, the importance of *novel facts*. In the paper considered to be his most important on the topic of scientific progress (1963, pp. 215–50)[9] *Popper identified independent testability exclusively with the prediction of novel facts*. He says (1963, p. 241), "we require that the new theory should be *independently testable*. That is to say, apart from explaining all the explicanda which the new theory was designed to explain, it must have new and testable consequences (preferably consequences of a new kind); it must lead to the prediction of phenomena which have not so far been observed." Popper admits that requiring the new theory to predict "what had never been thought of before" (p. 243) may "sound strange" (p. 247) because it means that whether or not evidence counts in favor of a theory depends critically on "whether the theory is temporally prior to the evidence" (1963, p. 247).[10]

---

merely have to connect it (conjunctively) in some way or other with any testable but not yet tested fantastic ad hoc prediction which may occur to us (or to some science fiction writer)" (1963, p. 244).

[9] And to a lesser extent in "The Aim of Science" (1972, pp. 191–205).

[10] Not everyone writing on Popper's transition from non-ad hocness to novel facts documents the transition in exactly the same way (see Musgrave, 1974, pp. 3–12; Watkins, 1978, pp. 33–6; 1984, pp. 288–300; and Worrall, 1978, pp. 45–51). Lakatos seems to argue (1978a, p. 172) that there was no transition at all, that Popper always subscribed to the view that non-ad hocness was equivalent to the prediction of novel facts.

Now *if* Popper's novelty requirement for non-ad hocness is strictly interpreted, it has the "unsatisfactory consequence" (Watkins, 1978, p. 34) that "known" evidence does not contribute to the confirmation of a theory, that is, that *only* novel facts matter.[11] It has been pointed out by a number of authors that such a novelty requirement is sufficient to rule out ad hoc maneuvers, but it is not necessary to do so.[12] For instance, in the previous example, if the evidence regarding inflation and governmental deficits were known before T'2 was proposed, those facts would not be novel and would not count as independent evidence for the new theory. Such implications have led several authors to propose new, less restrictive definitions of novel.[13]

In summary, then, for Popper good science is science that makes bold empirical conjectures and exposes these conjectures to severe tests. The ad hoc adjustment of a theory for the sole purpose of protecting it from such a refutation is precisely the opposite of what should occur in good scientific practice. Popper proposed independent testability as a requirement that would prevent such ad hoc adjustments. Because independent testability was associated with the prediction of novel facts, the two concepts, novelty and non-ad hocness, came to be regarded as synonymous.

II.   Ad hocness: Lakatos

In his presentation of the "Methodology of Scientific Research Programs" (hereafter, MSRP)[14] Lakatos defines a particular step in the development of a research program (a series of theories with shared hard-core metaphysical presuppositions and heuristic recommendations) as *theoretically progressive* if it "has some excess empirical content over its predecessor, that is, if it predicts some novel, hitherto unexpected fact" (1970, p. 118), and *empirically progressive* if some of these novel facts are actually confirmed. Lakatos defines a research program as *progressive* (nondegenerating) if it is theoretically progressive at each step in its development, and empirically progressive at least "intermittently" (1970, p. 134; 1968, p. 170). Notice two things about these definitions. First,

---

[11] Although this is not the only way that Popper's discussion of novelty can be interpreted, it is a quite common interpretation. For instance, Worrall (1978, p. 46) says, "the Popperian account of empirical support says that a theory is supported by any fact which it describes correctly and which was first discovered as a result of testing this theory; and that a fact which was already known before the theory's proposal does not support it."

[12] Musgrave (1974, p. 12) and Worrall (1978, p. 49).

[13] This changing view of novelty is discussed briefly in Hands (1985, pp. 6–7). Alternative definitions have been provided in Gardner (1982), Musgrave (1974), Watkins (1984), Worrall (1978), and Zahar (1973). Lakatos's emphasis on novelty (discussed in the next section) has been an important factor in the development of this literature.

[14] Lakatos (1968, 1970).

even theoretical progress requires the prediction of novel facts.[15] And second, Lakatos uses the expressions "predicts novel facts," "has excess empirical content," and "is independently testable" as perfect substitutes for one another.[16]

Although Lakatos's notion of progress is tied to the same testability/ novelty requirement that Popper used to eliminate ad hoc theory modifications, his actual use of the term differs significantly from Popper's. In fact, Lakatos uses the term "ad hoc" in at least three separate ways.[17] The first of these, which he calls "ad hoc$_1$," corresponds precisely to the way the term was used by Popper (and previously). A theory is ad hoc$_1$ if "there is no *independent test* possible for it" (1970, p. 175, note 2). Thus Popper's requirement for non-ad hocness is the same as Lakatos's requirement for nondegeneracy,[18] and the following equivalency holds: "non-Popperian ad hoc" = "non-ad hoc$_1$" = "theoretically progressive."[19] Lakatos, like Popper, makes non-ad hocness an essential component of his notion of progress in science.[20]

Lakatos's second definition of ad hocness, "ad hoc$_2$," is only a slight modification of ad hoc$_1$. He calls a theory (or problem shift) ad hoc$_2$ if it has excess content but *none* of this "excess content got corroborated" (1970, p. 175, note 2). This definition makes "non-ad hoc$_2$" = "empirically progressive."[21] Though requiring a theory to be non-ad hoc$_2$ is technically more stringent than requiring it to be non-ad hoc$_1$, the difference is only one of degree; ad hoc$_2$, like ad hoc$_1$, is fundamentally related to Popper's notion of ad hocness. Both requirements, theoretical and empirical progressiveness, represent ways to prevent the type of face-saving/

---

[15] Based on what Lakatos actually wrote, this is *not* literally correct. He says that a change is theoretically progressive *if* it predicts novel facts – he does *not* say *only if* it predicts novel facts. Thus the door is (formally) left open for other things that would be sufficient for theoretical progress. Although this *is* an interpretation that can be defended on the basis of what Lakatos actually wrote, it is certainly not the standard interpretation. The standard interpretation is (as above) that progress *requires* novel facts, that is, "if and only if" is read in rather than "if." The standard interpretation is probably more consistent with the overall spirit of the MSRP.

[16] For example, he says "produces novel facts (that is, it is 'independently testable')" (1970, p. 126) and "theories which had no excess content over their predecessors (or competitors) that is, which did not predict any *novel* facts" (1970, p. 175, note 2).

[17] This follows his presentation in (1978a), a paper originally published in 1968.

[18] Actually, of course, Popper requires some confirmation of this excess content (see note 8) and Lakatos requires at least intermittent confirmation.

[19] This equivalence is implicit in Lakatos (1968, 1970); it becomes explicit in later "Lakatosian" works such as Zahar (1973).

[20] "The problem of when a hypothesis-replacement is 'ad hoc', i.e., irrational, degenerating, bad, has never been discussed with more attention and detail than by Popper and myself" (Lakatos, 1978b, pp. 221–2).

[21] Actually, this identity requires a slight modification of Lakatos's definition; see Zahar (1973, p. 101, note 1).

content-decreasing/defensive behavior that Popper sought to exclude. This is not the case, though, for Lakatos's third notion of ad hocness.

Lakatos's third notion of ad hocness, "ad hoc$_3$," is related to the concepts of a research program's *positive heuristic*. According to MSRP, the hard core of the research program is the set of metaphysical (irrefutable) propositions that define the program and remain essentially unchanged throughout its evolution. The positive heuristic of the program is a set of rules that specify the research plan of the program and its relationship to the hard core.[22] The positive heuristic tells scientists working in the program what types of projects to work on, what empirical tests to perform, and how to interpret the results of those tests.[23]

Given this definition of the positive heuristic, ad hoc$_3$ is characterized as follows: "The theory is said to be *ad hoc$_3$* if it is obtained from its predecessor through a modification of the auxiliary hypotheses which does not accord with the spirit of the heuristic of the programme" (Zahar, 1973, p. 101).[24] The absence of such ad hoc$_3$ stratagems provides a dividing line "between 'mature science,' consisting of research programmes, and 'immature science,' consisting of a mere patched up pattern of trial and error" (Lakatos, 1970, p. 175). It also defines an *alternative type of progress;* "non-ad hoc$_3$ = heuristically progressive" (Zahar, 1973, p. 101, note 1). The motiviation for defining (and avoiding) this third type of ad hocness is that scientific progress should entail increasingly more unified and cohesive theories; it should not be achieved (though it could be if only ad hoc$_1$ and ad hoc$_2$ adjustments are excluded) "with a patched up, arbitrary series of disconnected theories" (Lakatos 1970, p. 175). Banning ad hoc$_3$ adjustments guarantees the continuity of science and preserves its "organic unity" (Zahar, 1973, p. 105). Thus, when scientific research *programs* are being considered, the previously discussed requirements for *progress* must be revised to include *heuristic progress.* "Within a given programme a theory represents progress if it satisfies three conditions: relatively to its predecessors, it should entail novel predictions; some of these predictions ought eventually to be confirmed; finally, the theory should be structured in accordance with the heuristic" (Zahar, 1983, p. 170).

[22] Lakatos (1968, pp. 170–3; 1970, pp. 134–8) and Worrall (1978, p. 59). Worrall (1978, p. 69, note 35) provides a partial list of the things that the positive heuristic might include.
[23] As an economic example, in Weintraub's (1985a) specification of the neo-Walrasian research program, the positive heuristic consists of propositions like "go forth and construct theories in which economic agents optimize" and "construct theories that make predictions about changes in equilibrium states."
[24] Zahar is quoted here simply because his statement is more straightforward than Lakatos's, which must be extracted from his discussion on pp. 174–7 and 182–7 of his 1970 paper.

This third type of ad hocness is clearly different from the type that concerned Popper (and was discussed previously).[25] It is apparent that even an empirically progressive (non-ad hoc$_2$) adjustment might still be ad hoc$_3$. For instance, it may be that T'2, proposed in the previous economic example, is ad hoc$_3$. Unless we know the macro research program the theory is embedded in, and can show that something in the hard core or positive heuristic of that program suggests that deficits should matter, T'2 could be accused of being ad hoc$_3$. Lakatos clearly considered program continuity to be extremely important and something that was not guaranteed by Popper's attempts to exclude ad hoc adjustments. For Lakatos, real progress occurs when a research program achieves theoretical/empirical progress "while sticking to its hard core" (1970, p. 187).

Thus there are two separate notions of ad hocness within the Popperian tradition. Ad hoc$_{1-2}$, or Popperian ad hocness, is the traditional notion of modifying a theory for the sole purpose of avoiding falsification. It can be prevented by requiring independent testability (or testing), that is, the prediction (or confirmation) of novel facts. The second notion, due to Lakatos, is ad hoc$_3$, and it pertains to the continuity of the program in which the theory is embedded. Ad hoc$_3$ adjustments can be avoided by requiring that any change be consistent with the core and positive heuristic of the program. Armed with these two concepts of ad hocness, let us now turn to the way the term is used in economics.

III.   Ad hocness in economics

The purpose of this section is to compare economists' use of the term "ad hoc" with its use in the philosophical literature: ad hoc$_{1-2}$ and ad hoc$_3$. In determining the way ad hocness is used in economics, two separate cases will be considered. The first is the way that *economic methodologists* use the term when appraising economic theories, and the second is the way that *economic theorists* (particularly recent theorists) use the term in theoretical discourse. In both cases, what is desired is a generalization regarding "the" representative or paradigmatic use of the term. Given the variety of ways the term is used, particularly among

---

[25] Though Popper did require a new theory to be "deeper," to have "a certain coherence or compactness" (1972, p. 197) or "simplicity" (1963, p. 241). Although these concepts are related to Lakatos's non-ad hoc$_3$, Popper was pessimistic about formalizing such requirements and never provided more than an intuitive discussion. Nor did Popper ever directly relate this coherence and simplicity to his notion of ad hocness. Recently, though, such concepts have been analyzed more rigorously (and related to ad hocness) by neo-Popperians, especially Watkins (1984).

theorists,[26] obtaining such a generalization is quite an empirical problem in itself. All that can be done in the current context is to posit a representative use and offer a few quotations/references in its defense. Hopefully this posit will prove to be an "empirically progressive generalization," that is, it will "anticipate" the way the term is used by (as yet) unexamined economic theorists.

There should be no controversy regarding the first group; the evidence clearly suggests that economic methodologists (and philosophers writing about economics) use the term in the traditional Popperian manner. For these authors, a theory is ad hoc if it is deliberately patched up to avoid falsification. For instance, Blaug (1980a) criticizes both human capital theory (p. 238) and the new economics of the family (pp. 242–3) as ad hoc in this traditional sense (despite Gary Becker's insistence to the contrary), and Hutchison accuses Marxists of making "*ad hoc* adjustments and qualifications" (1981, p. 18) to protect the Marxian theory of capitalist development from its predictive failures.[27,28] As yet another example, Rosenberg argues that most of the theoretical developments in the history of neoclassical rational choice theory amount of "largely *ad hoc* qualifications and restrictions that have preserved the theory against a series of failures to empirically substantiate it" (1980, p. 79).

Like methodologists and economic philosophers, economic theorists also use ad hocness in a defamatory way. It is not unusual in recent theoretical literature to find one economist condemning another economist or theoretical approach as ad hoc. This tendency is particularly pronounced in the rational expectations (or New Classical Macro) literature. In this controversial area it seems that "everyone calls the theory of the other ad hoc" (Klamer, 1983, p. 111). For example, in defending their use of the Lucas model, Sargent and Wallace state, "The advantage of Lucas's model is that ad hockeries are given much less of a role."[29] It is quite

---

[26] Not only economic theorists but natural scientists as well "use the term *ad hoc* to cover a multitude of sins. A theory may be called *ad hoc* because it is unaesthetic and clumsy, because it is arbitrary and uninteresting, or because it is wildly implausible" (Koertge, 1978, p. 267). Grunbaum (1976, p. 361) cites a quite extensive list of scientific uses of ad hocness (compiled by Holton).

[27] Similar criticisms of Marxian economics are made by Blaug (1980b).

[28] Although the ad hocness that concerns economic methodologists always seems to be of the Popperian type, it is interesting that Popperian methodologists such as Blaug, Hutchison, and Klant explicitly discuss the "disease" itself, that is, ad hocness, whereas Lakatosian methodologists are more likely to focus exclusively on the "cure," that is, "excess content" and "novel facts." In either case, there is seldom any recognition that the fundamental issue is the same.

[29] From T. Sargent and N. Wallace, "Rational Expectations and the Theory of Economic Policy," *Journal of Monetary Economics* 2, April 1976; quoted by Maddock (1984, p. 295).

common in surveys of this literature to hear that the assumption of rational expectations is compelling "in comparison with *ad hoc* alternatives" (Perry, 1984, p. 404) or that adaptive expectations, the principal alternative to rationally formed expectations, are simply "*ad hoc* rules" (Begg, 1982, p. 29). Keynesian alternatives to the New Classical Macroeconomics are said to rely on wage and price stickiness, which is "simply an *ad hoc* assumption" (Olson, 1984, p. 299), or they are based on "plausible – but you certainly could say ad hoc – disequilibrium dynamics" (Solow in Klamer, 1983, p. 139). In a few cases the accusatory arrow is even reversed; for instance, Hahn argues that it is the rational expectations theorists who "have chosen just that *ad hoc* model that delivers the goods" (1983, p. 60).

Although accusations of ad hocness seem to fly more freely in the rational expectations literature than in other theoretical areas, they are not exclusive to it. One of the other areas where it occurs is in traditional (Arrow–Debreu) general equilibrium theory. It has been known since the 1960s that in order to guarantee the stability or determinant comparative statics of a standard Walrasian general equilibrium system, it is necessary to impose quite restrictive mathematical properties on aggregate excess demand functions. Such restrictions are often called "*ad hoc* specializations of excess demand functions" (Fisher, 1983, p. 13) or "ad hoc assumptions, imposed directly on the excess demand system" (Hildenbrand's introduction to Debreu, 1983, p. 26).

How then are these economic theorists using the term "ad hoc"? Are they using it as methodologists do, as a claim that the accused theory has been deliberately modified solely to avoid an empirical refutation? The answer seems to be "no." Consider what immediately follows the Sargent and Wallace quotation cited previously. They say, "ad hockeries are given much less of a role and, consequently the neutrality proposition he obtains is seen to be a consequence of individual agents optimizing behavior."[30] Similar statements are made regarding the ad hocness of adaptive expectations. For instance, Begg states, "I argued that *ad hoc* rules such as Adaptive Expectations have the disturbing implication that they allow individuals to make systematic forecasting errors period after period" (1982, p. 29), and this "suboptimal use of available information is hard to reconcile with the idea of optimization" (1982, p. 26).[31] The previously mentioned Keynesian rigidities are not questioned empirically, but because the "assumption [of rigid wages or prices] is

---

[30] Ibid.
[31] In Begg's introduction to his own antirational expectations model he states, "we shall work with an ad-hoc specification of a macroeconomic model, rather than attempt to derive such a model from explicit microeconomic foundations" (1980, p. 294).

needed to generate the main Keynesian results, yet it is not derived from or supported by any analysis grounded in the motivational assumptions economists have found to be generally applicable" (Olson, 1984, p. 299). Even Solow's disequilibrium dynamics are potentially ad hoc because they are "certainly not the solution of some vast intertemporal optimization problem" (Klamer, 1983, p. 139). These statements do not indicate that nonrational expectations models are ad hoc because they lack empirical novelty or independent testability (though they might); rather, they are ad hoc because they are not derived from individual optimizing behavior. Nonrational expectations models are accused of being *ad hoc$_3$*, not *ad hoc$_{1-2}$*; according to their critics, the assumptions they require *do not follow from the core or positive heuristic of the neoclassical/individual optimization research program,* and that is the source of their ad hocness.

What about criticism going the other way, that is, what about theorists who accuse the rational expectations models of being ad hoc? Are they concerned with ad hoc$_3$ as well? Certainly this is the case for Hahn. The basis of Hahn's ad hocness charge is that Lucas-type models assume equilibrium but fail to explain the presence of that equilibrium on the basis of rational optimizing behavior. According to Hahn, "much importance is attached to rationality until it comes to price changes: then anything goes. For the Lucasians, prices change to keep Walrasian markets cleared by a mechanism that is entirely secret in the Lucasian mind" (1983, p. 54).[32] The accusation here, as in the case of nonrational expectations models, is that the theory in question fails to follow from the positive heuristic of the neoclassical research program, not that it is ad hoc$_{1-2}$.[33]

What about the situation outside of the rational expectations literature? Is the concern over ad hocness only a rational expectations phenomenon, or is it an economic theory phenomenon? Certainly if the

---

[32] Similarly, "I am in Lucas's methodological spirit when, instead, I propose that prices are flexible when there are no obstacles to price change when it is to someone's advantage to do so. More formally, prices in a given theory are flexible when their formation is endogenous to the theory. . . . Now as a matter of fact, prices in the Lucasian world are not properly endogenous to the fundamental theory, because there is no theory of the actions of agents that explains how prices come to be such as to clear Walrasian markets" (Hahn, 1983, p. 49).

[33] Following a time-honored Lakatosian tradition (Lakatos, 1971, p. 107), theorists who have "misbehaved" relative to the preceding reconstruction are confined to footnotes. One such case is Tobin (1980). In his discussion of Lucas's model, Tobin accuses (p. 42) it of being ad hoc in the traditional (ad hoc$_{1-2}$) sense. In response, Lucas fully admits that it is. "If ever there was a model rigged frankly and unapologetically, to fit a limited set of facts, it is this one" (1981, p. 563). The reader is reminded that the preceding argument tries to offer only an empirically progressive generalization about the way economic theorists use the term "ad hoc," not a claim that it is not used in any other way.

general equilibrium case cited previously is any indication, the concern is discipline-wide. Excess demand restrictions that guarantee stability and comparative statics (gross substitutes being the most common) are ad hoc because they do not follow from the standard assumptions on utility-maximizing agents, that is, they are not implied by the maximization of a strictly quasi-concave differentiable utility function subject to parametric prices. Since it is empirically obvious that not all goods actually exhibit properties like gross substitutability, it hardly seems possible that such assumptions were proposed to absorb a potential falsification. In addition, conditions like zero degree homogeneity and Walras's law are *not* considered ad hoc (though empirically questionable) simply because they *do* follow from the standard assumptions of consumer choice theory (and are therefore non-ad hoc$_3$ with respect to the neoclassical program).

Thus, for economic theorists, the sin of ad hocness seems to be infidelity to the metaphysical presuppositions of the neoclassical program rather than face-saving adjustments in response to recalcitrant data. Of course, this is not to say that economic theorists do not actually adjust their theories in an ad hoc$_{1-2}$ manner,[34] only that recent theorists seem to consider ad hoc$_3$ness to be a more damning criticism. The methodological implications of this result will now be examined.

IV.   Implications and conclusion

One response to the realization that economic theorists and economic philosophers use the term "ad hoc" in different ways is the so-called rhetorical response.[35] According to this view, these differences merely reflect the fact that methodologists and theorists are engaged in different types of discourse; they attempt to persuade different audiences and use different means to do so. Philosophers and methodologists are trying to persuade an audience convinced of the cognitive superiority of "science" that certain areas within economics do not measure up to those exacting standards. Economic theorists, on the other hand, are trying to persuade an audience convinced of the methodological superiority of the neoclassical approach that some particular economic theories do not measure up to its standards. Based on such a rhetorical view, the interesting things about ad hocness pertain to why certain individuals use it in certain ways, what it is about the conversational context that requires one use

[34] Thus, it may be that the preceding criticisms by economic methodologists are correct.
[35] Klamer (1984) provides such a rhetorical view. For him the rational expectations theorists' use of ad hoc$_3$ is an "epistemological argument" that serves "the new classical economists well to ward off the criticism that their assumptions are unrealistic" (p. 283).

over another, and what political/sociological/psychological factors influence the discourse of the two groups.

Although this rhetorical view seems fine as far as it goes, it does not exhaust the implications of the ad hocness issue. The differences among the various ways ad hocness is used have important methodological implications that go beyond these rhetorical concerns. For one thing, the preceding discussion can help economic methodologists provide a better rationalization of theoretical developments, particularly from a Lakatosian perspective. A good example of this is provided in Maddock's (1984) Lakatosian reconstruction of the rational expectations literature. At one point, Maddock notes an apparent "methodological inconsistency" in the work of Sargent and Lucas: "they rejected ad hoc adjustments to their models which could overturn the basic propositions, but made their own ad hoc adjustments in their endeavor to corroborate statistically those same propositions" (p. 301). This methodological inconsistency seems to dissolve when it is realized that different types of ad hocness are involved in the two cases. In the first case, the "ad hoc adjustments" rejected by rational expectations theorists are ad hoc$_3$ adjustments (discussed previously) that would introduce parameters not motivated by individual optimization. In the second case, where the rational expectations theorists "make their own ad hoc adjustments," the ad hocness is of the more traditional ad hoc$_{1-2}$ type. In this second case, as Maddock clearly documents, there was a rather blatant attempt to account for the empirical fact of "persistence" by adding a (thoroughly ad hoc$_{1-2}$) lagged unemployment (or income) term to the right-hand side of the Lucas supply function.

The two uses of ad hocness and the relative importance that theorists attach to each can also help explain Lucas's response to this apparent "inconsistency." Rather than provide a new theory that fits the data without being ad hoc$_{1-2}$, Lucas's response was to provide a formal general equilibrium model in which persistence could be derived from informational imperfections. As Maddock explains, "the introduction of a lagged income term into the aggregate-supply equation which had appeared ad hoc could now be justified as arising from within a consistent general equilibrium model with information differentials. As this paper stood it made no new empirical prediction, but it did lessen the impact of a criticism" (1984, p. 302). What it did, of course, was to lessen the criticism from other theorists that the supply function was ad hoc$_3$. Maddock claims that from a Lakatosian perspective Lucas's move was "defensive" (p. 302); but maybe not. The theory certainly didn't predict any novel facts, but maybe it was still "going forward" in a Lakatosian sense. What we have is a case where the lagged income term was both ad hoc$_{1-2}$ and ad hoc$_3$. According to Lakatos's MSRP, *both types* of ad hocness *must be eliminated* to avoid degeneracy.[36] Nothing Lakatos ever wrote specified which type of ad hocness should be addressed first.

This brings up a second but related point about the use of ad hoc$_3$ness in economics. Although heuristic progress (non-ad hoc$_3$ness) seems to be precisely what concerns economic theorists the most, it is almost never mentioned in the extensive literature that applies the MSRP to economics.[37] If heuristic progress were seriously considered, it might substantially change the nature of Lakatosian reconstructions in economics. On the positive side, as shown previously in the Lucas case, it may be possible to reconstruct certain theoretical developments as rational (or nondegenerating) by Lakatosian standards, where they would not be if only ad hoc$_{1-2}$ were considered. Lakatos *does* require heuristic progress, and it plays an important role in Lakatosian reconstructions of physical science.[38] If the profession's well-known infatuation with maximization can be reinterpreted as heuristic progress within a neoclassical research program that has individual optimization as a hard-core proposition, the entire history of economics may appear more progressive in Lakatosian terms. Also on the positive side, it seems that *economic theorists* have something like a general neoclassical research program clearly in mind. They seem to have already formed a hard core and positive heuristic, and to know when it is violated. This supports those economists attempting to reconstruct most of neoclassical economics as one big research program.[39] On the negative side, it seems that theorists' revealed preference for heuristic over theoretical/empirical progress (as Lakatos defines these terms) will make it hard to reconcile the history of economic thought with Lakatos's requirement that novel facts be predicted (though they need not be confirmed) at each stage in the program's development. This preference for heuristic progress may explain the paucity of novel facts in the history of economic thought.[40] It may be necessary to modify the MSRP to suit the

---

[36] "I define a research programme as degenerating even if it anticipates novel facts but does so in a patched-up development rather than by a coherent, pre-planned positive heuristic" (Lakatos, 1971, p. 125, note 36).
[37] A partial list is provided in Hands (1985), but many more works have appreared since that paper was written (for instance, Maddock, 1984, and Weintraub, 1985a).
[38] For instance, Zahar (1973) argues that Einstein's program superseded Lorentz's program because it was heuristically more progressive.
[39] Clearly, the best example is Weintraub (1985a).
[40] Although the absence of novel facts is a theme in Hands (1985), in all fairness it should be noted that "paucity" does not imply "nonexistence." Maddock (1984) and Weintraub (1985b), for instance, both do a very good job of finding novel facts in the economic programs they discuss.
  It may be just a humorous coincidence, but whenever philosophers in the Popperian tradition discuss authors who are critical of novel facts, that is, those who think that facts

needs of economics by "weighting" these two types of progress and finding an optimal way of making trade-offs between them. If this is to be
done in a way consistent with the actual practice of theorists, it seems
obvious that heuristic progress should be given a relatively large weight.
In any case, it appears that philosophers and economists taking a
Lakatosian approach to economics (as well as those criticizing it) should
seriously reconsider the question of heuristic progress (non-ad hoc$_3$ness)
and its role in the evaluation of economic theory.[41]

Finally, at the end of this discussion of implications (most of which
concern the Lakatosian interpretation of economics), it is important to
recall the discussion of Popper from Section I. Popper was concerned
with ad hoc$_{1-2}$, with the deliberate modification of a theory for the sole
purpose of avoiding a refutation. The concern with independent testability and novel facts only came about as a possible way of avoiding ad hoc$_{1-2}$
theory adjustment. In other words, novel facts are *not* fundamentally
interesting to Popper – they are only derivative; they are interesting because they help solve the problem of ad hoc$_{1-2}$ theory adjustment, a
problem that *is* fundamentally interesting. Thus, even if we accept Popper's concern over ad hoc$_{1-2}$ adjustments, novelty need not be as significant as recent work would indicate.[42] Of course, the elevation of novelty
to an independently interesting concept is due to Lakatos. Although
Lakatos's interest in novel facts initiated from the same basic concern as
Popper's, it seems to have turned into a novel fact fetishism that lost
sight of the original problem. It may be time, particularly in economic
methodology, to reexamine Popper's problem: the issue of ad hoc
theory adjustment in the traditional sense and what might prevent it. Do
traditionally ad hoc adjustments often occur in economics, and if so,
how are they problematic? Are there sufficient (or even necessary) conditions that would prevent such adjustments as they occur in economics?
Such questions would bring us back to the traditional issue of ad hocness
and Popper's problem, something that seems to have been lost in the
shuffle of recent methodological discussion.

are facts, regardless of whether they are "known" or "unknown," the two "philosophers" most often cited are J.S. Mill and J.M. Keynes (Lakatos, 1970, pp. 123–4; 1978a,
p. 183; Musgrave 1974, p. 2; Popper, 1963, p. 247).

[41] It is interesting to note that in Lakatos's few offhand comments about social science (for
instance, 1970, p. 176, note 1), he considers its immaturity, that is, its lack of heuristic
progress, to be its primary deficiency. It may be that economists' seemingly irrational
concern with "sticking with the program" (even at the expense of novel facts) is precisely
what makes economics the most mature of the social sciences.

[42] Recall (from note 4) that not all philosophers think that ad hoc$_{1-2}$ness is a real problem.
It can also be added that within the Popperian tradition, not everyone who thinks that
ad hoc$_{1-2}$ness is a problem believes that predicting novel facts is the way to solve it
(Koertge, 1978, p. 269).

References

Begg, D.K.H. (1980). "Rational Expectations and the Non-Neutrality of Systematic Monetary Policy," *Review of Economic Studies* 47:293–303.
  (1982). *The Rational Expectations Revolution in Macroeconomics.* Baltimore: Johns Hopkins University Press.
Blaug M. (1980a). *The Methodology of Economics.* Cambridge: Cambridge Univesity Press.
  (1980b), *A Methodological Appraisal of Marxian Economics.* Amsterdam: North-Holland.
Debreu, G. (1983). *Mathematical Economics: Twenty Papers of Gerard Debreu.* Cambridge: Cambridge University Press.
Fisher, F.M. (1983). *Disequilibrium Foundations of Equilibrium Economics.* Cambridge: Cambridge University Press.
Gardner, M.R. (1982). "Predicting Novel Facts," *British Journal for the Philosophy of Science* 33:1–5.
Grunbaum, A. (1976). "*Ad Hoc* Auxiliary Hypotheses and Falsificationism," *British Journal for the Philosophy of Science* 27:329–62.
Hahn, F. (1983). *Money and Inflation.* Cambridge, Mass.: MIT Press.
Hands, D.W. (1985). "Second Thoughts on Lakatos," *History of Political Economy* 17:1–16.
Hutchison, T.W. (1981). *The Politics and Philosophy of Economics.* New York: New York University Press.
Klamer, A. (1983). *Conversations with Economists.* Totowa, N.J.: Rowman and Allenheld.
  (1984). "Levels of Discourse in New Classical Economics," *History of Political Economy* 16:263–90.
Klant, J.J. (1984). *The Rules of the Game.* Cambridge: Cambridge University Press.
Koertge, N. (1978). "Towards a Theory of Scientific Inquiry," in G. Radnitzky and G. Anderson, eds., *Progress and Rationality in Science.* Dordrecht: Reidel, pp. 253–78.
Lakatos, I. (1968). "Criticism and the Methodology of Scientific Research Programmes," *Proceedings of the Aristotelian Society* 69:149–86.
  (1970). "Falsification and the Methodology of Scientific Research Programmes," in I. Lakatos and A. Musgrave, eds., *Criticism and the Growth of Knowledge.* Cambridge: Cambridge University Press, pp. 91–196.
  (1971). "History of Science and Its Rational Reconstructions," in R.C. Buck and R.S. Cohen, eds., *Boston Studies in the Philosophy of Science,* Vol. 8. Dordrecht: Reidel, pp. 91–136.
  (1978a). "Changes in the Problem of Inductive Logic," in *Mathematics, Science and Epistemology, Philosophical Papers,* Vol. 2. Cambridge: Cambridge University Press, pp. 128–200.
  (1978b). "Anomalies versus 'Crucial Experiments'," in *Mathematics, Science and Epistemology.* Cambridge: Cambridge University Press, pp. 211–23.

Laudan, L. (1977). *Progress and Its Problems.* Berkeley: University of California Press.

Lucas, R.E. (1981). "Tobin and Monetarism: A Review Article, *"Journal of Economic Literature* 19:558–67.

Maddock, R. (1984). "Rational Expectations Macro Theory: A Lakatosian Case Study in Program Adjustment," *History of Political Economy* 15:291–309.

Musgrave, A. (1974). "Logical versus Historical Theories of Confirmation," *British Journal of Philosophy of Science* 25:1–23.

Olson, M. (1984). "Beyond Keynesianism and Monetarism," *Economic Inquiry* 22:297–322.

Perry, G.L. (1984). "Reflections on Macroeconomics," *American Economic Review* 74:401–7.

Popper, K.R. (1963). *Conjectures and Refutations.* New York: Harper & Row.
  (1965). *The Logic of Scientific Discovery.* New York: Harper & Row.
  (1972). *Objective Knowledge.* Oxford: Oxford University Press.
  (1976). *Unended Quest.* La Salle, Ill.: Open Court.

Rosenberg, A. (1980). "A Skeptical History of Microeconomic Theory," *Theory and Decision* 12:79–93.

Tobin, J. (1980). *Asset Accumulation and Economic Activity.* Chicago: University of Chicago Press.

Watkins, J. (1978). "The Popperian Approach to Scientific Knowledge," in G. Radnitzky and G. Anderson, eds., *Progress and Rationality in Science.* Dordrecht: Reidel, pp. 23–43.
  (1984). *Science and Scepticism.* Princeton, N.J.: Princeton University Press.

Weintraub, E.R. (1985a). *General Equilibrium Analysis: Studies in Appraisal.* Cambridge: Cambridge University Press.
  (1985). "The Neo-Walrasian Program Is Empirically Progressive." Paper prepared for this conference.

Worrall, J. (1978). "The Ways in Which the Methodology of Scientific Research Programmes Improves on Popper's Methodology," in G. Radnitzky and G. Anderson, eds., *Progress and Rationality in Science.* Dordrecht: Reidel, pp. 45–70.

Zahar, E.G. (1973). "Why Did Einstein's Programme Supersede Lorentz's?" *British Journal for the Philosophy of Science* 24:95–123, 223–62.
  (1983). "The Popper–Lakatos Controversy in the Light of 'Die Beidn Grundprobleme Der Erkenntnis Theorie'," *British Journal for the Philosophy of Science* 34:149–71.

CHAPTER 4

Popper and the LSE economists

NEIL DE MARCHI

I

The usual student about to embark on a dissertation in economics is advised to find a tractable problem, produce a model, and test its implications in ways that shed light on the problem. It is accepted that data of the right sort are hard to find and yield only to trained pummeling (or caressing). Many compromises and judgments insert themselves between the theoretical and the empirical model ultimately adopted. Tests therefore are rarely satisfying and never conclusive, and the student learns to make do with conclusions as reticent as "The results do not warrant rejection of the hypothesis."

All of this is pretty much common wisdom. Testing is what we aspire to, and we think we know what it means to test. A mere thirty years ago, however, things were not so clear. Then, both the techniques and the methodology of testing were quite new. In 1955 there were just three texts in econometric methods available in English – Tinbergen (1951), Tintner (1952), and Klein (1953)[1] – and Friedman's essay espousing the testing of theory by checking its predictions was just two years old. Calculating technology, too, was very primitive for the majority. As an undergraduate I cranked out calculations on hand-operated Facit machines, and anything beyond a simple linear regression was unthinkable.

From the side of economic theory, too, there was a serious snag, although it is doubtful whether it was more than vaguely sensed by

I acknowledge gratefully the extraordinarily generous help I have received in trying to piece this story together from many of those involved. Richard G. Lipsey and Chris Archibald especially, but also Max Steuer and Kurt Klappholz, all gave liberally of their time to help me sort out nuances and factual details. Jack Wiseman, David Laidler, J.D. Sargan, W.W. Bartley III, Allan Sleeman, and Jeremy Shearmur also contributed valuable recollections and corrective suggestions. In the earlier stages of drafting I was helped, as always, by conversations with my colleague E. Roy Weintraub; and useful comments were received from Mark Blaug, A.W. Coats, D. Wade Hands, Bruce Caldwell, David Hendry, and Joop Klant. I also learned from conversations with Christ Gilbert, and a long weekend of intensive discussion with Arjo Klamer shaped in unusual degree the final form of the material. This chapter would not have come into being without the expert word processing assistance of Forrest Smith. My thanks go to them all.

[1] Davis's *The Theory of Econometrics* (1941) was an attempt to state economic theory in exact and quantifiable form. There was little in it in the way of econometric methods.

many. The dominant analytical tradition, advanced in the 1930s and 1940s by Robbins in the United Kingdom and Samuelson in the United States–the tradition of qualitative comparative statics–is one in which opportunities for testing are neither numerous nor discriminating. This manifests itself in several forms. There is likely to be more than one effect of a parameter change–for example, income and price effects–operating in opposite directions, so that theory alone has little to say about the outcome. This allows a theory to escape unscathed when results are not as expected. Moreover, economists are interested in policy; and, confronting, as they do, a lack of givenness about the parameter values of the equations that describe the behavior of "the" system, they are apt to resort to taxonomic analysis of possible cases. Here parameters function not as numerical but as algebraic constants. That is, "exogenous" parameters are deliberately assigned different values, so as to allow the exploration of different cases. Klant dubs this the "parametric paradox." Its effect is to render theory logically unfalsifiable (Klant, 1984, ch. 4, sect. 9, criticizing Samuelson). The same thing happens when, as rational expectationists suppose, the model structure, reflecting expectations, is not invariant to a supposedly exogenous parameter change. Here the important distinction between exogenous and endogenous variables simply breaks down. This is the basis of the so-called Lucas critique.

If we grant these constraints on testing from the side of economic theory, clearly measurement becomes of crucial importance. As Harry Johnson put it in a perceptive review of James Meade's *The Theory of International Economic Policy* (Johnson 1951, p. 827), referring to the first and simplest form of the difficulty: "the problems in which most theorists are interested require the specification of the direction of the net outcome of influences operating in opposite directions, and this in turn requires a specification of the magnitudes as well as the signs of the influences. For such problems, all that theory can do is to specify some (measurable) quantity on which the outcome will depend. *To determine the outcome in any particular case, however, it is necessary to measure the quantity*" (emphasis mine).

Making modern economics into an empirical science, however, has been a struggle. Rather, there have been many struggles: some in the realm of econometrics, some in economic theory, and at least one at the border where the two join. At that junction exact theoretical specification, quantification, and assessment all become pressing issues. I want to recount the story of a border skirmish in which precisely these things were fought over. It took place at the London School of Economics from 1957 to about 1963. There was a prior formative period during which lines

became drawn. The protagonists were Robbins, representing nonquantitative and logically unfalsifiable economic theory, and a group of unusu-
ally talented young members of the economics staff at the London School
of Economics (LSE), led by Richard Lipsey and Chris Archibald. They
were supported, in varying degrees, from the first by Kurt Klappholz,
Lucien Foldes, Maurice Peston, and Kelvin Lancaster. Bernard Corry
and Max Steuer joined later, on their appointment to the staff, as did Jim
Thomas, Miles Kennedy, and others. This group – really a palace guard,
since many had been students under Robbins and owed their elevation to
his influence – sought to recast economic knowledge in falsifiable form
and proclaim their independence from the dogma, in which they had been
schooled, that quantification is not only diffcult but unnecessary.

These may sound like sweeping aspirations, but the goal was actually
very specific: to replace Robbins's *Nature and Significance of Economic
Science* as the dominant source of methodological ideas for British
economists and to argue for the notion that theory alone cannot be a
sufficient basis for policy conclusions. Expressed positively, economics
should become a quantifed science. Initially, testing was not part of the
program. That came later as the group learned about Popper's ideas, at
first informally and then via *The Logic of Scientific Discovery,* which
appeared in 1959. The focus for the group's deliberations was a seminar
initiated by Lipsey in 1957 and called the "LSE Staff Seminar in Methodology, Measurement and Testing," or "M²T." The "T" for testing, to
repeat, was not in the original concept.

The story of this rather local struggle in the 1950s is full of interest. It
appears, for example, that Popper's views on methodology were cata-
lytic in some sense, but it is not immediately clear that it had to be *him*
or *his* ideas. Why not Hutchison, who had first introduced Popper to
English-speaking economists and was himself at the LSE until 1956? Or
Friedman, who had also stressed the empirical and had urged testing?
What exactly attracted the group to Popper?

It will emerge that personalities were very important in the evolution
of the group itself. Lipsey was its driving force. He took a leave from the
LSE for the academic year 1963–4 and moved in the fall of 1964 to a
chair at Essex. Almost at once the group dissolved, and the character
and direction of the seminar that succeeded M²T were quite different.
But even before Lipsey left, he and Archibald were moving away from
Popper. Why did this occur? The fact that Popper is more drawn upon
by economic methodologists than economists is not hard to understand;[2]

---

[2] This emerged from a check of references to *The Logic of Scientific Discovery* in the
"Social Sciences Citation Index." I am indebted to Lee Nussbaum for help in conducting
the check.

but if would-be practitioners of his approach so quickly abandon him, does this suggest that there are inherent difficulties in applying his ideas to economics?

I suggest that Popper has no compelling answers to the problem that economic theory alone yields few unambiguous predictions, the problem of the lack of fixed numerical parameter values characterizing economic systems, or the problem that exogeneity and endogeneity are sometimes less distinct than we would like. The LSE economists became disenchanted with falsifiability as a criterion when they began to discover the force of these difficulties for themselves. They also fairly quickly concluded that economic propositions that are quantified will necessarily involve an error term. But this raises the question, how good is a "good" fit? Popper's idea that we should try to refute hypotheses in isolation is weakened – as he himself recognized – when the propositions are expressed as probability statements. Some of the LSE group in fact moved toward a different criterion, comparative predictive power (anticipating Lakatos's notion of "excess content"), as the weakness of the Popperian injunction became clear to them. Finally, they discovered that to apply Popper's critical rationalism actually involves a change of style in terms of the way economists engage in debate. It calls for an attitude of "come, let us reason together" (and work to tease something testable out of *both* our theories). But that demands a combination of commitment plus personal indifference, which makes its way slowly and fitfully at best. The LSE economists discovered this painfully when Archibald invited Chicago to reconsider imperfect competition and was rebuffed. Friedman and Stigler brusquely refused to engage Archibald in debate. If we look beyond the language, it is plain that they were pitting the demonstrated survival value of the competitive modeling research tradition against the claims of an isolated theory. There are dimensions to economic argumentation that take us far beyond Popper's precept of rational (critical) discussion, the central idea of which is that we try as hard as possible to overthrow our own hypotheses.

By exploring these issues, we shall grasp something of why working economists have relatively little use for Popper. The LSE struggle offers a perfect context. Our order will be to look more closely first (Section II) at the stage and the players. In Section III, we shall work through a sample of the research work of the LSE group related to Popperian themes. Section IV looks at the reasons why Archibald and Lipsey abandoned Popper. Finally, the threads comprising the evidence for the several lines of argument just mentioned will be drawn together.

II

Lipsey entered the LSE as a research student in 1953 and two years later was appointed an assistant lecturer. He had attended Robbins's seminar as a student and continued to do so as a staff member. Robbins was Professor of Economics, Analytical and Descriptive, and his seminar was the focus of theoretical endeavor within the School. The style of the seminar was the then common one of analytical dissection. Theory was regarded as "a method of classifying the universe of possible cases" (Johnson, 1951, p. 826; cf. Lange, 1944). Models were examined for the realism of their assumptions and for internal consistency.[3] Results might be tested for robustness (to assumptions change) but were rarely subjected to quantification using actual numbers. Overall assessment was made by an economic-linguistic test – is it economically meaningful? – or according to a largely undefined notion of relevance: Has light been shed? Insight gained?

Lipsey and Archibald's famous 1958 paper, "Monetary and Value Theory: A Critique of Lange and Patinkin," is in this genre. Arising out of discussions of Patinkin's *Money, Interest, and Prices* in Robbins's seminar, their paper was a thorough examination of out-of-equilibrium processes versus equilibrium conditions in models with a real-balance effect. Through a refinement of the stock-flow distinction, the authors discover that "full" classical "equilibrium" conditions do not require the presence of a real-balance effect and that models embodying this effect cannot "invalidate" Keynesian claims about less than full employment "equilibrium." Notice all the terms that require quotation marks. Was this merely a terminological dispute – a "sorting out," as Lipsey has referred to it (notes to the author, 7 June 1985)? Was that how economics advanced? Lipsey felt at the time the implied objection: "I was never quite sure if this exercise was of purely scholastic interest" (ibid.). What Lipsey and Archibald did conclude with confidence was that "one model cannot be used to invalidate another" (1958, in Thorn, ed., 1966, p. 320). This made it a question of circumstances or problem context as to which model is preferable. And that question, as they correctly pointed out, "is one for empirical rather than *a priori* investigation" (ibid.).

Robbins, though, had little truck with empirical investigation. Read-

---

[3] Cf. Harry Johnson's remark about Cambridge in the 1950s: "the examination of the realism or unrealism of analytical assumptions as a test of the validity of a theory . . . provided a basic technique of British theoretical discourse in the 1930s and on well into the 1950s" (1978, p. 158).

ers familiar with *An Essay on the Nature and Significance of Economic Science* will recall his lofty dismissal of " 'Quantitative Economics', 'Dynamic Economics', and what not" (1952 [1935], p. 112), and his rough handling of the fictitious Dr. Blank and his researches into the elasticity of demand for herrings (ibid., pp. 107–8). There are just too many variables, and they are altogether too variable. "Is it possible reasonably to suppose that coefficients derived from the observation of a particular herring market at a particular time and place have any *permanent* significance. . .?" (ibid., pp. 108–9). Given the changeableness of economic parameters, one might, of course, respond by claiming that this is all the more reason to measure. Robbins acknowledged this possible response in a reply to his critics (1938, p. 351). Equally, however, one might argue, as Keynes did, that although measuring provides useful information, we miss the point of economic logic and model building if we try to quantify parameters with any suggestion that the numbers will be of general validity. Robbins took his stand on that side of the issue.[4] In practice, this put a damper on measuring.

That, then was how matters stood in the mid-fifties at the LSE. Robbins was skeptical about quantification. Among his junior colleagues there was a growing, if still somewhat vague, sense that this was wrong; that there must be something more to economic science than (as Steuer has rather nicely put it: letter to the author, 14 May 1985) "the discovery of irresistible truth through logical manipulation of a few self-evident postulates." However, the issue was not just quantification in the abstract; it was how you bring economic analysis to bear on policy questions. Harry Johnson, in the review of Meade cited previously, elaborated a position that appealed to several at least among the eventual members of M²T: "if economic theory is to be applied to problems of economic policy, this can most usefully be done within the context of a particular problem occurring in a particular environment. Only so will full justice be done to the complexities of policy problems, and adequate attention paid to the necessity of economic measurement" (1951, p. 828). In contrast to this view, Robbins was perceived as invoking "scientific" economics – pure deductive analysis, without measurement – directly in support of a noninterventionist policy stance.[5]

---

[4] There is a striking similarity between Robbins's convictions on this point and Keynes's. (See Keynes's letter to Harrod, 16 July 1938, in Keynes's *Collected Writings*, Vol. XIV, p. 299).

[5] This is the interpretation that was placed on Robbins's basically negative judgment on setting aggregate demand policy by a commitment to full employment; see his *Money, Trade and International Relations* (1971a, pp. 2–3 and ch. II) and his *Autobiography of an Economist* (1971b, pp. 230–1). His enthusiasm for Patinkin's work, too, seemed to be linked to the view that the logical consistency of the full employment equilibrium had

To Lipsey and Archibald, what needed to be done was clear. Lipsey was bothered about the general methodological issue of validation – how we judge the "correctness" of economic theories – and he knew that he wanted to look for answers in the empirical rather than the a priori direction. The very last sentence of Lipsey and Archibald's critique of Patinkin makes this perfectly plain (Thorn, 1966, p. 320). The introduction to Lipsey's *An Introduction to Positive Economics*, begun in 1961 and published in 1963, is an affirmation along the same lines. More than this, if we may read back from the *Introduction to Positive Economics*, it is clear that he had a strong sense that quantification is desirable. This is a well-developed theme in the book, starting with the very serious quotation from Beveridge that precedes the table of contents. It also informs his answer to Robbins in the methodological introduction. There he argues that the numerical inconstancy of the "givens" of economic theory causes added difficulty in generating evidence but does not mark economics off as unscientific (p. 6). Again, he acknowledges that individual behavior is difficult to predict; but it is not true, at least as applied to groups, that human behavior is "utterly capricious" (p. 10). The proper question to be addressed in the face of these difficulties is a quantitative one: *How much* stability is there (ibid.)? Later in the book, following a discussion of the unfortunate Dr. Blank's problem, Lipsey expresses himself even more forcefully: "the theory of demand and price can have few applications to the real world without some empirical observations of quantitative magnitudes. Empirical measurements are critical to [the use of] economic theory" (p. 161).

Quantification, then, was one need. Another was how to generate testable implications and conduct tests of economic theory. If quantification was Lipsey's mission, reconsidering theory with an eye to testing was Archibald's. The two, of course, merge; but in the beginning they were two distinct concerns.

Hutchison had spoken of testability (1938). Archibald, however, in a 1959 review of the state of economic methodology, concluded that it was not clear from Hutchison's discussion just what or how we test (1959a, p. 60). Hutchison's work dated from the 1930s, when he felt it necessary to attack "mystical" economics, or propositions with purported empirical consequences but for which there is no apparent transformation that would render them empirically checkable (1938, ch. 1, passim.). Perfect foresight economics, for instance, may be all very well, but we should understand that it is fundamentally distinct from an economic analysis of

been demonstrated afresh in *Money, Interest, and Prices*. I am indebted to David Laidler and Allan Sleeman for alerting me to the political aspect of the opposition to Robbins among junior members of staff at the LSE.

real–that is, uncertain–worlds. A first step, therefore, before concerning ourselves with how "realistic" an analysis is, is to make sure that we have "assumptions" that are not empty but capture some relevant aspects of empirical reality (p. 119). Robbins's "impressionistically *a priori*" style of theorizing (p. 120) was one object of Hutchison's ire, and he ought to have been seen as an ally by the LSE junior staff. But this apparent concern with realistic assumptions, and his stress on using *ceteris paribus* only together with strongly verified empirical generalizations (p. 46), led his potential supporters at the LSE to believe that he was urging some kind of naive inductivism. This, plus an aversion to the logical positivist underpinnings of his position, canceled out the appreciation evoked by his courageous attack on Robbins.[6]

Two other factors helped to guarantee Hutchison's relative neglect. One was the fact that he offered so little guidance in showing how economics could be done in an empirical manner. Samuelson's *Foundations,* with its discussion of ways to make equilibrium propositions operational, held out a promise of getting beyond both Robbins and Hutchison. The *Foundations* greatly influenced Lancaster and Archibald (see, for instance, Lancaster, 1962, and Archibald, 1961, 1964, 1965). In a 1961 presentation to M²T, Archibald argued that comparative statics has the advantage over studying equilibrium properties in that we can so rarely observe equilibrium (abstract of a paper presented to M²T, October 25, 1961, and November 1, 1961; minutes taken by Bernard Corry). Earlier, in helping to develop a theoretical foundation for Lipsey's Phillips Curve research (Lipsey, 1960, esp. pp. 13–14), Archibald had silently invoked Samuelson to move the identification problem out of the way. Suppose that supply and demand functions are both shifting about. We may know both what is in the *ceteris paribus* pound and that the demand and supply relations are normal. Then we would be in Hutchison's preferred position and would be a step beyond tautological propositions. But we would still be a long way from testability. Archibald showed that in such a situation we can proceed by using the notion of *excess* demand or supply without observing the *ceteris paribus* conditions. We need only add a subsidiary assumption about speed of adjustment and adopt an empirical proxy for "excess."

The other intervening factor was the appearance of Friedman's 1953 essay arguing for the testing of implications, combined with the appearance of *A theory of the Consumption Function* (1957). Friedman's empha-

---

[6] These judgments emerged in my conversations with members of the LSE group. Machlup's 1955 designation of Hutchison as an "ultra-empiricist" possibly influenced the way he was read by them. See Machlup (1955) and Hutchison's reply (1956), both in Caldwell (1984).

sis on predictions held a natural appeal to the LSE group, impressed as they were with comparative statics analysis à la Samuelson. Moreover, Friedman espoused the view that "[f]actual evidence can never 'prove' a hypothesis; it can only fail to disprove it" (1953, p. 9). This, together with his rejection of realism of assumptions as a test of theory, meant that the problem of induction could simply be skirted. To clinch the appeal, Friedman not only addressed methodological concerns, he also showed – much more so than Samuelson – how theory could be combined with quantification: *A Theory of the Consumption Function* was quickly embraced by the economics profession as an exemplar of quantitative economic analysis.

Not that the LSE economists were Friedmanites. Lipsey held that if an assumption is wrong yet a theory predicts well, there must be at least one other wrong assumption, negating the impact of the first (notes to the author, 7 June 1985). Friedman's position, thus interpreted, implied a naive instrumentalism that was hard to accept. Archibald (1959a, p. 61) complained that Friedman had not shown any more clearly than Hutchison just how we test, nor what are the criteria of a "good" test. He protested too, as did Klappholz and Agassi in an important survey of works on economic methodology, "Methodological Prescriptions in Economics" (1959), that Friedman stressed testing almost to the exclusion of any other sort of critical examination. This might be stultifying, which is bad enough. Yet Friedman also accepted large chunks of economic theory without actually offering any evidence of their having been tested (Archibald, 1959a, p. 62; Klappholz and Agassi, 1959, pp. 66, 67–8). This latter characteristic seemed to betray a strong and contradictory verificationist residue in Friedman's methodology. It did not sit well with the young LSE economists, who by this time had discovered Popper.

In describing Archibald's concern with testing and the reasons why Friedman failed to convince, I have run ahead of events. As things stood a year or so after Lipsey's appointment to the LSE staff – say, in early 1957 – the situation was as follows. Lipsey was itching to get into combat against Robbins and other old-line liberals such as Plant and Paish. His restlessness, shared by others, was based on political and technical dissatisfaction.[7] Neither Hutchison nor Friedman quite met their battle needs,

---

[7] Not only was Robbins accused of downplaying quantification and elevating pure theory to a role of crucial importance in guiding policy, but his negative reaction to Harry Johnson's 1951 review of Meade's *Theory of International Economic Policy* is said to have led to his opposing Johnson as Meade's successor in the Commerce Chair in 1957. Johnson was somewhat older than the junior LSE staff and had begun to be looked up to by them as something of a mentor. He took an active part in the London-Oxford-Cambridge seminar, and in this forum and as an editor of the *Review of Economic Studies* in the late 1950s and early 1960s exerted an influence on the M²T group and helped publish their work. I am grateful to David Laidler for alerting me to Johnson's role. Letter to the author, 27 November 1985.

but they were eager to be satisfied. Although they were not wholly gullible, then, it was only a matter of time before appropriate weaponry would be found.

Enter Popper. He had been in the Philosophy Department at the LSE since returning to Europe from wartime teaching posts in New Zealand in 1946. His ideas were not a matter of daily conversation among the economists, but neither were they entirely unknown to them. In the late 1950s there was an optional logic and scientific method course available to Part One B.Sc. (Econ.) students at the LSE, and some good undergraduates who took it—David Laidler and Maurice Peston among them—brought to their economics teachers in the final year of specialization bits of what Popper was saying.

In the spring or early summer of 1957 Lipsey gathered the group of his concerned young colleagues into an informal seminar, outside of the Robbins seminar. They met to discuss how to get out from under the Robbins incubus. As it turned out, they soon found themselves receiving instruction in Popper's ideas. For Klappholz had got to know Joseph Agassi, a graduate student of Popper's, who later became his research assistant. Agassi was keen to proselytize. He became mentor to the economists and, as Lipsey recalls it, over about half a year they "learned, and came to accept, much of Popper's views on methodology" (letter to the author, 17 May 1985).

This almost suggests mass conversion, and the group may well have regarded themselves as disciples at first. Certainly, after their initial instruction in Popper's views, they felt charged up and eager to go out and apply them to economics. At this point they constituted themselves formally as the LSE Staff Seminar on Methodology, Measurement, and Testing, with Lipsey as chairman. The title of the seminar reflects their confidence that at last they knew how to advance beyond Robbins.

What was it that Popper gave the group? Three things stand out. First, he imparted an impetus to formulate theory in testable form. This was picked up by Archibald, as I have already indicated, but he brought Lipsey and others along. Notice that in supplying this impetus, Popper legitimized the theoretical enterprise but made theorists accountable. Neither Hutchison nor Friedman could have given quite this feeling of comfort to a group whose upbringing as economists, we must remember, was essentially in a pure theoretical tradition.

Second, Popper did not just urge testable theory; he actually issued some guidelines on how to pursue testing. As Steuer has put it (in conversation, 1 July 1985), with Popper "you had a tight procedure to guide you through the maze of the fact–theory mess." It is often forgotten how central to Popper's thought is the notion of methodological conventions. Here are several of his obiter dicta that bear on testing:[8]

> A refutable theory is one that denies something.
> More pointed predictions deny more and are therefore more refutable.
> Testing should be "severe."
> Stratagems for saving the hypothesis when evidence is unfavorable are to be avoided.
> Theoretical progress involves accounting for what we know and explaining new facts.

These pieces of advice add up to a set of test criteria. They too go beyond anything to be found in Hutchison or Friedman.

Third, Popper exalted criticism above the idea that we can ever know with certainty. What could be better for a band of would-be revolutionaries?

Despite their eager embracing of Popper, the LSE economists were never undiscriminating in their commitment, and the ways in which they drew on his work became more selective as their early broad concerns gave way to more precisely formulated problems.

It is time to consider this next phase in more detail, which we shall do by looking at some of the research spawned by the M²T seminar.

III

A quite remarkable number of published articles and notes can be traced directly to the seminar, not to speak of Lipsey's best-selling *Introduction to Positive Economics* (over 1.5 million copies sold to date in thirteen languages). These can be listed,[9] but it is probably more revealing to note the distinct motivations and roles played by key individuals in the work of the group. That means chiefly Lipsey and Archibald.

Lipsey was the acknowledged leader, and he set both the pace and the tone. The *Introduction,* which he began in 1961 and thought of as an expression of the thinking of the M²T seminar, was his answer to Robbins. It stressed methodological awareness from the outset and resolutely subjected established theories to criticism. Virtually every part ended with a whole chapter either criticizing received theory or drawing its empirically testable implications. Not infrequently he had to conclude

---

[8] An overlapping but longer list, with references, is to be found in Mark Blaug's *The Methodology of Economics* (1980), p. 19.
[9] Items in my list of references that should be regarded as M²T-related work are given an asterisk.

that the theory being considered did not yield a large number of testable predictions (e.g., pp. 221, 239, 326); or that testing it seemed to be extraordinarily difficult (p. 326); or simply that it yielded few implications about questions of interest (pp. 265–6, 325 n. 2, and 326). But even conclusions like these were discoveries. Nobody before had undertaken this exploration.

It is not clear whether, at the time, Lipsey was disturbed that economic theory seemed to be so little "positive."[10] At any rate, his zeal was undiminished. The essential message remained: "economic theory is unable to produce something out of nothing" (p. 239). If we know no facts or cannot or do not measure parameters and relations and judge their stability quantitatively, "we cannot use economic theory to make useful predictions about the real world" (p. 161). Methodologically speaking, that is to say, there was no excuse for Robbins's attitude that we needn't bother to measure just because so many things are happening and the numbers are bound to alter anyway (1952 [1932], pp. 107ff.), and certainly no basis for leaping to policy from pure theory. Furthermore, since a main reason why so few predictions seemed to emerge from accepted theories was that the theories themselves were so poorly informed – they assumed almost no knowledge of the real world – this very poverty of quantitative information was a kind of self-condemnation. These critical points are well taken. It remains true, though, that Lipsey's constructive harvest was scanty and he could only express a plausible optimism: "Generally, the more things we do know . . . the more likely it is that we shall be able to deduce interesting and possibly unsuspected consequences from these facts" (*Introduction*, 1963, p. 239).

In being concerned with getting quantitative knowledge, Lipsey ran a risk of being accused of pursuing measurement without theory. His major empirical preoccupation was a detailed reconsideration of Phillips's work on the relation between unemployment and the rate of change of money wage rates (Lipsey, 1960). This work occupied the seminar for a full six months. Lipsey thought it important "to quantify Phillips' results,"[11] discovering, for example, just how much of the variance in nominal wages is explained by unemployment and its rate of change. He also wanted to test Phillips's subsidiary hypotheses in a systematic way. And he thought that alternatives to Phillips's explana-

---

[10] We do know that when he set out in 1959–60 to learn some econometrics, he was naive about the amount of existing quantitative work. He recounts that he set an assistant to work cataloguing past work, and expected that this might take a month or two at most (notes to the author, 7 June 1985).

[11] Here too there was a political undercurrent. Supporters of Labour among M²T members took Phillips's results to be a useful antidote to Robbins's fear of cost-push inflation.

tion should be tested too (1960, p. 1). This sounds admirably Popperian in its repeated stress on testing. In fact, however, Lipsey's stated ideal order of proceeding was somewhat inductive and reminds one more of Friedman: The researcher first discovers what phenomena need explaining and then builds a model to rationalize these data. Finally, further implications or out-of-sample implications of the model are tested. Lipsey's penchant (not only in this instance: see Brechling and Lipsey, 1963) was to put in most of the work at stage one, since to build up a clear picture of the explicanda "a rather elaborate treatment [of the data] is required" (ibid.).

There was also a theoretical modeling stage in this Phillips Curve work. A model was inserted at Archibald's insistence (Lipsey, 1960, p. 12, n. 1). He was the analytical alter ego to the LSE group. Lipsey, it need hardly be added, thoroughly welcomed his interventions. As he himself explained the desirability of having a model (I paraphrase very liberally from ibid., pp. 12, 21 n. 2, 23):

1. General relations between variables ($\dot{W}$, U, $\dot{U}$, for instance) are open to more than one interpretation, some of them *mis*interpretations. The only way to avoid the latter is to spell out fully the model underlying the relations.
2. What if a relation ceases to hold or changes? Without a model, all we can conclude is that it has ceased to hold or has changed. We do not know why; hence we can learn nothing from observation.
3. An empirical model that is theoretically embedded (not ad hoc) will contain further testable predictions, the actual testing of which will increase our understanding because they relate to data other than those used to construct the initial predictions.

Lipsey here comes over as being not only utterly antipathetic to Robbins's style but also very commonsensical in his approach to methodological issues. In this respect he seems as close to Friedman as to Popper, and one is reminded that it was Archibald who stressed testable *theory*, whereas Lipsey pushed ways to measure and to capture what is in the data. The contrast between the essentially empirical and the essentially theoretical emerges very clearly in two subsequent and separate papers generated by these two extending the early Phillips Curve work: Lipsey and Parkin (1970) and Archibald, Kemmis, and Perkins (1974).

Archibald, for his part, worked much on the theory of the firm and on market structure. At least some of his determination to write out fully specified and testable models arose out of a disappointment with Friedman and Chicago on these subjects – not with Friedman's message, note, but with what seemed to Archibald to be a complacent attitude, possibly stemming from too lightly assuming that orthodox price theory had been tested and was firmly established (Archibald, 1959a, pp. 61, 63; 1961, pp. 3, 5).

There is an unmistakable tendency in Friedman to slip into a priori defenses of propositions such as profit maximization (Archibald, 1961, p. 3; Hirsch and de Marchi, 1985). As noted previously, there is as well a distinctly un-Popperian theme in Friedman's essay, and one strikingly at odds with his apparent acceptance of falsification. He speaks repeatedly of our "confidence" in and evidence *for* a hypothesis, even of "our confidence in [its] validity," and of testing as if its function is to verify (!) validity (1953, pp. 9, 12, 22, 23, 28, 40). Whereas Popper tests for truth "by eliminating falsehood" – a negative construction that fits his critical view of knowledge (Popper, 1963, p. 81) – Friedman seeks to strengthen confidence by accumulating positive instances. Friedman, for all his verbal deference to the asymmetry thesis, is not a critical rationalist. Archibald picked up the point. In "Chamberlin *versus* Chicago" (1961) he accused "Chicago" of having asked "what do we know?" without having asked "the inquiring, scientific [Popperian] question: What don't we know?" (p. 5).

We noted earlier Archibald's complaint that Friedman had failed to explain how we test and what is meant by a good test (1959a, p. 61). In the context of the theory of the firm, the complaint could be made fairly specific. How do we test a purely static theory at all? We cannot in general observe equilibrium conditions; and in the absence of detailed quantitative information about functions, which mostly we do not have, we apply qualitative comparative statics. But to do this successfully requires, at a minimum, that we specify in advance which things are to be regarded as constants in the hypothesis under test, and that we ensure that they are observables (1959a, p. 61; 1961, p. 9).[12] All of this presupposes an explicit model, "loose" enough to allow change away from equilibrium but "tight" enough to yield qualitative predictions that are refutable. Archibald attempted in a series of papers on aspects of the theory of the firm (1961, 1963a, 1964, 1965), and also in isolated attempts to reformulate the implications of welfare economics and the marginal productivity theory of distribution (1959b, 1960), to state models with testable consequences. He accused Friedman, in not having bothered to do likewise, of having actually discouraged "that sceptical reexamination of the allegedly obvious that is the prerequisite of prog-

---

[12] Archibald felt attracted by Papandreou's stress on structure in his approach to testing, but despaired of the very abstract way in which he was content to talk about the environment ("social space") within which a test might be specified (Papandreou, 1958, 1963; Archibald, 1963b).

ress" (1959a, p. 62). Archibald's cajoling of Lipsey to specify models in his own work may have been motivated in part by a desire to save him from Friedman's failing.

Archibald saw Lancaster's work on "The Scope of Qualitative Economics" (1962) as complementing, at a higher level, his own efforts "to know what models have qualitative content, and, where they do not, to know why" (Archibald, 1964, p. 21). Since Archibald was trying to apply critical rationalism, it is worth pausing to record his total lack of success in engaging the Chicagoans in the constructive enterprise of seeing what, if any, testable propositions monopolistic competition theory could be made to yield. No episode illustrates better, by positive example and by default, what it might mean to be a critical rationalist economist.

Archibald ran at Friedman and Stigler head on in his "Chamberlin *versus* Chicago," asking both what predictions one might derive in a monopolistic competitive framework and why the Chicagoans had not bothered to explore this themselves, in view of Friedman's methodological precepts. He set up a model of the individual firm allowing for advertising and for quality variation, and a model of the group. His approach was to consider monopolistic competition within what he called the "Robbins–Samuelson qualitative comparative statics tradition," checking to see if as many clear empirical implications emerge as in the case of competition and monopoly.

The results were disappointing, but for reasons Archibald thought it useful that we understand. At the fairly high level of generality adopted (physical returns eventually diminish, as do returns to advertising; demand curves slope downward), not much could be expected. Qualitative comparative statics analysis of the effects on the firm of advertising outlays yielded no unambiguous implications, simply because there were too few restrictions on the relations between variables and parameters.[13] This was unlike the case of competition, where there are very convenient cost and demand restrictions, or monopoly, where the number of variables is small (two!). One methodological moral drawn is familiar from what was said previously about Lipsey's *Introduction to Positive Economics:* "we must give theory some facts to help it to predict more facts" (1961, p. 15). The model of group response to postulated changes in demand, costs, tax rates, and so on proved to be just as empty, for the reason that the relationship between the share-of-the-market demand curve (Chamberlin's DD') and the "partial" demand curve (dd') is in-

---

[13] The reasons are clarified in Archibald's brilliant paper, "The Qualitative Content of Maximizing Models" (1965, in Morishima, 1973); see esp. p. 76 and n. 7. See also Section IV, this chapter.

completely specified. Subsequently, Archibald tried introducing an additional restriction, that price is taken as given by individual firms (Archibald, 1964). It turned out, however, that even such a strong assumption did not eliminate the need for a knowledge of cross-partial derivatives linking firms, knowledge that we cannot pretend to have.

The Chicago response to Archibald must have been as frustrating to him as the exercise itself. He deliberately adopted the Popperian position that one criticizes a theory most effectively if one tries first to "make the best of it." Chicago did not want to play by those rules. Both Stigler and Friedman in effect defended their a priori assessment of Chamberlin. Since, in their view, no operational meaning could be attached to the notion of "group," no testable implications could be expected from monopolistic competition theory and none need be sought. In short, Archibald had wasted his energy. They seemed content with competitive and monopoly models, although, as Archibald noted in a rejoinder, if each of these models applies only in certain cases, by implication other cases would refute them (1963a, p. 69). This apparently didn't bother Stigler or Friedman. Stigler commented that methodological discussion – by implication, points of the sort raised by Archibald – is useless and that he knew good work when he encountered it (Stigler, 1963, p. 63). Friedman acknowledged that one needs to know where each model applies, though he gave no criteria for knowing (cf. Friedman, 1953, p. 25). These attitudes exemplify the complacency – one might say, presumption – of which Archibald had complained initially.

Quite aside from this response, Archibald must have regretted that critical rationalism as applied to monopolistic competition theory foundered because of a degree of complexity that qualitative comparative statics could not handle. Was Popper's methodology at fault, or was the economic technique simply unfruitful in this instance? More on this in a moment. Clearly, the methodology stood above and was unscathed by the outcome of this particular application, and Archibald's methodological attack on Chicago verificationism was certainly warranted from his Popperian point of view. Nonetheless, serious questions were raised about the practicality of testing. And the victory was in any case pyrrhic: The Chicagoans were able to brush off the methodological attack because Archibald had not come up with any point of substance to show their a priori judgment wanting.

In addition to Lipsey's measuring and Archibald's striving to be critically rational, they or other members of the M²T seminar fired off salvos at the folly of methodological prescriptions other than "to argue critically" (Klappholz and Agassi, 1959),[14] and at the wooliness of thinking that enabled some economists to purport to be able to deduce empirical implications from models involving identities (Klappholz and Mishan, 1962). There was also a note of support sounded for Popper's objective "propensity" interpretation of probability as against the psychological "potential surprise" analysis of Shackle (Foldes, 1958). Lancaster, early on, in a review of Hicks's *Revision of Demand Theory,* had expostulated against armchair theorizing (Lancaster, 1957), and he showed how certain propositions of welfare theory could be expressed in refutable form (Lancaster, 1958). And there were careful efforts to encourage *discriminating* (i.e., critical or "severe") testing: Lipsey and Steuer (1961) on Kaldor versus Phillips on the relation between U and $\dot{W}$; and Archibald (1960) on Stein on the predictive accuracy of marginal productivity theory.

Even this gives only a hint of the range of problems tackled by the members of the M²T seminar. The records of the meetings themselves would convey more accurately the scope, and the fervor, of the discussions, but sadly almost none seem to have survived.

Without attempting complete coverage, however, it is clear that there were four lines of approach taken by the participants in the M²T seminar. Some tended to what we may call "Popperian purism": One may use only refutable statements. One may not prescribe in methodology, but can only aspire to and therefore should confine oneself strictly to critical argumentation. Agassi, Klappholz, and Ralph Turvey, who sometimes attended, took Popper seriously enough to have inclinations in this direction. Others maintained a primary interest in economic analysis but wanted to see how far theories could be rendered testable: Archibald, Steuer, and, at a distance, Lancaster. Lipsey was open to this but for himself simply wanted to be thoroughly empirical: to quantify; to gain some acceptance for those willing to work with data. Finally, there were some who were more eclectic. Theory has many uses, only one of which is to generate testable implications (Peston, minutes of M²T meeting, November 1, 1961). Alternatively, there are parts of economics that lend themselves to direct testing – some of the relations of macroeconomics, for example – and some that are better regarded as falling under the head of ideal types. The theory of profit maximization is of this latter sort. This was Laidler's view ("Some

---

[14] Klappholz and Agassi were surveying recent economic methodological literature and were at pains to show that making oneself vulnerable to criticism is all there is. There is no guarantee that good methodology will issue in good economics, although one has no alternative but to be critical. The others in the group were shocked by this at first.

Reflections on the Testing of Economic Theories" [1960 or 1961], paper circulated among members of M²T).[15]

Given these different understandings of what could be accomplished, and how to do it, it is not surprising that tensions developed. There was always a danger, from the side of the purists, that proscription would be practiced. It never was, but there was some difficulty in maintaining a free flow of papers for the seminar. After Lipsey handed over to Max Steuer in 1963, the name was changed; it became simply "the Wednesday Seminar." Any current research could be presented there; it did not have to conform to a certain mold. In contrast to the M²T seminar, there was no shortage of papers offered.[16] The eclectics eventually carried the day; yet even while Lipsey and Archibald were still at the center of things (Archibald followed Lipsey to Essex in 1964), they began to see difficulties in Popper's approach.

IV

Difficulties arose from both of their respective directions. Archibald had found it virtually impossible to derive testable predictions from marginal productivity theory before he ever turned to the theory of imperfect competition. The problem with every test he could devise was that it involved making important subsidiary assumptions. If there are too many of these, it becomes impossible to pinpoint what has gone wrong in the event of a refutation. Moreover, some assumptions, like "price equals marginal revenue," imply competitive equilibrium conditions that are hard to observe. One way or another, then, the attempt to state refutable propositions seemed to lead into a maze of "alibis" (Archibald, 1960, pp. 210–13).

Now these look like practical difficulties that one might try to minimize by keeping to just a very few restrictions (subsidiary conditions) on the one side, and making the context as fully observable as possible, on the other. This last might be achieved by looking not just to equilibrium conditions but to the comparative static content of models as well. This was exactly what Archibald did in trying to rehabilitate monopolistic competition theory. The results in terms of testable predictions were dismal, as we have already noted in passing. What was wrong? As Archibald reflected on the matter, he perceived a more fundamental difficulty.

[15] Laidler was a temporary assistant lecturer at the LSE in 1961–2.
[16] Steuer recalls (conversation, 1 July 1985) that in M²T there was often the question, "Which theory should we test next week?" In its successor, the problem was to select from among the many papers offered.

The probem may be put this way. Frequently we would like to be able to conduct an experiment in which we alter one parameter (call it *a*) of a system in equilibrium and emerge with a clear prediction about the direction of change in variables of interest to us $(x_1, \ldots, x_n)$. It turns out that we can never sign more than one of the *n* expressions dx_i/da unless the cross-partials among the variables are either zero or we have specific information about them. Moreover, we cannot even sign that one element if parameter *a* appears in more than one equation (Archibald, 1965, in Morishima, 1973, pp. 71–4). This second condition results in a form of the "parametric paradox."

Think of a simple case of "second best," an example Archibald himself used.[17] We wish to alter a tax rate k_g and observe the impact on a utility function. Knowing the sign of dU/dk_g will tell us whether the tax rate should be raised or lowered.

Now

$$\frac{dU}{dk_g} = \sum_{i=1}^{n} U_i \frac{dx_i}{dk_g};$$

but we have two problems: the sign of

$$U_i \frac{dx_i}{dk_g}$$

is unpredictable unless interfirm or interindustry effects of the change in k_g are zero or known in detail; and not even dx_g/dk_g can be signed if the parameter k_g appears in more than one equation. We know that it will, however, in all cases involving some degree of monopoly control over price. Let there be a wedge, k_i, between price and marginal cost in the *i*th industry – this is the departure from Pareto optimum conditions that puts us in a second-best situation to start with. It will not do, as a welfare-improving policy change, simply to impose the same *k* in all other industries. For if in the *i*th industry there is monopoly power, the profit-maximizing k_i will be a function of all the other *k*'s (pp. 77–9).

Samuelson, in introducing qualitative comparative statics in its mathematical form, had argued that there is no serious loss of generality because of the conditions necessary for unambiguous signing (*Foundations*, p. 33; cited in Archibald, 1965, in Morishima, 1973, p. 71). Archibald's explorations showed that Samuelson was mistaken, and in a way that had very serious consequences for deriving testable predictions by this method. There are almost no unambiguous qualitative predictions, or predictions "in general," when one is trying to assess the effect of a parameter change, if the change also alters other parameters.[18]

[17] In what follows I draw heavily on Archibald.
[18] Archibald notes a single exception: Derived demand curves slope downward (1965, in Morishima, 1973, p. 84).

As Klant notes, this sort of thing renders theory logically unfalsifiable. Archibald stressed rather the practical difficulties mentioned at the outset of this discussion. One may always impose restrictions so as to lessen the generality of theory and thereby generate predictions. The cost of this has been mentioned. One is not sure where to look if things go wrong. Alternatively, we may impose "reasonable" signs on the cross-partials to help sign expressions of interest. This reintroduces potential falsifiability. But even this gain is illusory since, as Archibald notes, "In this sort of situation . . . we can always 'rig up' the unobserved bits to make the theory predict as we wish, but, by so doing, we render the theory unfalsifiable" (Morishima, 1973, p. 76). A third alternative exists in principle. We might try to obtain information of the sort needed on cross-partials. This, however, in Archibald's judgment, would require "empirical investigation of a sort at present almost unknown" (1964, p. 22).

So much, then, for Popper's "tight procedure to guide you through the maze of the fact–theory mess" (see Steuer's comment in Section II). In economics, matters turn out to be more complex. To the degree to which relational interdependence is a problem, virtually no falsifiability is possible.

Lipsey, too, fairly quickly concluded that falsifiability is a nice ideal but difficult to translate into practice. He was interested primarily in finding empirical models that characterize the data; hence he became sensitive to the problem of errors of observation.[19] Errors, he had concluded (by the time he completed the first edition of the *Introduction to Positive Economics*), "may always be present" (2nd ed., 1966, pp. xx, 51). This means that all empirical hypotheses really are statistical (probabilistic) (p. 52n.). But statistical hypotheses necessarily admit of exceptions (pp. 10, 24–5, 52)–they do not absolutely prohibit anything. He concluded from this that stochastic propositions are not strictly refutable (p. 51).

Popper, of course, was well aware of the difficulty, even acknowledging that physics is based on probability statements (1959, pp. 189–90, 191, and Section 68). What he advised was the adoption of statistical conventions along lines that have become quite familiar (e.g., specify confidence limits). To Archibald, who became involved in these issues too, what seemed to be called for was nothing less than a new demarcation criterion.

In "Refutation or Comparison?" (1966), Archibald argued that con-

---

[19] He believed that the error term includes both omitted factors and errors of observation, but stressed the latter.

ventions are inevitably somewhat arbitrary; but more than that, they represent a marked departure from refutability in the sense of a relation between a universal and a singular statement (1966, pp. 280, 287, 190). However, he held that it is not economic inquiry that should be jettisoned as unscientific, but Popper's demarcation rule that should give way. "My own judgment is that many of the irrefutable hypotheses in economics are important, that they are incurably irrefutable for good and fundamental reasons [here Lipsey's kinds of reasons], and that the activity of comparing them with observation is useful (too practically useful to be acceptably called metaphysics)" (p. 279).

Archibald advocated demarcation by comparison. We should compare the predictive success of extant rival theories. If we exhaust these critical experiments, naive hypotheses rivaling the more successful theory can be constructed, subject to sensible restrictions such as that they have no fewer degrees of freedom than the serious rival (p. 291). Archibald's proposed demarcation rule was the following: "that we call a statement – or hypothesis – scientific if we may, at least in principle, compare its probable truth or falsity with that of another statement by appeal to observation (reference to facts)" (p. 293). Having empirical content thus meant "being potentially comparable" (with preexisting rivals, with constructed rivals, or with the null hypothesis and, in every case, with facts).

This new rule carried serious consequences. For Popper, "there are sea-serpents" is confirmable but not refutable (we may always find one if we maintain the search), and hence metaphysical. For Archibald, "there are sea-serpents" is a comparable hypothesis (pp. 293, 294). Similarly, "inductive confirmation," a phrase that would horrify a Popperian (cf. Boland, 1982, ch. 1), seems, on Archibald's new view, a perfectly sensible way to convey a sense of the comparison procedures actually followed by scientists and inherent in statistics (pp. 294–5).[20]

It is not clear that Archibald's new rule represents quite the advance upon Popper that he intended (or that Popper would seriously object![21]). It embraces all the conventions of statistical hypothesis testing

---

[20] Archibald pointed out that even the familiar R^2 is a comparative measure: "it tells us how much better our fitted relationship predicts the independent variable than does its own mean" (p. 282).

[21] As Blaug notes, Archibald was in fact "knocking against an open door" (1980, p. 122, n. 30). It seems almost as if Archibald was looking for a reason to break with Popper. For it is clear that Popper himself was busy with ways to *reconcile* falsifiability and probability. He writes: "*How is it possible* that probability statements – which are not falsifiable – can be *used* as falsifiable statements? (The fact that they can be so used is not in doubt: the physicist knows well enough when to regard a probability assumption as falsified.)" (1959, p. 204). In particular, he was concerned to argue that "accepted basic statements may agree more or less well with some proposed probability estimate; *they may repre-*

that he also regarded as arbitrary. What is important about it, however, is that it marks the end of an infatuation with Popper in no uncertain terms. Archibald had already just about given up on trying to squeeze testable implications out of microeconomics (1964, p. 22; 1965). His example in "Refutation or Comparison?" is the Keynesian macro-model. This, he frankly admits, is irrefutable (but comparable). Despite strenuous efforts to portray himself as still within the pale, he had in fact abandoned Popper's refutability for something that looks like a rationalization of economists' practices, with all the rough edges and philosophical fuzziness that surround them.[22] As if to underscore what had happened, he noted (it is not clear whether with regret or mild surprise): "I used to accept Popper's doctrine of sea-serpents

sent better, or less well, a typical segment of a probability sequence" (ibid.; emphasis added).

It doesn't take much to see in this an intuitive groping for what the British econometrician David Hendry calls "tentatively adequate conditional data characterizations." Hendry has spelled out a number of decision rules that may usefully be applied in the process of designing "satisfactory" empirical models. [For an excellent statement of his views, see Gilbert, (1985a).]

What prevented Archibald from taking a more tolerant view of Popper's tentative exploration in this direction? The main barrier was that the M²T group on the whole expected rather little from econometrics. This was partly a function of the arrangements for teaching at the LSE. Statistics was pursued and purveyed *outside* the Economics Department, so there was a natural barrier to be overcome by any economist wishing to explore what the statisticians had to offer. (Lipsey, recall, taught himself econometric techniques.) Moreover, there was a strong feeling among the economists that there was not much that they could learn from statisticians/econometricians, so far as *testing* was concerned. The econometricians, Archibald recalls, "seemed never to report a refutation" (cf. Gilbert, 1985a, p. 2: the goodness of fit or "Average Economic Regression . . . view of econometrics"). This led easily to a sense that "one didn't need econometrics to be a good Popperian scientist" (Steuer, conversation, 1 July 1985).

This is just one of the extraordinary ironies that seem to surround this episode (others are discussed in the concluding paragraph of this chapter). Denis Sargan joined the LSE in 1963 and was quickly brought – by Phillips – into the Economics Department. Sargan taught the methodologically sophisticated econometrics that had been developed at the Cowles Commission and is singlehandedly responsible for changing the focus and the methodological sensitivity of British econometricians (for more on this, see Gilbert, 1985b). In retrospect, it seems likely that Popper might have found even more fertile ground among the students of Sargan than he did among the economists; but by the time a sufficient group had emerged, it was to Lakatos rather than to Popper that nonphilosophers in search of a framework were looking.

22 Friedman and Meiselman had recently published the results of exactly the sort of statistical comparison, between Keynesian and quantity theory, that Archibald advocated (Friedman and Meiselman, 1963). It settled nothing, provoked a good deal of controversy, and eventually led to a debate about reduced-form models, from which it emerged that considerable observational equivalence is to be expected. This has become familiar to economists. Archibald was not unaware of the potential for inconclusiveness in comparisons (1966, p. 295). Laidler's "Reflections" paper (Section III, this chapter) also embodied the notion of comparing theories for their predictive content. He acknowledges the influence of Friedman and Meiselman, whose approach was being discussed in the Chicago Money Workshop in 1960–1.

quite uncritically" (p. 293). Lipsey's way of saying the same thing (in notes introducing the second edition of his textbook) was more blunt: "I have abandoned the Popperian notion of refutation" (*Introduction*, 2nd ed., 1966, p. xx). A little further on he writes: "The choice is not one between theory and observation but between better or worse theories to explain our observations" (p. 14).

V

How close did members of the seminar get to resolving the concerns of their pre-Popperian youth? And what does their experience reveal about why Popper so captivated them initially, but not for long? A brief recapitulation of developments will help us toward clear answers.

1. Lipsey led the group in revolt against Robbins and self-evident truth in economics. They were feeling their way toward empirical testing when Agassi showed them Popper. Popper gave more direction to their efforts than they could have gleaned from Hutchison or from Friedman's essay. From Popper they learned that testing is for refutation; that it must be severe; and that there must be no attempt to cover up failures.

2. One way to derive testable predictions in the absence of detailed quantitative knowledge is via qualitative comparative statics. Archibald chose this route in order to test the theory of maximizing behavior and especially the theory of the firm. It proved a disappointment in all but familiar and uninterestingly simple cases. Parameter interactions threatened to undermine the falsifiability of qualitative theory, and there seemed to be no way to get around the need for detailed quantitative information in more closely conditioned predictions.

3. Lipsey insisted on the importance of obtaining knowledge of parameters, elasticities, and functional stability to answer "how much" kinds of questions. To do otherwise and follow Robbins in *not* measuring would be to concede that economics is of limited practical value (or to accede to Robbins's alleged use of pure theory for policy prescription). Lipsey maintained strong convictions that economics is useful, Archibald's skepticism about falsifiability within the qualitative calculus notwithstanding.

4. Both Lipsey and Archibald became convinced that economic hypotheses must be expressed in statistical terms. Testing therefore inevitably involves probability distributions, not point observations of absolute import. Popperian testing they under-

stood to mean getting a proposition into a form in which it strictly forbids something. They substituted comparability for this sort of strict refutability as a way to "save the phenomena" (economics!). This may also have saved Archibald from complete despair; and certainly it allowed Lipsey to report a much richer scientific content to economic theory in the second edition of his *Introduction to Positive Economics*.

5. In trying to apply Popper, it may be said that Archibald experienced a double failure. There was the failure with qualitative comparative statics. And there was his inability to convince Stigler and Friedman that critical rationalism is a game worth playing. This pointed to an unresolved conflict in Popper's approach. Agassi taught the LSE economists quite clearly that the fact that something is refuted does not mean that you throw the theory away.[23] But nor did Popper offer very much advice about what to do in such cases. Friedman, however, hinted at a way, in arguing that competitive theory, tested or not, must be viewed and judged against alternatives "over a long period" (1953, p. 23).

The logical next step for the LSE group, having substituted comparison of theories for confrontation between theory and observation, would have been to adopt Lakatos's notion of comparisons between connected sequences of theories. Lakatos was at the LSE from 1959 on, and some of the economists knew of his remarkable *Proofs and Refutations* from seminar presentations prior to its publication (in article form) in 1963–4. Lipsey, however, was preoccupied with his textbook and had got involved in governmental advising. Archibald was trying to absorb the discovery that economic theory does not lend itself to Popper's refutability. In short, the moment was not right for grasping the significance of Lakatos's startling tale of how progress occurs in mathematics.

Thus Popper gave the LSE group a procedure, but it led nowhere. There were in some cases logical barriers to falsifiability in economics. There turned out to be a need for detailed information of a sort whose availability was not guaranteed in cases where the qualitative calculus was subjected to enough restrictions to make it yield predictions. Over and above these problems, Popper's refutability quickly came to seem too rigid for statistical propositions.

That Popper's ideas flourished at all among the LSE economists is thus somewhat surprising and may be attributed in large measure to circumstances that were quite time- and space-specific. Firstly, a revolt

---

[23] Klappholz, conversation, 2 July 1985.

(against Robbins) was brewing independently, but a manifesto was lacking. *The Logic of Scientific Discovery* supplied this need. There was, secondly, a critical mass of interested individuals, partly attracted by Lipsey's own dynamism – his career catapulted him from graduate student to full professor in six years. Popper didn't create the group spirit; Lipsey did. Once again, however, the group had a target but lacked slogans and arguments. Popper helped focus the group's energies by giving it certain shibboleths and the ideal of testing. These proved up to galvanizing revolutionary zeal but, because of internal weaknesses, not up to sustaining substantive research. Not, it might be added, that the agenda of M²T was itself sustainable, whatever the dependence – or lack of it – on Popper. Archibald's part in the program presupposed a level of mathematical sophistication that went far beyond the requirements for undergraduates at the LSE, whereas Lipsey's could not be carried through satisfactorily without more in the way of econometrics than he or anyone else in the group could claim.[24]

One final note. There is irony in the group's using Popper as a stick with which to beat Robbins. Politically they were on the same side. They were also, as Bill Bartley points out (letter to the author, 9 September 1986), at one in things having to do with the LSE. Robbins even lent his enormous abilities to compensate for Popper's inexperience in matters (including appointments) involving the LSE administration. Finally, as Klant reminds us, Popper, in *The Poverty of Historicism* (1957, p. 143), came close to excepting economics and the rationality principle from the requirement of testability. The reason given was that in economics "the parameters are themselves in the most important cases quickly changing variables" (ibid.). The author of the article from which Popper drew this argument was none other than Lionel Robbins (Robbins, 1938)![25]

References

Adorno, T.W., et al., eds. (1976). *The Positivist Dispute in German Sociology.* Trans. G. Adey and D. Frisby. New York: Harper & Row.
*Agassi, J. (1959). See K. Klappholz and J. Agassi, "Methodological Prescriptions in Economics," *Economica* n.s. 26:60–74.
*Archibald, G.C. (1959a). "The State of Economic Science," *British Journal for the Philosophy of Science* 10:58–69.

[24] I am indebted to David Laidler for these reminders.
[25] Allan Sleeman introduces yet another twist to this, however, in pointing out that by the time he, as an undergraduate, attended Robbins's famous "History of Economic Thought" course in the autumn of 1959, Robbins was introducing his material by recanting his 1935 position and advocating a Popperian testing approach. Letter to the author, 20 November 1985.

164   **de Marchi**

* (1959b). "Welfare Economics, Ethics, and Essentialism," *Economica* 26:316–27.
* (1960). "Testing Marginal Productivity Theory," *Review of Economic Studies* 27:210–13.
* (1961). "Chamberlin *versus* Chicago," *Review of Economic Studies* 29:1–28.
* (1963a). "Reply to Chicago," *Review of Economic Studies* 30:68–71.
* (1963b). "Discussion (of Papandreou)," *American Economic Review* 53:227–9.
* (1964). "Profit-Maximising and Non-Price Competition," *Economica* 31:13–22.
* (1965). "The Qualitative Content of Maximizing Models," *Journal of Political Economy*. Reprinted in Morishima (1973), pp. 70–84.
* (1966). "Refutation or Comparison? *British Journal for the Philosophy of Science* 17:279–96.
* Kemmis, R., and Perkins, J.W. "Excess Demand for Labour, Unemployment and the Phillips Curve: A Theoretical and Empirical Study," in Laidler and Purdy (1974), pp. 109–63.
Blaug, M. (1980). *The Methodology of Economics*. Cambridge: Cambridge University Press.
*Brechling, F.F.R., and Lipsey, R.G. (1963). "Trade Credit and Monetary Policy," *Economic Journal* 73:618–41.
Boland, L.A. (1982). *The Foundations of Economic Method*. London: Allen & Unwin.
Caldwell, B. (1984). *Appraisal and Criticism in Economics. A Book of Readings*. Boston: Allen & Unwin.
Davis, H.T. (1941). *The Theory of Econometrics*. Bloomington, Ind.: Principia Press.
De Marchi, Neil (1985). See Hirsch and de Marchi (1985).
*Foldes, L. (1958). "Uncertainty, Probability and Potential Surprise," *Economica* 25:246–54.
Friedman, M. (1953). "The Methodology of Positive Economics,"in *Essays in Positive Economics*. Chicago: University of Chicago Press.
(1957). *A Theory of the Consumption Function*. Princeton, N.J.: Princeton University Press.
(1963). "More on Archibald versus Chicago." *Review of Economic Studies* 30:65–7.
and Meiselman, D. (1963). "The Relative Stability of Monetary Velocity and the Investment Multiplier in the United States, 1897–1958," in *Stabilization Policies*. Englewood Cliffs, N.J.: Prentice-Hall, pp. 165–268.
Gilbert, C.L. (1985a). "Professor Hendry's Econometric Methodology." Mimeo.
(1985b). "The Development of the British School of Economics." Mimeo.
Hirsch, A., and de Marchi, N. (1985). " 'The Methodology of Positive Economics' as *Via Media*." Mimeo.
Hutchison, T.W. (1938). *The Significance and Basic Postulates of Economic Theory*. London: Macmillan.

(1956). "Professor Machlup on Verification in Economics," *Southern Economic Journal.* Reprinted in Caldwell (1984), pp. 118–25.

Johnson, E.S., and Johnson, H.G. (1978). *The Shadow of Keynes.* Oxford: Blackwell.

Johnson, H.G. (1951). "The Taxonomic Approach to Economic Policy," *The Economic Journal* 61:812–32.

Klant, J.J. (1984). *The Rules of the Game.* Cambridge: Cambridge University Press.

(1985). "The Natural Order." Mimeo.

*Klappholz, K., and Agassi, J. (1959). "Methodological Prescriptions in Economics," *Economica* 26:60–74.

* and Mishan, E.J. (1962). "Identities in Economic Models," *Economica* 29:117–28.

Klein, L.R. (1953). *A Textbook of Econometrics.* Evanston, Ill.: Row, Peterson.

*Laidler, D.E.W., and Purdy, D.L., eds. (1974). *Inflation and Labor Markets.* Manchester: Manchester University Press.

Lakatos, I. (1976). *Proofs and Refutations. The Logic of Mathematical Discovery,* ed. J. Worral and E. Zahar. Cambridge: Cambridge University Press.

*Lancaster, K. (1957). "Revising Demand Theory," *Economica* n.s. 24:354–60.

* (1958). "Welfare Propositions in Terms of Consistency and Expanded Choice," *Economic Journal* 68:464–70.

* (1962). "The Scope of Qualitative Economics," *Review of Economic Studies* 29:99–123.

*Lange, O. (1944). *Price Flexibility and Employment.* Cowles Commission for Research in Economics, Monograph no. 8. Bloomington, Ill.: Principia Press.

*Lipsey, R.G. (1960). "The Relation between Unemployment and the Rate of Change of Money Wage Rates in the United Kingdom, 1862–1957: A Further Analysis," *Economica* 27:1–31.

* and Steuer, M.D. (1961). "The Relation between Profits and Wage Rates," *Economica* 28:137–55.

* (1963). See Brechling and Lipsey (1963).

* (1966). *An Introduction to Positive Economics,* 2nd ed. London: Weidenfeld and Nicholson.

and Archibald, G.C. (1958). "Monetary and Value Theory: A Critique of Lange and Patinkin," *Review of Economic Studies* 26:1–22.

* and Parkin, J.M. (1970). "Incomes Policy: A Re-Appraisal," *Economica* 37:115–38.

Machlup, F. (1955). "The Problem of Verification in Economics," *Southern Economic Journal* 22:1–21.

Meiselman, D. (1963). See Friedman and Meiselman (1963).

Mishan, E.J. (1962). See Klappholz and Mishan (1962).

Morishima, M., (1973). *Theory of Demand.* Oxford: Oxford University Press.

Papandreou, A.G. (1958). *Economics as a Science.* Chicago: Lippincott.

(1963). "Theory Construction and Empirical Meaning in Economics," *American Economic Review* 53:205–210.

Patinkin, D. (1956). *Money, Interest, and Prices. An Integration of Monetary and Value Theory.* New York: Harper & Row.

Popper, K. (1959). *The Logic of Scientific Discovery.* London: Hutchinson.

(1960 [1957]). *The Poverty of Historicism.* London: Routledge & Kegan Paul.

(1962 [1945]). *The Open Society and Its Enemies,* 2 vols. London: Routledge & Kegan Paul.

(1963). *Conjectures and Refutations.* New York: Harper Torchbooks.

(1976a [1961]). "The Logic of the Social Sciences," in Adorno et al. (1976), pp. 87–104.

(1976b). *Unended Quest. An Intellectual Autobiography,* Fontana Ed. London: Fontana/Collins.

Robbins, L.C. (1952 [1935]). *An Essay on the Nature and Significance of Economic Science.* London: Macmillan.

(1938). "Live and Dead Issues in the Methodology of Economics," *Economica.* n.s. 5:342–52.

(1971a). *Money, Trade and International Relations.* London: Macmillan.

(1971b). *Autobiography of an Economist.* London: Macmillan.

Samuelson, P.S. (1947). *Foundations of Economic Analysis.* Cambridge, Mass.: Harvard University Press.

*Steuer, M.D. (1961). See Lipsey and Steuer (1961).

Stigler, G.J. (1969). *Five Lectures on Economic Problems.* Freeport, N.Y.: Books for Libraries Press.

(1963). "Archibald versus Chicago," *Review of Economic Studies* 30:63–64.

Thorn, R.S., ed. (1966). *Monetary Theory and Policy. Major Contributions to Contemporary Thought.* New York: Random House.

Tinbergen, J. (1951). *Econometrics.* Trans. Van Olst. New York: Blakiston.

Tintner, G. (1952). *Econometrics.* New York: Wiley.

PART III

Falsification and trying to do without it

CHAPTER 5

The case for falsification

TERENCE W. HUTCHISON

I

The preceding title and subtitle, as formulated by the authors of the draft program, seem to correspond reasonably well with what I have discovered that I want to say. But a little further clarification may not, perhaps, be superfluous.

Any significant case for adopting, or "striving after," a methodological principle must rest ultimately on some ethical, moral, or political argument (as Popper emphasized in the debate with Habermas and elsewhere). Insofar as methodological principles are critical principles, then, the criticism they contain, or imply, must rest on some kinds of normative standards or presuppositions. Moreover, I would like to emphasize, at the start, how closely the real questions of economics, much more than is the case with any other subject, scientific or otherwise, are constantly and intimately involved with controversial political, indeed party-political, issues, an involvement that gives rise to persistent and perennial problems in applying economic knowledge to policy.

Anyhow, it is with such ultimate ethical or political meta-arguments for the (or a) falsification and falsifiability principle that this chapter is concerned.

II

I want to start from, and take as far as it will go, Professor Johannes Klant's analogy or comparison between the methodological principles of economics and the "rules of the game." Personally, however, I would not want to emphasize at all appreciably the two definite articles. It may seem that the main problems arise from the fact that a number of different games, or types of gamesmanship, are going on at the same time (some more like chess, and some more like a game of academic oneupmanship). Anyhow, a game, including the "Scientific Economics Game" or the "Economic Theory Game," is not *given,* in a particular form, so that its rules and codes can be discovered and formulated if we search and analyze far enough.

So, before one can usefully discuss the rules of the game, one must start by asking about the aim of the game (or of playing the game) or about *why* the players are playing it (beyond, that is, simply trying to win).

The aim of a game, as a purely amateur pastime, is, presumably, simply the enjoyment of the players. For many or most players, for a game to be enjoyable, a code of more or less agreed-upon rules is necessary. To employ Mark Blaug's analogy of playing tennis with the net down (and possibly with no lines to demarcate the court), this is widely held to be less enjoyable than playing with a net and court in accordance with the standard dimensions and demarcations, and to be more enjoyable than with no net or with a net, say, twenty feet high. Many or most players of games find that "anything goes" does not, generally, make for enjoyment.

When, however, a game becomes a professionalized spectator sport, and the players are paid to play, the immediate enjoyment of the players may not be the sole or most important factor, or justification, for whatever rules are adopted. The rules of the game will have to be formulated with regard to the enjoyment of the paying customers, spectators, or televiewers, for whose enjoyment considerable modifications in the rules may be required – if not in the basic code, at any rate in what may be called the "by-laws" for particular matches. Such modifications in the rules regarding, for example, the timing and length of matches, designed to increase the enjoyment of the paying public, might well be quite unacceptable to unpaid amateurs.

III

Sir John Hicks remarked:

There is much of economic theory which is pursued for no better reason than its intellectual attraction; it is a good game. We have no reason to be ashamed of that, since the same would hold for many branches of pure mathematics. (1979, p. VIII, quoted by Hutchison, 1981, p. 266).

I think that this highly authoritative observation must be accepted as substantially correct regarding the pursuit of much of economic theory today. But I would also estimate that, despite his great authority, very few of the players of the Economic Theory Game (ETG) would accept Sir John's description of what they are doing and why they are doing it.

Let us assume, however, for the moment, that the "good game" of much of economic theory was being played simply as an amateur pastime (as perhaps it actually was by some gentlemanly performers in the eighteenth and nineteenth centuries) – that is, without financial complications arising from the sponsoring of the game by some outside body representing spectators. Then, surely, any rules of the ETG would, and should, be settled by the players alone, simply with a view to maximizing their own enjoyment. Of course, various forms of the game, with different rules, might coexist side by side, as with the various codes of football, providing for differing tastes or national traditions. Anyhow, one may sometimes derive the impression that the principle applicable to purely amateur games – that the enjoyment of the players should be the sole justification for any rules, codes, or demarcations – is enthusiastically adhered to by many contemporary players of the ETG.

IV

The ETG, however (even if it were a game), is certainly not today a purely amateur game or pastime (whatever it may have been for some gentlemen in times past). The players today are nearly all full-time, paid professionals, the paying public being, in many or most cases, the taxpayers, consideration of whose enjoyment or utility might be regarded as of some importance in deciding on any rules or demarcations. But for the ETG today, the paying public, far from being appreciative spectators, are largely incapable of understanding what the players are doing. (Indeed, to some extent, it may seem that the players of the ETG, in the interests of their professional status, may be intent on rendering their performance more and more incomprehensible to the paying public).[1] Today, the only people resembling critical, and to some extent knowledgeable, spectators may be the small band of those (also paid professionals) who are concerned with the method and history of the ETG.

Incidentally, I am not competent to discuss Sir John Hicks's comparison of the ETG with pure mathematics, which he also describes as a "good game" – though, of course, it is hardly one that can be appreciated by much of a spectator public. Anyhow, the question remains as to just how and where, the professional players of the ETG, or of the Pure Mathematics Game, may reasonably and honestly expect to find their financial support: from some body, public or private, resembling a Natu-

---

[1] In a recent penetrating study, it has been stated that already a century ago, Alfred Marshall "wanted economists to be trained in a body of theory which – without excessive grief – he recognized would be inaccessible to laymen" (Moloney, 1985, p. 2). This may not be entirely fair regarding Marshall, who, in any case, certainly wanted economists to provide guidance for policy. But whether or not the inaccessibility of economic theory to laymen can be described as an aim of Marshall, the vast jungle growth of this inaccessibility over roughly the last half-century must surely be regarded as at least highly acceptable professionally, and not entirely unwelcome or unintended.

ral Science Research Council? From an Arts, Literature, and Rhetoric Council? Or from a Sports Council (such as we have in Britain)? In any case, however, as paid performers and not self-financed amateurs, the players of the ETG can hardly reasonably expect that the rules of their game should be formulated purely and simply with a view to the enjoyment of the players.

V

By now, some of the limitations are apparent of the comparison between the methodological principles, or disciplinary demarcations, of economics and economic theory, and the rules of a game, as played either by amateurs or by professionals. This comparison may suggest some relevant questions, but it fairly soon becomes inapplicable.

On the question of *aims,* doubtless the aims of economists are, and always have been, extremely mixed and various for doing what it is economists do. But it might be interesting to draw up a questionnaire on the subject to be addressed, perhaps, to all the living economists, included in Mark Blaug's invaluable work of reference. Here we may simply set down two alternatives, or questions, regarding aims or motives from what should, of course, be a much longer and much more refined list. The first alternative (I) would be on Hicksian lines and ask whether economic theory was being, or should be, pursued mainly for its intellectual attraction as a good game. The other alternative (II) might be formulated roughly as follows: Is economic theory being pursued (or should it be) mainly or primarily with the aim of contributing, more or less directly or ultimately, to the guidance of policy, public or private?

I would be extremely surprised if a large majority of economists did not answer in favor of II rather than I, indicating that the, or a, main aim of economic theory should be to provide guidance, directly or indirectly, for policy. I would, moreover, assert that an even greater majority would answer in the general direction of II rather than I, if it were possible to take account of the views of the great economists of the past, by inviting experts in the history of economic thought to answer on their behalf. From the medieval philosophers, through the mercantilists, the English classicals, the historicals, the Marxians, the Keynesians, and even, I would maintain, the early neoclassicals like Jevons, Marshall, and Walras, guidance for policy was predominantly *a,* or usually *the,* main aim of what economists were doing. The tendency toward an increasing remoteness from policy relevance, and even from any real-world processes, might be traced back to the neoclassical period. But it is only in the last 30 or 40 years, with a vast mushrooming of the number and proportion of academic economists around much of the world, and with the growth of a colossal worldwide academic economics industry, that the pursuit of economic theory as, in Sir John Hicks's description, a good game (though not usually admitted to be such), has achieved the significant dimensions that it has.

VI

We are not, of course, attempting any very precise formulation of our alternative II, which we are claiming would receive the greatest support from economists as a description of the (or a) main aim of economics and economic theorizing. But the phrase about "the guidance of policy, more or less directly or ultimately," should be briefly qualified or elaborated.

Admittedly, it may sometimes be difficult or impossible to assess, or predict, whether or not some piece of apparently quite abstract analysis or theory may not ultimately turn out to possess significant real-world relevance, such as might be applicable to the guidance of policy. Examples have been cited, from the history of the physical sciences, of refinements in pure mathematics (perhaps originally elaborated as a good game), which have subsequently turned out to have important real-world applications and even vast technological uses. Doubtless this possibility would often be invoked to justify much of the ETG. But multiplying highly abstract formulas or models on the possibility that one day some kind of real-world application *might* (one never knows) turn up does not seem to be a convincing additional justification for an activity that was otherwise, or initially defended as a good game.

Some limited concession might, however, be made. But before any such is granted, it would be reasonable to ask for convincing examples from the history of economic thought, which do not seem easy to find. In fact, what is much more frequent in the last hundred years are examples of precisely the opposite process: Highly abstract "models" have been elaborated, initially aimed and claimed as eventually to acquire some real-world applicability, which, after many decades, has never actually emerged. Optimistic claims that, by successive approximations, the abstract scaffolding will eventually be removed have not been fulfilled, for if it was, nothing would be found behind the scaffolding of abstraction that would stand up on its own.

VII

It might be widely agreed that the, or a, prime aim of economic theorizing has been, and is, to assist in the guidance of policy. But the question then arises as to what this implies regarding any rules of the game, or any code or demarcations, for whatever kind of activity economists are engaged in. Politicians, journalists, and sometimes ordinary citizens are concerned with economic policies and sometimes present their views at great length, orally or on paper. But politicians, journalists, and ordinary citizens, when pronouncing on economic policy, do not have to submit to rules or demarcations other than those laid down in the laws of their country regarding libel, national security, and so on. So why should there be any different or additional rules for economists beyond those obtaining for politicians, journalists, and ordinary citizens? Why, on the subject of economic policies and processes, shouldn't "anything go" for economists just as for anyone else?

The answer to such a question obviously depends on whether economists have made, or do make, any claims that their conclusions on economic processes and policies generally differ, in some significant qualitative respect, from those of noneconomists. If economists renounce any such claims regarding their pronouncements on economic policy, as compared with those of politicians and journalists, then obviously no additional rules or code need be applicable.

I would, however, maintain that over the last hundred and fifty years or so, since, for example, the time of James Mill, many economists have put forward considerable claims for what they have had to say on economic policies, in particular, as possessing a certain measure of *authority*. So what can be the source of such authority? It would not seem that it can justifiably be regarded as deriving simply from the much larger amount of time and effort that they have spent on the specialized study of economic processes and policies. A kind of labor theory of value hardly seems to work. The proof of the puddings cooked up by economists cannot lie simply in the number of socially necessary hours of labor applied by the cooks.

Moreover, as already maintained, economists do not only make claims for the authority of their pronouncements; they also apply for, and obtain, financial support for their research. The further question follows, therefore, as to what kind of claims for their subject economists' applications for research funding are based on, or what kind of rules, discipline, or demarcations are claimed to obtain. It is possible that economists' applications for financial support might not have been as successful as they have been if it had been evident that the kinds of claims for the subject on which these applications were based resembled those of physicists and natural scientists much less than they did the kinds of claims relevant for applications for sponsorship from artists, poets, rhetoricians, or games players and sportsmen of one kind or another.[2]

VIII

Even those subjects described as "sciences" (as economics usually has been by its practitioners) differ very widely and importantly, not only in the kind of subject matter with which they are concerned but also in what may be called their "institutional" or "political" relations or setting. Disregard of such differences often render unsatisfactory or inadequate many of the generalizations of philosophers and others about "scientific method," in that no account is taken or appreciation shown of the special, peculiar characteristics or relationships of a particular subject like economics.

To return to what was mentioned in passing in the opening paragraph, a peculiar characteristic of economics and political economy has always been its special relationship with politics – and, indeed, with the central controversies of party politics – an involvement, these days, more constant and more intense than that possessed by any other science or subject. Obviously, for subjects like geology, astronomy, or entomology, such issues of applied methodology are hardly serious. But for economics, this constant and intense involvement raises significant issues for any methodological rules, by-laws, or demarcations for practitioners of the subject. These issues were a main theme of Max Weber's great essay, "Wissenschaft als Beruf," which I shall not attempt to reargue here.

---

[2] I think it would be quite reasonable to describe a, or the, main aim of economic theory as improved, or less inaccurate, prediction; though I would not want to insist that economists, as such, can only provide guidance for policy insofar as they can reduce the inaccuracy of the relevant predictions below what it would be without any contribution from economics. It is not easy to see how the large numbers of economists working for governments, banks, and private firms could be earning significant salaries if it was not believed that somehow their work improved, marginally and on the average, the predictions on which decisions had to be based. It therefore seems incongruous and disloyal for some academics to keep insisting that economists "cannot predict," and should not try to, while many of the brightest products of economics departments are constantly and successfully answering advertisements for economists sought to engage in prediction. Possibly this demand for qualified economists for purposes of prediction is now falling off, judging by a report (*New York Times*, 3 September 1985) that a major bank has "announced the elimination of its economics department, dismissing or transferring 40 people." Personally, I regard it as entirely credible that slightly, and on the average, economists can and sometimes do improve important predictions, in one way or another and that, when they do, they would be well worth considerable salaries (cf. Hutchison, 1977, pp. 8ff).

Not only is economic policy undoubtedly today the most important
and controversial aspect, or part, of policy and policy making in most
countries. It might also reasonably be maintained that in contemporary
democracies such as exist in the Netherlands, Britain, and the United
States, economists should not only make (what they claim to be) a
disciplined contribution to the substantive discussion and assessment of
economic policies, but attempt, as far they can, by any example they set,
to raise the level of debate or, at least, to counter deterioration in that
level. Insofar as this is or should be one of the aims of practitioners of a
subject, it is one that may have significant implications for any methodological principles or rules that they wish or claim to observe. In particular, insofar as a country's institutions and policymaking procedures are
based on the principle of far-reaching freedom of discussion, it seems
doubtful how far economists should seek to base their methodological
principles, and any significant conclusions, on dogmatic, unquestionable
assumptions or a priorist axioms for which scientific or apodictic certainty is claimed.[3]

IX

We have now discussed the claims of economists to some kind of authority for their subject in the field of economic policy, based partly on their
theories. We have also referred to the claims of economists for the
funding of their research from public and private sources, and to the
kinds of grounds on which such funding could reasonably be claimed.
Finally, we have mentioned the possible methodological issues raised by
the intense involvement of economic theory with political issues, and the
problem that arises if some demarcation or distinction is to be claimed

---

[3] A priorism rejects fundamentally the falsifiability principle (FP) and all empirical testing. Insofar as no restrictions seem to be formulated regarding the initial axioms, a
priorism amounts to a form of "anything goes." Long supported in economics by
Misesians (including very briefly, in the thirties, Hayek, who soon began to abandon it),
a priorism has now found support among Marxians (politically quite naturally).
Misesians and Marxians presumably claim authority, and reject all testing and falsifiability, for quite different, perhaps flatly contradictory, fundamental axioms. As Johannes
Klant has remarked: "It is remarkable that those who are so fond of appealing to self-
evidence and intuitive recognition make no attempt to make it clear why it is that so
many are lacking in the lucid insight that they must intuitively have" (1984, p. 76). The
political implications are alarmingly hostile to freedom of economists, or of any group or
authority, claiming infallibility, or "apodictic certainty," for selected axioms, and conclusions deduced from them that are claimed to possess significant economic content, but
for which testing and falsifiability are comprehensively rejected. The FP, on the other
hand, is a truly libertarian principle because, in demanding testing and falsifiability, it is
based on human fallibility and denies the infallibility claimed by the a priorists,
Misesian, and Marxian.

between the functions in economic policy making of the economist and those of politicians, journalists, and members of the public.

It may now be time to discuss briefly the principle of falsification and falsifiability, and its relevance for attempts to meet the three questions raised previously. The falsification and falsifiability principle may be summarized as recommending that theories, and predictions based on them, should be testably formulated, and that the fundamental importance should be recognized and upheld of observing the threefold distinction, or trichotomy, between (1) theories that have stood up to serious tests, (2) theories that are testable but have not yet been adequately tested, and (3) those that are not conceivably or remotely testable.

This threefold distinction marks an important demarcation, though this demarcation certainly need not be described as one between sense and nonsense or between metaphysics and science. In debating issues of economic policy, however, it would seem highly desirable to achieve as much clarity as possible on whether the various theories and predictions involved in a discussion of policy are testable or untestable, conceivably or practically, and on what actual tests, if any, they have survived. Just as it may be held desirable that the public should at least be informed, regarding some new drug that is being put on the market, of whether or not it has undergone any serious tests for its effects, so it may be held that, when discussing the adoption of an economic policy, an economist might reasonably be expected to state what tests the theory or predictions underlying this policy had survived. As Professor Koertge has remarked:

It is extraordinary that people who would not dream of taking a medicine which had not been thoroughly tested are quite willing to swallow educational, psychological, or political theories which not only have not been tested but which, as actually formulated, are not even in principle testable. (1979, p. 79, quoted by Hutchison, 1981, p. 303)

It is not, however, for one moment being suggested that any legal enforcement or sanctions, such as obtain with regard to the marketing of drugs, are possible or desirable with regard to the testing of economic theories and predictions. Needless to add, the falsification and falsifiability principle is not comparable with legislation, but must be put forward simply as a voluntary code, upheld, as far as it can be, by seriously critical opinion.

X

In reviewing objections to the falsification and falsifiability principle (FP) the observation need not long detain us that, in fact, in economics not much attention is paid to it (though a good deal of lip service *is* paid). But insofar as lip service is not translated into action, so much the worse for economics. Anyhow, we are concerned here with norms and standards and not with actual behavior. A backward glance, however, at the longer-term history of the subject may suggest that the disregard by economists of testing, falsification, and empirical evidence may have been considerably exaggerated. From a longer-run perspective, there does often seem to have been a significant correlation between the rise and decline of theories and a kind of loose historical testing. Important turning points in the history of the subject do seem to have coincided with the falsification of orthodox theories, such as the hard-line Malthusian doctrine in mid-Victorian Britain and, even recently, of the more confidently unqualified versions of Keynesian and monetarist theories. Indeed, one might shudder at the kind of intellectual spectacle that the subject would present, and would have presented, if the FP had been more completely disregarded than it actually has been.

Anyhow, it is important to appreciate that an economic theory that has been falsified should not necessarily be regarded as finally eclipsed and relegated to the status of a historical curiosity. For the historical and institutional conditions that originally lent support to an economic theory, though subsequently superceded or transformed, may, with further historical change, come back again to restore support. There is a vital difference here with regard to the finality of the elimination of theories in the natural sciences, as compared with the falsification and elimination of theories in the social sciences.

We have thus already partly answered a *second* objection to the FP: that its application would have appallingly destructive consequences. If that were really the case, so be it. The destruction of a lot of intellectual clutter in economics, which is unable to survive reasonable testing, surely need not be ranked among the major intellectual tragedies of our time. But again there seems to be much exaggeration in the more alarmist objections of this kind. For, because a theory fails a test, it need not be regarded as finally destroyed or eliminated. A test may well reveal grounds for caution about a theory and predictions based on it, though for purposes of policy making, it may still be regarded as the least weak theory available.

What would, indeed, be threatened by an effective body of critical support for the FP would be the more dogmatic forms of opinion mongering regarding economic processes and policies based on untested, and perhaps untestable, theories. For the falsificationist code enjoins *witholding judgment* regarding theories and, of course, policies based on them, which have not survived reasonably critical testing. Certainly a much greater readiness to withold judgment might be required, by effective support for the FP, than might be palatable to some economists.

For a politician, withholding judgment is more or less an occupational impossibility, as it may be even for an ordinary citizen when it is his or her duty to cast a vote. But, far from being an impossibility for an academic, there should be nothing intolerably difficult about it, and it is bound – at any rate, according to the FP – to be a frequent and regular duty. Not that the academic economist would be left with no role in the discussion of economic policy. Far from it. There would be an ample role for academic economists in criticizing economic policies and predictions, and the theories on which these were partly based, for the untested and sometimes untestable hypotheses on which they may rest. This kind of criticism would serve to raise the level and standards of the public discussion of economic policy, and would counter the extravagant claims and excessive optimism with which politicians seek to sell their policies to the public, and which tend to result in dangerous public disappointment and disillusionment with democratic policies. As a supporter of the FP, I would simply reaffirm the recommendation put forward in the concluding sentences of Johannes Klant's book:

It behooves the economist to behave modestly when he does not know the answer. If he is not able to do so, let him say openly to all concerned: I am a philosopher, an ideologist, a politician. . . . (1984, p. 187)

XI

As an attempt to formulate criteria of adequacy or a demarcation principle, the Popperian FP was by no means a fundamentally new departure. Attempts at demarcation could be traced back to Hume, who was specifically concerned with marking off and laying foundations for the moral, or social, sciences. Moreover, the classical and neoclassical writers on scope and method were centrally concerned, from Senior and Cairnes to J.N. Keynes and Robbins, with trying to lay down demarcation principles. Should the FP and its predecessors now be abandoned as too restrictive? If so, can some milder and more permissive version be formulated, or should all such attempts in this long tradition be abandoned and "anything goes" be recognized as the overriding methodological principle of economics?

The most notable recent attempt to soften up the Popperian FP was that of Imre Lakatos. It should be noted that the work of Lakatos (like that of Popper) was primarily concerned with what is an extreme case in the methodology of science, that of physics. In the field of social studies,

Lakatos opposed what he called "Polanyite autonomy" and vigorously rejected outright permissiveness, or "mob rule." Moreover, his denunciation of Marxism for its falsified predictions and protective stratagems followed closely on lines originally struck out by Popper, whose influence on Lakatos, here and at other points, remained important (cf. Hutchison, 1981, pp. 18–21).

Unfortunately, however, Lakatos also left behind him some grounds for Feyerabend to claim him as a supporter of ultrapermissiveness and for maintaining:

Scientific method, as softened up by Lakatos, is but an ornament which makes us forget that a position of "anything goes" has in fact been adopted. (Lakatos and Musgrave, eds., 1970, p. 93)

His tragically premature death forestalled any explicit confirmation by Lakatos (or any reconciliation, if necessary) of his hard disciplinary line regarding social subjects (or some of them) and his very soft, permissive line regarding physics, amounting to "anything goes." Nor were any explicit suggestions left by Lakatos as to where economics should be placed in the spectrum of the sciences. But in their actual application and interpretation of the Lakatosian innovations, some writers seem to have accepted enthusiastically methodological parity between economics and physics, and to have come down strongly on the side of "anything goes" for economists, or of providing "ornaments" (or fig leaves) for concealing the outright abandonment of discipline. A kind of covert anarchism seems to have become fashionable, purveying a flattering permissiveness. At the same time, the illusion is fostered that *some kinds* of disciplinary principles are being maintained, while actually, attempts to formulate and retain such principles are dismissed as naive, outmoded "positivism." Such writings on the methodology of economics usually proceed in lofty, almost utopian abstraction from the sordid, real-world problems for practitioners of the subject, regarding the intense involvement of economics with political controversy and the question of financial support.

Moreover, a kind of superhuman utopianism seems to prevail, even regarding economists themselves, who are urged to disregard all rules except "honesty, clarity and tolerance" (McCloskey, 1983, p. 482). Of course, if we were all intellectually superhuman, capable unaided of upholding impeccably all the intellectual virtues, and never inclining toward crooked, obscure, or intolerant thought or expression, there might well be no role for critical codes of discipline, demarcation, and adequacy. For we would be living in an intellectual utopia. But for those of us concerned with the discussion of economic processes and policies in the real world, within a reasonably free democratic framework, a vital role may always remain for critical principles and criteria of adequacy, such as the FP. For, among those of us who, however lofty our intentions, are liable sometimes to fall below the level of the purest intellectual honesty, clarity, and tolerance, the FP may be supported as helping usefully to reduce our shortcomings.

References

Hicks, Sir John. (1979). *Causality in Economics*. Oxford: Basil Blackwell.
Hutchison, T.W. (1977). *Knowledge and Ignorance in Economics*. Chicago: University of Chicago Press.
 (1981). *The Politics and Philosophy of Economics*. New York: New York University Press.
Klant, J. (1984). *The Rules of the Game*. Cambridge: Cambridge University Press.
Koertge, N. (1979). "Braucht die Sozialwissenschaft wirklich Metaphysik?" in H. Albert and K.H. Stapf, eds., *Theorie und Erfahrung, Beitrage zur Grundlagenproblematik der Sozialwissenschaft*. Stuttgart: Klett-Cotta, p. 55ff.
Lakatos, I., and Musgrave, A., eds. (1970). *Criticism and the Growth of Knowledge*. Cambridge: Cambridge University Press.
McCloskey, D. (1983). "The Rhetoric of Economics," *Journal of Economic Literature* 21:481–517.
Maloney, J. (1985). *Marshall, Orthodoxy and the Professionalisation of Economics*. Cambridge: Cambridge University Press.

CHAPTER 6

John Hicks and the methodology of economics

MARK BLAUG

Sir John Hicks's career in economics spans more than fifty years, in the course of which he has published fourteen books, including six collections of almost one hundred essays. In some of these, particularly *Value and Capital* (1939) and *A Revision of Demand Theory* (1956), there are hints of Hicks's general attitude to the nature of economics, but it is only recently that he has become more explicit about his views on the methodology of economics. A 1976 essay on ""Revolutions" in Economics" voiced doubts about the applicability of Lakatos's philosophy of science to economics; the opening and closing chapters of *Causality in Economics* (1979) threw up similar doubts about the wider question of empirical testing in economics; and, finally, an essay written in 1983 with the pointed title of "A Discipline Not a Science" decisively parted company with all varieties of empiricism, Popperianism, falsifiability, or call it what you will, in economics.

1.   Economics as a discipline not a science

After observing that economic theories can offer no more than "weak explanations" for economic events because they are always subject to a *ceteris paribus* clause – a feature that he appears to believe is unique to economics – Hicks concludes:

it becomes clear that they cannot be verified (or falsified) by confrontation with fact. We have been told that "when theory and fact come into conflict, it is theory, not fact, that must give way" [a quote from R.G. Lipsey]. It is very doubtful how far that *dictum* applies to economics. Our theories, as has been shown, are not that sort of a theory; but it is also true that our facts are not that sort of fact. (1983, pp. 371–2)

Economic facts, he goes on to say, are not the data produced by replicable, controlled experiments but the testimony of observers in historical time. For that reason alone, economic facts are frequently defective.

A lack of consilience between theory and fact, in economics (when that cannot be ascribed, or readily ascribed, to the weakness of the theory . . .) is most commonly due to a lack of correspondence between the terms in which the theory runs, and the terms in which the fact is described. . . . When that clash occurs, it may be that theory should be improved, so as to run more closely in the terms in which the relevant facts are commonly described but it may also be that the description of the facts should be improved, so that we may think about them more clearly. I believe it is this last . . . which is the special function of economic theory. Though the concepts of economics (most of the basic concepts) are taken from business practice, it is only when they have been clarified, and criticized, by theory, that they can be made into reliable means of communication. Now once one recognises that this is what economic theory very largely is doing, one sees that the use of models, which are themselves quite unrealistic, may be extremely defensible. . . . I might indeed go on to maintain that the *Value and Capital* model, of General Equilibrium under Perfect Competition, can be defended in much the same way . . . it is a laboratory, in which ideas can be tested.

I have quoted this statement at length because it is simply astonishing, both in its general drift and in its careful choice of words. First, we are told that when there is "a lack of consilience between theory and fact," that is, when an economic theory appears to be refuted by the evidence, this can sometimes be ascribed to the "weakness" of that theory. Now I would have thought instead that it can sometimes, and even frequently, be ascribed to the falseness of that theory. Second, we are told that a much more common reason for the failure of theory to agree with the facts is the lack of an adequate specification of what philosophers of science call "correspondence rules" for translating the analytical variables of the theory into the terms in which observational data are expressed; improving this translation, refining the specification of "correspondence rules," is, according to Hicks, "what economic theory very largely is doing." Now, again, I was under the impression that what economic theory very largely is doing is providing causal explanations of the workings of the economics system, so as to enable us accurately to predict the effect of a change in an exogenous variable on one or more of the endogenous variables of the theory.

When economic theory comes into conflict with the facts, such as they are, let us by all means reexamine the quality of the data and the correspondence rules that must be employed to compare the implications of the theory with the data. These are points well worth making provided that we are reminded that there may come a point when the clash between theory and data cannot be explained away in these terms. Unless we are prepared to admit that all economic theories may be false and may have to be abandoned eventually, we are furnished with an unqualified license to theorize as we like. But Hicks is silent throughout this essay on economics as "A Discipline Not a Science" on the crucial question of whether we are ever permitted to place any bars on the proliferation of possible economic theories, or indeed how we are to choose between them. If the improved "description" of the facts is, as he says, "the special function of economic theory," it is not clear to me how one would decide whether one theory contributes more to this end than another, since apparently all economic theories are equally true.

But of course truth, substantive truth, has nothing whatever to do with it. Economics, Hicks is telling us, is a game, a disciplined game played according to certain formal rules – logical consistency, simplicity, elegance, and generality – but still a game, and truth does not come into it.[1] Such a methodological standpoint immediately reminds us of Keynes's famous declaration in the introduction to the *Cambridge Economic Handbooks*, which Hicks indeed quotes with approval:

the Theory of Economics does not furnish a body of conclusions immediately applicable to policy. It is a method rather than a doctrine, an apparatus of the mind, a technique of thinking, which helps its possessor to draw correct conclusions. (Hicks, 1983, p. 375)

Keynes never did tell us how one would know that a conclusion drawn by an economist was correct – and neither does Hicks.

2.   Realism as a desideratum of economic models

Although economic theories cannot be verified or falsified, they must nevertheless satisfy standards of "realism." This is a theme to which Hicks frequently returns. Thus, in his prefatory remarks to the reprint of his essays on *Money, Interest and Wages,* he observes:

All models are simplifications of reality; they leave out things which are judged to be unimportant, for the purpose in hand, in order to make it possible to think more clearly about the things that are retained. What is left out, and what is to be retained, is chosen with reference to the problem in hand. It is perfectly proper to use some sort of model for one purpose, and another for another. (Hicks, 1982, p. 218).

We are not told how to judge whether a particular model is appropriate to "the problem in hand," but we are warned not to confuse the question

---

[1] Since we are gathered here to celebrate Johannes Klant's retirement as Professor of the Methodology and History of Economics at the University of Amsterdam, it may be worth adding that his book, *The Rules of the Game,* does not endorse Hicks's view of economics as "a discipline not a science." Klant is perfectly aware of the inherent difficulties of achieving falsifiable general theories in a subject like economics, and he makes no bones of the fact that economics contains a generous mixture of metaphysics and purely formal models. But he is also convinced that economics has achieved some "reasonably confirmed falsifiable hypotheses" and that economists should not abandon the aim of continually striving to achieve falsifiable theories (Klant, 1984, pp. 184–5).

of the inner logic of an economic model with "the question of applicability of the model to particular empirical data–whether in relation to those data, it is a good model or not" (Hicks, 1982, p. 219). But if economic models cannot be verified or falsified, how are we supposed to relate them to empirical data? The only criterion that Hicks ever offers is that of choosing among models in accordance with the "realism" or descriptive accuracy of their assumptions.

For example, growth models incorporating neutral technical progress are rejected because "The real world is not in a steady state, never has been, and (probably) never can be" (Hicks, 1965, pp. 183, 201; 1977, pp. xv–xvi; 1983, p. 109); Chamberlin's tangency solution in the theory of monopolistic competition "does correspond with a certain region of reality" (Hicks, 1983, p. 141); scale economies are of sufficient importance in the modern world to make perfect competition a useless standard for judging optimum organizations of production (Hicks, 1983, p. 153); income effects for finely defined commodities are likely to be small, so that "in strictness the law of demand is a hybrid; it has one leg resting on theory, and one on observation" (Hicks, 1956, p. 59); the factor-price-equalization theorem is largely irrelevant to the determination of international prices because "a general tendency to increasing returns to scale would seem to be nearer the facts" (Hicks, 1983, p. 231); the fact that market structures in modern economies are increasingly characterized by price-making rather than price-taking behavior is "verified by the most common observation," thus justifying the use of "fixprice" rather than "flexprice" models (Hicks, 1977, p. xi; 1982, pp. 225, 229, 234–5); the phenomenon of reswitching–a fall in the rate of interest leading to a substitution of labor for capital instead of the other way around–is dismissed as "being on the edge of things that could happen" because it would involve the improbable situation in which the lower construction costs of a new technique are offset by its longer construction period and higher operating costs (Hicks, 1973, pp. 44–6; 1977, p. 9); finally, the view that the labor market is a special kind of market in which a sense of "fairness" about wages directly affects efficiency, in consequence of which money wages exert an independent influence on the volume of employment, is correct "both as a matter of theory and as a matter of history" (Hicks, 1963, p. 318).[2]

Such casual empiricism likewise colors Hicks's retrospective judgment

---

[2] I have found only one example in all of Hicks's writings in which he faults an economic theory because its implications, rather than its assumptions, are refuted by the evidence. Thus, he notes, the expectations theory of the term "structure of interest rates" has been "tested against the facts; and it has usually been found that it does not fit the facts very well" (Hicks, 1974, pp. 45–6).

of some of the great economists of the past. Thus, the classical conceptions of flexible wages and fixed coefficients of production are defended
as realistic in the circumstances of the day (Hicks, 1967, p. 147; 1979, p.
47), and the decline of Ricardian economics in the second half of the
nineteenth century is attributed to the waning importance of the scarcity
of land (Hicks, 1983, p.38). In the same way, Keynes's assumption of an
exogenous money wage is deemed to be justified by the facts of the
1930s (Hicks, 1977, p. 81), but changes in methods of collective bargaining and in monetary institutions have rendered Keynes's analysis increasingly obsolete (Hicks, 1983, p. 38). Because the "facts" of economics are
subject to continual, nonrepeatable change, economic theories are for-
ever doomed to be valid only for the historical circumstances in which
they are born. Therefore, if there are "revolutions" in economics, they
are merely changes of attention because what Kuhn called "loss of content" in successive "paradigms" is considerable. It would seem, therefore, that every "well-chosen" economic theory is true for its time
(Hicks, 1981, p. 233), and the job of the historian of economic thought is
to make sense of these well-chosen ideas in the light of their historical
context. Such "relativism" is, of course, perfectly defensible if only we
were given some help in distinguishing the well-chosen from the ill-
chosen theories of the past. If Ricardo was correct for his time, was
Malthus also correct for the same time even when he argued in diametri-
cal opposition to Ricardo?

3.   Positive versus normative economics

Hicks has always upheld the distinction between positive and normative
economics, and of course, a great deal of his output has been concerned
with normative economics of the cost-benefit variety in which problems
of true or false take second place to problems of good and bad. Nevertheless, his writings on questions of positive economics seem to me to suffer
from a continuous unwillingness to face up to the question of how it is
that we ever discover whether a piece of positive economics is true or
false. On the one hand, we are asked not to regard economics as a
science but only as a discipline, a form of applied logic without any
empirical content. Without worrying too much about the honorific label
of "science," Hicks's object in calling economics a discipline rather than
a science is, as we have seen, to discourage attempts to knock out
economic theories by empirical testing. At the same time, we seem to
come equipped, according to Hicks, with considerable background
knowledge about the workings of economic systems that enable us to
know when assumptions about economic behavior or the operation of

economic institutions are realistic or not. But arguments employed to throw cold water on empirical judgments about the implications of economic theories surely apply with equal force to empirical judgments about the assumptions of economic theories.

On the one hand, "There is much economic theory which is pursued for no better reason than its intellectual tradition; it is a good game . . . [like] pure mathematics" (Hicks, 1979, p. viii) but, on the other hand, "What we want, in economics, are theories which will be useful, practically useful" and "I have always held (as I said in the preface to *Value and Capital*) that theory should be 'the servant of applied economics' " (Hicks, 1983, pp. 15, 361). So, presumably, there are well-chosen economic theories embodying realistic assumptions that somehow illuminate the workings of real-world economic systems even though they can never be validated with reference to empirical evidence. If we should ever find ourselves in the situation in which we are confronted with two such competing economic theories, each purporting to address the same "problem situation," such as Keynesian fiscalism and Friedmanian monetarism, we may apparently choose between them in terms of the respective degrees of realism of their assumptions (Hicks, 1975, p. 4). Unfortunately, it is easy to show that theories with patently unrealistic assumptions *may* be true and that, contrariwise, theories with extremely realistic assumptions *may* be false. To hold that economic theory should be practically useful and yet to deny that there is any place for empirical testing in economics is simply inconsistent.

Moreover, the Robinson-Keynes-Hicks description of economics as *merely* a "box of tools" is incompatible with the Hicksian claim that the ultimate purpose of economic theorizing is to devise optimum or, at any rate, superior economic policies. If economics cannot aspire to any substantive knowledge of economic relationships, it cannot speak with authority about questions of economic policy. It may be true to say, after Marshall, that economics is "not a body of concrete truth, but an engine for the discovery of concrete truth," but if economics is to be practically useful, we do well to underline some of the concrete truths we have discovered. In other words, either economics is simply an intellectual game or else it is something more than just a "discipline."

Take, for example, the simple policy question of whether a specific tax on a commodity will raise its price, but by less than the amount of the tax. The relevant "discipline" is the Marshallian cross of demand and supply, but by itself, this cannot give us any answer to the question we have posed. To answer it, we must assume that the demand curve for the commodity is negatively inclined and the supply curve positively inclined. But those assumptions imply knowledge of "concrete" truths and therefore go beyond the "engine" on its own. Thus, even on so simple a question, it is not enough to take our stand on economics as merely a technique of thinking.

4.   Causality in economics

One problem is that Hicks constantly evades fundamental questions of economic methodology even in works that appear on the surface to be directly concerned with them. *A Theory of Economic History* (1969) raised high hopes that light would be thrown on the famous question of the nature of historical explanation and, in particular, on how historical explanations differ from the explanations afforded by economic models. But it soon turned out that the term "theory" in this book denoted a general, nondeterministic scheme of social evolution within which different forms of economic life may be distinguished; it is something like a stage theory, but not in the strict sense that endogenous developments are relied on to account for the passage from one stage to another. Hicks gives great prominence to the growth of markets and market exchange via the emergence of middlemen and merchants, and employs various "models" to explain some of the specific changes within particular stages of development, such as the "lag of wages behind industrialization" during the Industrial Revolution due to the dramatic switch from circulating to fixed capital. At no point, however, does he raise the question of whether any of these models are true, or rather, how one would find out if they are true. His "theory of economic history" is simply another "story"; it is a plausible and possibly significant story but, like so many of the other stories of historians, we are given no aid in choosing between it and a large number of other equally plausible accounts of the same set of historical events.

Similarly, *Causality in Economics* (1979) appeared in its opening pages to deliver the goods we had long been waiting for:

> All experimental sciences are, in the economic sense, "static." They have to be static, since they have to assume that it does not matter *at what date* an experiment is performed. There do exist some economic problems which can be discussed in these terms; but there are not many of them. . . . The more characteristic economic problems are problems of change, of growth and retrogression, and of fluctuation. The extent to which these can be reduced into scientific terms is rather limited. . . . As economics pushes on beyond "statics," it becomes less like science, and more like history. (Hicks, 1979, p. xi)

Having emphasized the temporal nature of all economic phenomena in contrast to "science," in which the passage of time is rarely critical – but what of biology, geology, and astronomy? – Hicks moves on to observe that economics is also unique in being concerned with the consequences of purposive individual decisions. One might have imagined that this would lead on naturally to a consideration in intentional modes of causal explanation – the reasons of economic agents are the causes of their action – methodological individualism, *Verstehen* doctrine, and the like. For instance, there is the question that cannot fail to worry a macro-economist: If aggregate economic outcomes are frequently and perhaps invariably the unintended consequences of individual actions, can such outcomes be reduced to individual action and, if not, what becomes of methodological individualism? But Hicks does not stop to raise such questions, and instead moves on to observe that most effects in econom-ics are produced by a multiplicity of causes and hence that causality always involves the implicit or explicit use of counterfactuals (the *modus tollens* form of logical reasoning according to which if A is the cause of B, then non-A implies non-B). Thus, theorizing is necessarily involved in every causal assertion in economics. This is perfectly true and might have been employed to question Friedman's as-if, empty-box interpreta-tion of economic theories but, again, this is not the route chosen by Hicks.

The point about counterfactuals leads straight on to the final point, which is indeed the main thesis of the book, that causation in economics is not necessarily Humean in character, cause always preceding effect in time; it may be "static" if cause and effect exist more or less permanently or "contemporaneous" if the relevant time period connecting cause and effect is stretched out. Much is made of the concept of "contemporane-ous causality" – "the characteristic form of the causal relation in modern economics" – in the middle chapters of the book dealing with Keynesian economics, but the concept seems at best a new word for "simultaneous determination." The purpose of Hicks's distinction between three types of causality seems to fit general equilibrium theory into the language of causality, whereas past practice has been to refuse to give general equi-librium theory a causal interpretation. It is true that there is something very peculiar about general equilibrium theory, namely, that it is com-patible with any and all economic events, but I doubt that we learn very much by calling simultaneous determination "causal determination" in a special sense of the word "cause."

The last chapter of *Causality in Economics* questions the applicability of Neyman-Pearson techniques of statistical inference to economics be-cause the time-series observation that econometricians commonly em-ploy are not random drawings from a known population. This is, of course, the now almost standard justification for the replacement of Neyman-Pearson techniques for Bayesian methods of inference. But this is not how Hicks's argument proceeds. Both Neyman-Pearson and Bayes depend on cardinally measurable probabilities. Many economic events occur with a frequency, argues Hicks, that cannot be expressed in cardinal numbers and sometimes not in any numbers at all; there is both Knightian uncertainty and true ignorance about the occurrence of many economic events. If so, that certainly kills off any notion of econometric testing as a court of last resort for choosing between competing economic theories. Unfortunately, it also kills off the idea that well-chosen models with realistic assumptions will somehow throw light on the real world and prove useful to policymakers, which, as we have seen, is one of Hicks's abiding beliefs.

I have probably been very unfair to what I regard as the rather thin philosophical content of *Causality in Economics*. However, I have summarized it fairly[3] and others must judge its significance for themselves. What is clear, however, is that it was written in apparent ignorance of the simply enormous literature on the difficult philosophical concept of causality, not to mention an even larger literature on the problem of causal explanation in the social sciences.

For example, it is a mistake to suppose that causal statements are decisively tested by counterfactual statements. When events have multiple causes, as they usually do in the social sciences, the truth of a counterfactual statement is neither necessary nor sufficient for the truth of a causal statement: if A is not *the* but simply *a* cause of B (but so is C, D, etcetera), the statement that A is a cause of B may be true even though the statement that the nonoccurrence of A implies the nonoccurrence of B is false (Elster, 1983, pp. 34–40). Mackie's (1975, p. 62) INUS condition for causality – A is a cause of B if A is an Insufficient but Necessary part of a condition that is itself Unnecessary but Sufficient for B – comes much closer to the sorts of causal propositions we often encounter in economics. Addison et al. (1984) illustrate the INUS condition by examining the well-known proposition that investment is a cause of economic growth: This proportion may well be true, and yet we can get economic growth even without extra investment; investment by itself

---

[3] Helm (1984) gives a sympathetic account of Hicks's views on methodology and compares them favorably with those of Friedman. He sums up (p. 124):

> Hicksian causality is the central building block of his non-positivistic methodology. . . . There are three components to his account of causality. The first relates to weak predictions and the *ceteris paribus* clauses mentioned above, and is his distinction between strong and weak causality. The second is his counterfactual account. The third is his relation between temporal ordering and his three possibilities: static, reciprocal, and contemporaneous.

See also Addison et al. (1984), who are less sympathetic but focus entirely on Hicks's account of "static" causality.

is insufficient, but it is a necessary part of a larger set of conditions (such as entrepreneurship, an efficient financial system, a stable government, etcetera) that is sufficient and yet not strictly necessary to produce growth. How we test the truth of an INUS causal statement is, of course, another story, but suffice it to say that we cannot refute it simply by considering counterfactuals.

5.   The younger Hicks and the older Hicks

In a perceptive review of Hicks's *Economic Perspectives*, Leijonhufvud (1979) noted the peculiar relationship between Hicks the Younger – the Hicks who reformulated the orthodox theory of consumer behavior in terms of indifference curves, interpreted Keynes in terms of the IS-LM apparatus, and revived and refined general equilibrium theory – and Hicks the Older, who has come to be increasingly skeptical of general equilibrium theory and indeed of all static analysis that is not "securely in time," who insists that all labor and most commodity markets are fixprice markets, and who contends that useful economic theory must incorporate stylized institutional facts. The Younger Hicks is widely read and constantly cited, while the Older Hicks is generally neglected and rarely cited, all of which is to say that the Older Hicks undermines the achievements of the Younger Hicks in opposition to the prevailing mainstream of professional opinion that the Younger Hicks had done so much to establish.[4]

But a deeper reason for the relative neglect of the Older Hicks is the deeply private tone of much of Hicks's recent writings, a dialogue in fact with his former self, which we are invited to sample but perhaps not fully to share. Thus, there are frequent references to Keynes, Hawtrey, Robertson, Hayek, and Wicksell, all major figures in pre–World War II economics, but current writers like Friedman, Lucas, and Tobin are rarely mentioned even when he is discussing macroeconomic issues of inflation and the formation of expectations. Moreover the illusiveness of Hicks's laconic literary style – "I am no longer convinced"; "it is not as persuasive as it once appeared to me"; "one may now have grave doubts"; etcetera – makes it difficult to pin down the criteria he employs to arrive at his judgments. I am not at all sure, therefore, that I have succeeded in capturing the standards he implicitly invokes in appraising economic the-

---

[4] As Hicks said himself in later years: "They gave me a Nobel prize [in 1972] for my work on "general equilibrium and welfare economics" . . . work which has become part of the standard literature. But it was done a long time ago, and it is with mixed feelings that I found myself honoured for that work, which I myself felt myself to have outgrown" (1977, p. v).

ories. For example, there is his frequently expressed admiration for Keynes with "his keen nose for the actual, the current actual" (Hicks, 1977, p. 141n), and this despite the fact that Hicks finds Keynes's arguments in some respects inconsistent and even incoherent (Coddington, 1979, pp. 979–80). But what is not clear is the grounds on which Keynesian economics is given such high marks by Hicks. Is it because Keynesian economics "illuminated" the depression in the 1930s? Is it because it implied "correct" policy conclusions? Is it because it was well corroborated by empirical evidence? Or is it instead, as I suspect, because Keynesian economics provided a simple, elegant, and robust economic model with dramatic policy implications, which moreover proved fruitful in the quantification of economic data? After all, Hicks wrote a textbook in economics, *The Social Framework* (1942), which was clearly inspired by the balance-sheet approach of the Keynesian schema. Nevertheless, and despite the numerous occasions on which Hicks has returned to probe the foundations of the Keynesian system, I have been unable to discover the precise basis for Hicks's high opinion of Keynes. And what is true of his judgment of Keynes is also true of many of his other theoretical appraisals.

6. By way of conclusion

What is clear is that Hicks generally attaches greater importance to certain formal criteria for appraising economic theories – consistency, simplicity, elegance, and generality – than to empirical criteria, particularly in relationship to the implications rather than the assumptions of economic models. I am not the first to have noticed this (e.g., Maes, 1984, p. 180). It is also clear that, whatever his misgivings about empirical testing in economics before World War II, such misgivings have become much stronger in recent years, culminating in the explicit condemnation of all attempts at economic testing in his 1983 *Collected Essays on Economic Theory*.

I once made the bold assertion that most modern economists are "innocuous falsificationists," that is, they pay lip service to the Popperian view that the validity of economic theories must be judged *in the final analysis* by the accuracy of their predictions, and occasionally they even practice what they preach (Blaug, 1980, p. 127). Evidently, Hicks is an exception to this characterization and, considering his enormous influence on the shape of modern economics, his is no minor exception.[5]

[5] As Lindbeck (1985, p. 42) notes: "it is indeed remarkable how strong the intellectual influences of these four theorists [Hicks, Samuelson, Arrow, and Debreu] has been on our profession – by influencing not only the choice of issues and methods but also the 'style' of analysis and exposition."

Yes, indeed, some would say, and this only goes to demonstrate the
sterility of *pre*scriptive Methodology with a capital M and the importance of *des*criptive methodology with a lowercase m: We need to study
what economists actually do and not what they should do (McCloskey,
1983). It is, however, impossible rigidly to divorce the two, and even
those who profess to be totally open-minded about the best practice in
economics find themselves driven to criticize actual practice (Caldwell
and Coats, 1984).[6] Besides, I have been preoccupied in this chapter less
with what Hicks does than with what he says he does. What Hicks says is
that economic theories cannot be tested for their truth value, and yet he
does not deny, or at least he does not appear to deny, that economic
theories have truth value: They are not merely conventional instruments
for organizing our background knowledge but genuine causal explanations of what does happen and why it so happens. Moreover, some
economic theories are said to be better than others even though we are
somehow precluded from ever comparing them in terms of their power
to account for empirical evidence. There is nothing wrong with such a
position, but it does lead inevitably to the conclusion that economic
theory is a subject precisely like pure mathematics, an intellectual game
to be justified in its own terms. And that position is incompatible with
the notion of economics as the handmaiden of economic policy, which
Hicks has consistently upheld. I conclude, therefore, that it is impossible
to extract any coherent methodology of economics from the writings of
Hicks.

References

Addison, J.T., Burton, J., and Torrance, T.S. (1984). "Causation, Social Sci-
ence and Sir John Hicks," *Oxford Economic Papers* 36(1):1–11.
Blaug, M. (1980). *The Methodology of Economics*. London: Cambridge Univer-
sity Press.
Caldwell, B.J., and Coats, A.W. (1984). "The Rhetoric of Economics: A Com-
ment on McCloskey," *Journal of Economic Literature* 22(2):575–8.
Coddington, A. (1979)."Hicks's Contribution to Keynesian Economics," *Jour-
nal of Economic Literature* 18(3): 970–88.
Elster, J. (1983). *Explaining Technical Change. Studies in Rationality and Social
Change*. Cambridge: Cambridge University Press.
Helm, D. (1984). "Predictions and Causes: A Comparison of Friedman and

---

[6] Both in his 1983 paper and in his 1985 book, McCloskey is much concerned with the bad
rhetoric of significance tests in econometrics, arguing for Bayesian in preference to
Neyman-Pearson methods. Actually, if the methodology of falsificationism, or what he
calls "modernism," is as silly as he makes out, it is difficult to see why he is so concerned
about econometric practice.

Hicks on Method," *Oxford Economic Papers* 36(suppl.):118–34; reprinted in *Economic Theory and Hicksian Themes,* eds. D.A. Collard et al. Oxford: Oxford University Press, 1984.

Hicks, J. (1956). *A Revision of Demand Theory.* Oxford: Oxford University Press.

Hicks, J. (1965). *Capital and Growth.* Oxford: Oxford University Press.

(1967). *Critical Essays in Monetary Theory.* Oxford: Oxford University Press.

(1969). *A Theory of Economic History.* Oxford: Oxford University Press.

(1973). *Capital and Time.* Oxford: Oxford University Press.

(1974). *A Crisis in Keynesian Economics.* Oxford: Oxford University Press.

(1975). "What Is Wrong with Monetarism?" *Lloyds Bank Review,* 118:1–13.

(1977). *Economic Perspectives.* Oxford: Oxford University Press.

(1979). *Causality in Economics.* Oxford: Blackwell.

(1981). *Wealth and Welfare, Collected Essays on Economic Theory,* Vol. I. Oxford: Blackwell.

(1982). *Money, Interest and Wages, Collected Essays on Economic Theory,* Vol. II. Oxford: Blackwell.

(1983). *Classics and Moderns, Collected Essays on Economic Theory,* Vol. III. Oxford: Blackwell.

Klant, J.J. (1984). *The Rules of the Game. The Logical Structure of Economic Theories.* London: Cambridge University Press.

Leijonhufvud, A. (1979). "Review of J. Hicks *Economic Perspectives,*" *Journal of Economic Literature* 17:525–8.

Lindbeck, A. (1985). "The Prize in Economic Science in Memory of Alfred Noble," *Journal of Economic Literature* 23(1):37–56.

Mackie, J.L. (1975). *The Cement of the Universe. A Study of Causation.* Oxford: Clarendon Press.

Maes, I. (1984). "The Contribution of J.R. Hicks to Macroeconomics and Monetary Theory." Ph.D. thesis, Katholieke Universiteit te Leuven.

McCloskey, D.N. (1983). "The Rhetoric of Economics," *Journal of Economic Literature* 21(2):481–517.

McCloskey, D.N. (1985). *The Rhetoric of Economics.* Madison: University of Wisconsin Press.

PART IV

The missing chapter: empirical
work and its appraisal

CHAPTER 7

Finding a satisfactory empirical model

MARY MORGAN

It is commonplace criticism that econometricians never refute a model that they set out to "test" in the sense that they never reject the underlying theoretical model they have used. It has been argued that refutations cannot be expected from econometrics for various reasons of a logical or philosophical nature. The less kindly, more casual observer might note that econometricians sometimes blame the paucity of data or problems with the estimation method or computing power, rather than reject a theory; in other words that, as bad workers, they blame their tools.

Without wishing to detract from the sound philosophical arguments about the inability to test economic theories, and ignoring the unkind aspersions on econometricians, I want to argue from a different viewpoint – an historical viewpoint. This viewpoint suggests that although econometricians have described their activity as that of testing economic theories, this testing should not be understood in quite the same terms as methodological discussions about falsification and verification. In my view, econometricians have been primarily concerned with finding satisfactory empirical models, not with trying to prove fundamental theories true or untrue.

Historically, econometricians sought applied counterparts to theory that "worked" with reference to observed data. This involved not only the translation of theory into empirical models but also the parallel development of criteria for labeling empirical models "satisfactory." The range of criteria formed a sort of qualitative assessment with questions centered on the issue "How well does the empirical model work with reference to the data?" This chapter examines the problem of finding an empirical model and the development of testing criteria in the early history of econometrics. The quality control idea of testing that

My thanks go to the discussant and participants at the Klant conference and to Margaret Schabas for their helpful comments on the ideas expressed in this chapter. Much of the historical material in the chapter is drawn from an extended study of the history of econometrics, initially funded by a grant from the ESRC (Grant 6727) and reported in detail in Morgan (1984).

emerges in this "pre-Popper" period contrasts with the right or wrong, true or untrue, type of assessment that seems to pervade methodological debate on theory testing in economics.

I.   Empirical models

In the late nineteenth century, both in discussions about methodology and in economic practice, economists saw statistical and mathematical methods as two different tools operating in separate spheres. The role of mathematics was to aid in the task of deductive theorizing, whereas the role of statistics was to help in the empirical task of measuring economic laws, verifying or testing theories, and even suggesting theories.[1] Modern economic practice comes close to this original vision, with mathematical economists and econometricians operating in separate, or at least sequential, areas of interest. In contrast, between the early twentieth century and the 1950s, econometrics emerged as a distinct activity in which mathematical and statistical methods were united in a single practice within economics.

The initial aim of econometricians was to use mathematics and statistics to make economic theories "concrete" and measure the constant parameters of those laws. They were faced with immediate problems. First, theories were expressed in words, rather than in mathematical form; the relationships between the variables were often poorly defined, and the variables themselves might not be measurable. Second, although economic theories were taken to be fundamentally true, econometricians found that they were not necessarily readily applicable to any real data set. In response to these difficulties, econometricians of the 1920s and 1930s tried to bring about a closer correspondence, or matching, between theory and data (Morgan, 1984). Since the theoretical models themselves could not be measured, finding empirical models that could be subjected to measurement was the first task in this program. This required the translation of the theory into a more usable form and the development of the appropriate approximations to be applied to the basic economic theory for each particular set of circumstances.[2] Analogous problems and activities occur in all sciences; for example, in apply-

---

[1] While the methodological point of view is given, for example, by Keynes (1891), Jevons's work gives the prime practical example of the separation of the two tools.
[2] In discussing this aspect of empirical model building, I have been much influenced by Nancy Cartwright's provocative book *How the Laws of Physics Lie* (1983), in which she argues that the fundamental theoretical laws of physics are true in some fundamental sense but that for any given real circumstance, they are false.

ing Boyle's law, the chemist has to rely on a set of empirically derived approximations for each substance, and these have been gathered over the years by applied chemists. Similarly, engineers have developed the relevant approximations for physical theories to be applied, for example, in building a bridge.

In economics, finding an empirical model to match the theory involved making the theory operational in several ways:

1. Translating the verbal theory into mathematical form, and deciding in what form variables should be used and on the functional form for each theory.
2. Finding ways of dealing with the *ceteris paribus* clauses under which the theory is assumed to hold (for example, choosing homogeneous periods).
3. Finding the correct model for time and space: specifying the time adjustment/dynamic processes for each theory and taking into account local specific factors (e.g., institutional features such as price-setting mechanisms).

If we take as an example the development of demand studies in the interwar period (when the field of econometrics was young but developing fast), we see that the preceding three requirements were interwoven. Translating the simple downward-sloping law of demand into a mathematical equation linking price and quantity seemed easy enough, but before the coefficient of this "law of demand" could be measured, it was necessary to find some way of keeping the other disturbing factors constant in line with the *ceteris paribus* clauses of economic theory. This was, in turn, part of the need to deal with the gap between the theory, which was static, and the data, which were usually in the form of time series.

Econometricians initially dealt with the disturbing factors that changed over time (but were assumed constant in theory) by methods that preadjusted the data before the relationships of interest were fitted. One method was to adjust the quantities demanded to remove the effect of population growth before fitting a demand curve (Lehfeldt, 1914). Toward the end of the 1920s, it was suggested that it would be better to incorporate these disturbing variables in the empirical demand relationship because they were precisely the other variables that influenced demand (Smith, 1925; Schultz, 1928). This, in turn, was linked to the task of deciding which other variables of the many suggested by theorists were actually relevant in the empirical model: for example, which other prices from the "all other prices" of demand theory were the influential ones (Ezekiel, 1933).

At the same time in the late 1920s and the early 1930s, there was a discussion within econometrics about how to deal with the time dimension of the theoretical relationships in these models. Econometricians adopted different ways of introducing dynamic aspects into empirical models. One method involved introducing time lags of various lengths into the model to capture the delays between causes and effects. Another path was to add new forms of the theoretical terms into the model to capture a more complex behavior than simple response to current prices. These were not necessarily independent approaches; their use would often depend on whether the starting point was mathematical or statistical work.

The cobweb model provides a good illustration of the first path to dynamic models. In the cobweb model, price responds to this year's quantity demanded, while supply is determined by the previous year's price. This model was first used by Moore in 1925 to model what he called a "moving equilibrium" of demand and supply. Moore gave no particular reason for this choice of model, although he might have rationalized it on the basis of knowledge of the particular market. The model formulation was analyzed and applied again in the early 1930s in three different publications by Schultz, Leontief, and Tinbergen (Ezekiel, 1938). Tinbergen (1930), for example, expressed reservations about the model because he saw that under a certain range of parameter values the model implied a path diverging away from an equilibrium solution, giving an exploding cobweb pattern. The suggestion that such a divergent path could form the basis of a crisis model was made by Evans in 1931, and in 1938 Ezekiel proposed it as an alternative explanation of the malaise of the 1930s economies: that is, the economies had adjustment processes that led away from full employment. The lagged adjustments or responses in crucial relationships that characterized the cobweb model could also, in certain circumstances, produce cycles in the variables. This version of the model entered econometric business cycle literature in the early 1930s – for example, in Frisch's propagation and impulse model of 1933 – and soon became an essential element in mathematical theories of the business cycle.

In this story, the cobweb model started off in the mid-1920s as an approximation for the time relationships of an empirical demand model, but by the mid-1930s it had become an essential element of empirical cycle models and thence of cycle theory. This rapid assimilation, from an empirical approximation to an essential element in theory, was no doubt due to the integrated nature of econometrics during this early period, when those who were undertaking empirical work were also responsible for developing satisfactory mathematical versions of verbal theories. It provides a good example of how econometric work played a role in theory development.

An example of the second way of formulating dynamic models is given by the work of Roos and Evans. Roos was an econometrician who became the director of economic research of the National Recovery Administration under the New Deal initiative in the United States and the first research director of the Cowles Commission (whose research program during the 1930s was purely econometric). He left academia in the late 1930s to form perhaps the first econometric consulting company. Evans was primarily a mathematician, and consequently his role was in the development of mathematical formulations and adaptations of economic theory. The mathematical demand models developed by Roos and Evans all involved quantity as the dependent variable and incorporated as explanatory variables a simple current price term, a term depicting the influence of past prices (the integral over past prices), a term incorporating the rate of change of prices (a differential term), and lastly, a linear time trend. They combined these terms in different ways: For example, the differential term was thought to be particularly appropriate in modeling speculative demand in wholesale markets, while the time trend was a commonly used approximation to cover influential trending variables. Roos adapted these to empirical models and applied them to individual commodities in a substantial monograph in econometrics entitled *Dynamic Economics* (1934). Roos's influence is less easy to trace than his career. Nevertheless, a study of the literature shows that the Roos–Evans equations were used in discussions of demand by Schultz (1938), whose work was highly influential, and by many others.

The use of past values and rates of change to help explain present values of variables and delayed responses within economic relationships was a fairly general development. Adjustment processes were used to model not only the past but also the future. Roos touched on the problem of expectations in his attempt to model speculators' demand by the rate of change of prices. Tinbergen (1933) attacked the problem of expectations more directly in trying to assess the planning horizons and reaction times of agents to unforeseen changes.

In general, the adaptations that econometricians made to verbal theories (whether justified by rationalizations of a semitheoretical kind or not) were designed to produce models with empirical relevance. This meant formulating a model that had the "correct" theoretical properties (e.g., equilibrium tendencies) but that also incorporated elements to make the model relevant to the particular real circumstances. The latter involved several possibilities. It could mean introducing elements to match some general observed features of data, such as cycles, or more specific observed features such as those seen in the market for a particular commodity. Above all, an empirical model must be one that is measurable. This translation of theories into empirical models that can be fitted to statistical data was described earlier as making theories "operational." This term was used deliberately, for Percy Bridgman was the only philosopher of science whose work was referenced by those involved in the econometric work of the period. Both Roos (1934) and Schultz (1938), important figures in econometrics, expressed admiration for Bridgman's ideas and used their books to try to introduce operationalism into economics. As Klant (1984) points out, Bridgman's ideas on operationalism had considerable influence on economists in the 1930s.[3]

These early econometricians were open and direct about their desire to translate theory into empirical models. Within the demand field, for example, there was some discussion about the relative roles of theorists (meaning nonmathematical economists) and of econometricians in developing such models. The econometricians blamed the theorists for their failure to develop adequate models to cope with the problem of time, and the consequent necessity for their own development of such models (Gilboy, 1930; Stigler, 1939). Some economists clearly resented what they saw as statisticians interfering in economic theory. For example, Keynes's famous critique (1939) of Tinbergen's work accused him of plucking lag lengths out of midair. Such criticisms were unfair, for as any econometrician of the period well knew, theorists just did not supply such information in their theories.

II.   Satisfactory models

Achieving a satisfactory level of correspondence between economic data and economic theory involved not only developing appropriate empirical (measurable) models but estimating these models (measuring the parameters of the relationships) and then deciding whether they were satisfactory or not. The assessment of models as "satisfactory" depends, of course, on the purpose of the empirical models. Early econometricians had many ideas about the purposes of their models and about assessing whether their models were satisfactory, but these ideas were rarely expressed clearly.

[3] For example, Klant reminds us that Samuelson's *Foundations of Economic Analysis* was written in 1937 under the title *The Operational Significance of Economic Theory.*

Their aims and criteria ranged over the following set of ideas:

1. To measure theoretical laws: Models must satisfy certain theoretical requirements (economic criteria).
2. To explain (or describe) the observed data: Models must fit observed data (statistical or historical criteria).
3. To be useful for policy: Models must allow the exploration of policy options or make predictions about future values.
4. To explore or develop theory: Models must expose unsuspected relationships or develop the detail of relationships.
5. To verify or reject theory: Models must be satisfactory or not over a range of economic, statistical, and other criteria.

Often econometric work covered several of these aims.

The main purpose of the earliest work, in the 1910s and 1920s, was to measure the parameters of empirical models based on theoretical laws that were assumed to be true. These were assessed by criteria based on economic theory. The primary criterion was whether the measured parameters had the "correct," that is, the expected, theoretical sign (Lehfeldt, 1915), and the size of the parameter was secondary. By the 1930s the purposes of empirical models and their assessment were widening. Other criteria were being developed, for example, parameter constancy when the empirical model was fitted over different time periods. Statistical criteria, which were external to economic theory and concerned with measures of fit to data, were introduced very gradually.

Two examples of applied work from the 1930s give an idea of how econometricians assessed whether their empirical models were satisfactory. These are not representative examples, for both economists were more coherent about their assessment strategies and used more criteria than most of their fellow econometricians of the period. Whitman (1936) was a product of the pragmatic U.S. school of econometricians; he developed the work of Roos and Schultz in the case of the demand for steel. His aim was not entirely clear, but he seemed to have been seeking a more detailed and applicable version of the theory of demand. He used the Roos–Evans empirical models (discussed previously) and estimated three models (rejecting Roos's integral variable as unmeasurable in favor of Evans's variable involving the sum of lagged prices). Each model was fitted for three different time periods, chosen because he believed that each period was reasonably homogeneous. He compared the models on the basis of (1) the "rationality" of the implied theoretical explanation; (2) the signs of the parameters (whether they were "correct"); (3) the sizes and stability of the parameters over the three time periods and their standard errors; and (4) the degree of statistical explanation achieved by the model (corrected R^2). He described the empirical models that were most satisfactory according to these criteria as "fairly good demand equations."

Whitman's comparison of alternative empirical models did not involve choosing between different fundamental theories but rather between different empirical models of the same theory involving different dynamic processes. He was not seeking to prove one of these models as the true one, but to find the most satisfactory of the different versions. His comparison used a relatively sophisticated assessment process for the period, for it tested the models' consistency with both theory and statistical data in a coherent way. Those that performed better on the tests were better models, but for Whitman they still held the interim status of "hypotheses" pending further econometric investigation.

Tinbergen was a product of the more mixed European tradition, also pragmatic in its way. In his macroeconometric modeling of the late 1930s (1937 and 1939) Tinbergen was, as always, modest and cautious in his work, though he did claim to "test" theories. He stated his belief on testing clearly: that statistical work cannot prove a theory correct, though it can go some way toward proving a hypothesis incorrect. Because of the difficulties involved in building and estimating a large macro-model, Tinbergen used graphic means to help choose the variables in the equations and assemble the empirical model. This method seemed to involve ad hoc adjustments and manipulations, but the work gained rather than lost from Tinbergen's willingness to be open about the problems involved. One of his aims was to use the final macro-model to simulate different policy options and to assess which policy would be most useful in reducing unemployment. He found that he could indeed use his empirical models for this task.

Tinbergen was one of the few econometricians to develop a well-defined testing program, using every possible criterion that had been developed in econometrics by the late 1930s to assess his empirical models. First, he considered the consistency of his results with economic theories in respect to the individual relationships and then in terms of the implied dynamic process of the system. He used statistical criteria to assess how well his model characterized the data set and to test whether assumptions about the technical properties required by the statistical method held true. (For example, he tested for constancy of the equations' parameters over different subperiods.) He also used historical criteria to see whether his empirical model explained certain peculiar historical features of the period such as the 1929 Great Crash. The information from these testing criteria was used to help him to reformulate his empirical model in an iterative process, for Tinbergen kept refining his model to find one that was more satisfactory than the last.

Consistency with theory, satisfactory fit to the data, sensible explanations of the history, and satisfactory fulfillment of the conditions and assumptions of the econometric method were the criteria that the empirical model must satisfy, and Tinbergen was sufficiently happy with the results of his assessment to claim "statistical verification." By this, he meant that his empirical model satisfactorily explained the statistical/historical data. During the process of building his model, Tinbergen had rejected some theories, or elements of theories, on the grounds that his empirical models of these theories did not explain the data. It was noticeable that formal ways of rejecting models using statistical tests were still lacking in econometrics. The introduction of more rigorous formal ideas of theory testing in econometrics was due to the work in the 1940s of Haavelmo, who introduced the probability approach into econometrics and placed the subject more firmly on its statistical foundations (Morgan, 1987). This change was established with the help of econometricians at the Cowles Commission.

Haavelmo (1944) stated that in the absence of an experimental framework in economics, econometrics must act on both the theory and the data, making adjustments on both sides in order to get satisfactory models. He also stated that a theory became a hypothesis that could be tested only when it was associated with a design of experiments that showed how to measure the variables and make the necessary approximations to get an empirical model. This was, of course, what econometricians in the 1920s and 1930s had already been doing in formulating empirical models. According to Haavelmo, all theories should also be formulated as probabilistic statements, for any theory formulated as an exact equation (one with no probabilistic or random element) was useless from the point of view of economics; it would always be rejected by observations (Haavelmo, 1943). What was required was some way of allowing true theories to be accepted most of the time and false theories to be rejected most of the time when they were tested against data. Probability theory, together with Neyman–Pearson testing methods, seemed to offer such a procedure. Using this framework, econometricians could throw out theories that often failed the statistical tests; but they might be left with many theories that were compatible with the same observed data set, and it was impossible to prove which of these theories were true. Since Haavelmo had already stated that tests could be made only after a theory had been formulated as a probabilistic empirical model, in effect he gave econometricians a formal procedure for rejecting empirical models.

Following Haavelmo's introduction of the probability approach to econometrics in 1944, a much fuller use of statistical techniques, and in particular Neyman–Pearson testing methods, came into econometrics. It is important to note the emphasis Haavelmo placed, not only on the probabilistic theory formulation and associated testing mechanism, but also on the "design of experiments" role of econometrics. The role of econometrics in designing the correct approximations or additions to theory is a strong current going back through the empirical work of the 1920s and forward to post–World War II econometrics.

III.   Testing

The testing developed by the early econometricians involved an idea of quality control and quality ranking. In the first place, a range of criteria were applied to empirical models to distinguish those that were satisfactory from those that were not. If the empirical model exhibited a basic set of qualities (satisfied the criteria), it was considered satisfactory. This set of qualities included both economic theory criteria and data criteria because the empirical models that econometricians worked with were a sort of halfway house, formed to capture the correspondence between theory and data, and thus needed to satisfy both sides. When empirical models failed to work according to the given set of quality indicators, the usual response of econometricians in the 1930s was to use a different set of approximations – that is, an alternative empirical model – rather than an alternative fundamental theory. In the second place, the tests provided a sort of ranking of empirical models: The model that performed best on the set of quality control indicators was considered the most satisfactory.

A study of the history of econometrics suggests that prior to Popper, there were ideas about testing in economics that were rather different in aim and meaning from the usual notions of refutation, confirmation, verification, or falsification. Present-day econometricians apparently focus their energies more explicitly on testing theories than earlier workers in the field, and the language of econometrics is now in a sense more Popperian, for models are typically rejected or not rejected. This change of emphasis and language in econometrics masks a continuity of both thought and practice with earlier work, for the testing notions adopted from the 1920s to the 1940s have naturally left a legacy.

It is easy to find examples of this legacy. In the process of finding satisfactory empirical models, the early econometricians built up a fund of empirical models or models with empirical relevance. Modern econometricians have continued this practice and now have access to a library of empirical models and approximations to which new ones may be added and from which old ones can be borrowed, applied, and comparisons made. For example, present-day econometricians can use one of a range of dynamic adjustment processes varying from the cobweb model or Irving Fisher's distributed lag model (both dating from 1925) to the more modern error correction models popularized by Davidson et al. (1978).[4] The presence of this set of ready-made approximations does not mean that any one of them will be automatically correct, but only that they have been found to work in similar circumstances. Indeed, such approximations go into the theory, as in the cobweb model, and sometimes become the source of theoretical argument in themselves – for example, whether expectations are adaptive or rational.

The quality control idea of testing can also be helpful in understanding and interpreting present practice in econometrics. For example, Gilbert (1986) compares British and American attitudes toward the presence of serial correlation. For both groups of economists, serial correlation is an unsatisfactory quality to find in an empirical model, but their response varies. Gilbert describes how the Americans see serial correlation as a "pathological" symptom of failure in the econometric model, whereas the British consider it an indication of how the empirical model needs to be reformulated to obtain a model with a better set of qualities. The latter approach shows that the notion of quality control testing is still to be found in the work of some current econometricians who, despite differences in language, share the same concerns as their predecessors.[5]

References

Cartwright, N. (1983). *How the Laws of Physics Lie*. Oxford: Clarendon Press.
Christ, C. (1966). *Econometric Models and Methods*. New York: Wiley.
Davidson, J.E.H., D.F. Hendry, F. Srba, and S. Yeo (1978). "Econometric Modelling of the Aggregate Time-Series Relationship between Consumers' Expenditure and Income in the United Kingdom," *Economic Journal* 88:661–92.
Evans, G.C. (1931). "A Simple Theory of Economic Crises," *Journal of the American Statistical Association* 26:61–8.

[4] See, for example, textbooks in econometrics, the survey article by Griliches (1967), or the recent listing of dynamic model formulations by Hendry and Richard (1982, Section 3).
[5] See, for example, Hendry (1983) for a very recent, relatively nontechnical discussion of empirical models and their evaluation that is close to the ideas discussed here. An earlier example of a similar approach is given by Carl Christ's text (1966).

Ezekiel, M. (1933). "Some Considerations on the Analysis of the Prices of Competing or Substitute Commodities," *Econometrica* 1:172–80.

(1938). "The Cobweb Theorem," *Quarterly Journal of Economics* 52:255–80.

Fisher, I. (1925). "Our Unstable Dollar and the So-Called Business Cycle," *Journal of the American Statistical Association* 20:179–202.

Frisch, R. (1933). "Propagation Problems and Impulse Problems in Dynamic Economics," in *Economic Essays in Honour of Gustav Cassel*. London: Allen & Unwin.

Gilbert, C. (1986). "The Development of British Econometrics, 1945–85." Applied Economics Discussion Paper No. 8, Institute of Economics and Statistics, Oxford.

Gilboy, E.W. (1930). "Demand Curves in Theory and Practice," *Quarterly Journal of Economics* 44:601–20.

Griliches, Z. (1967). "Distributed Lags: A Survey," *Econometrica* 35:16–49.

Haavelmo, T. (1943). "Statistical Testing of Business Cycle Theories," *Review of Economics and Statistics* 25:13–18.

(1944). "The Probability Approach in Econometrics," *Econometrica* 12 (suppl.).

Hendry, D.F. (1983). "Econometric Modelling: The Consumption Function in Retrospect,"*Scottish Journal of Political Economy* 30:193–220.

and Richard, J.F. (1982). "On the Formulation of Empirical Models in Dynamic Econometrics," *Journal of Econometrics* 20:3–33.

Keynes, J.M., and Tinbergen, J. (1939 and 1940). "Professor Tinbergen's Method," *EJ* 49:558–68. Review of J. Tinbergen (1939): *Statistical Testing of Business Cycle Theories*, Vol. I. Geneva: League of Nations. "A Reply" by Tinbergben and "Comment" by Keynes, *Economic Journal* 50:141–56.

Keynes, J.N. (1891). *The Scope and Method of Political Economy*. London: Macmillan.

Klant, J.J. (1984). *The Rules of the Game*. Cambridge: Cambridge University Press.

Lehfeldt, R.A. (1914). "The Elasticity of the Demand for Wheat," *Economic Journal* 24:212–17.

(1915). "Review of H.L. Moore: *Economic Cycles: Their Law and Cause*," *Economic Journal* 25:409–11.

Marschak, J. (1942). "Economic Interdependence and Statistical Analysis," O. Lange, F. McIntyre, and T.O. Yntema, eds., *Studies in Mathematical Economics and Econometrics – In Memory of Henry Schultz*. Chicago: University of Chicago Press.

Moore, H.L. (1925). "A Moving Equilibrium of Demand and Supply," *Quarterly Journal of Economics* 39:357–71.

Morgan, M.S. (1984). "The History of Econometric Thought," Ph.D. thesis, London School of Economics. Forthcoming as *The History of Econometric Ideas*. Cambridge University Press.

(1987). "Statistics without Probability and Haavelmo's Revolution in Econometrics," in L. Krüger, G. Gigerenzer, and M.S. Morgan, eds., *The Proba-*

bilistic Revolution, Vol. II: *Ideas in the Sciences.* Cambridge, Mass: MIT Press.

Roos, C.F. (1934). *Dynamic Economics.* Cowles Commission Monograph 1. Bloomington, Ind.: Principia Press.

Samuelson, P.A. (1947). *Foundations of Economic Analysis.* Cambridge, Mass.: Harvard University Press.

Schultz, H. (1928). *Statistical Laws of Demand and Supply with Special Application to Sugar.* Chicago: University of Chicago Press.

(1933). "A Comparison of Elasticities of Demand Obtained by Different Methods," *Econometrica* 1:274–308.

(1938). *The Theory and Measurement of Demand.* Chicago: University of Chicago Press.

Smith, B.B. (1925). "The Error in Eliminating Secular Trend and Seasonal Variation before Correlating Time Series," *Journal of the American Statistical Association* 20:543–45.

Stigler, G.J. (1939). "The Limitations of Statistical Demand Curves," *Journal of the American Statistical Association* 34:469–81.

Tinbergen, J. (1930). "Bestimmung und Deutung von Angebotskurven," *Zeitschrift für Nationalökonomie* 1:669–79. (English summary, 798–99.)

(1933). "The Notion of Horizon and Expectancy in Dynamic Economics," *Econometrica* 1:247–64.

(1937). *An Econometric Approach to Business Cycle Problems.* Paris: Hermann.

(1939). *Statistical Testing of Business Cycle Theories,* Vols. I and II. Geneva: League of Nations.

Whitman, R.H. (1936). "The Statistical Law of Demand for a Producer's Good as Illustrated by the Demand for Steel," *Econometrica* 4:138–52.

CHAPTER 8

The neo-Walrasian program is empirically progressive

E. ROY WEINTRAUB

Economists and philosophers agree that general equilibrium analysis is important, but they disagree with each other, and among themselves, on its role in the growth of economic knowledge (see, for example, Hahn, 1973; Coddington, 1975; Blaug, 1980; Hausman, 1981; Kotter, 1983; Klant, 1984; Hands, 1985; Rosenberg, 1986).

In a number of recent studies (Weintraub, 1979, 1985a, 1985b) I have presented the view that general equilibrium analysis is associated with a scientific research program in the sense of Lakatos, and that the Arrow–Debreu–McKenzie model (which many economists and philosophers take to be general equilibrium theory) is an instantiation of the hard core of what I have called "the neo-Walrasian research program." I have argued that the development of existence proofs is an example of the "hardening" of the hard core of that program. I have also suggested that the hard core of the program guides work in the protective belts of the program, and that work in the belts is appropriately appraised by asking questions about both theoretical progress and empirical progress; within the neo-Walrasian program, the positive heuristic connects formal theory to empirical work. If the neo-Walrasian program is roughly coextensive with neoclassical economics, general equilibrium analysis shapes a research agenda for applied economic analysis.

This claim has drawn some attention, not all of it sympathetic (Rosenberg, 1986). In particular, Rosenberg has argued that although this set of ideas reconstructs the core of the program, the real issues concern the role of the theories in the protective belts. He has suggested that insulating general equilibrium theory from criticism, by identifying it as a programmatic core, does not deal with the central issue of whether the program is explanatory. Rosenberg suggests that most criticisms of economic analysis are criticisms of the theories that are presumed to lie, in my construction, in the belts. He thus argues that the Lakatosian "consolation" provides no real answer to those critics of economics who claim that the failures of economics are truly explanation failures in the belts.

This chapter has been improved as a result of some very useful comments by Neil de Marchi, Bruce Caldwell, Alex Rosenberg, Arjo Klamer, Wade Hands, Craufurd Goodwin, and Dan Hausman.

In Lakatosian language, Rosenberg is claiming that the neo-Walrasian program fails tests for progressivity.

If indeed general equilibrium analysis is unrelated to applied work, so that there is no process of empirical testing, corroboration, and falsification, then economic theory, general equilibrium theory more specifically, is necessarily a branch of formal logic or applied mathematics. (This is exactly the view expressed in Rosenberg, 1983, prefigured in 1980.) It is with such arguments that I disagree.

To make my own case, I shall argue as follows: General equilibrium analysis guides the construction of theories in the belts of the neo-Walrasian program, since the heuristics of the program shape the theory sequences in the belts; the heuristics may be used to evaluate claims of theoretical progress; applied economics is associated with empirical analysis (corroboration and falsification) of the claims to theoretical progress; it is easy to document claims that there is empirical progress in the belts; the philosopher who wishes to understand progress in economics must understand empirical work in economics.

The neo-Walrasian program

A Lakatosian scientific research program, recall, is a complex of linked theories. Each theory must be falsifiable in principle and have some corroborating instances. The program idea suggests that each theory is linked in specific ways to all the other theories in the program. Each shares certain elements; each can be developed from a "theory generator" called the "hard core" of the program. This hard core consists of the "rules" for constructing theories. The rules and shared presuppositions of all the linked theories, together with those theories, constitute the research program. (See Leijonhufvud, 1976; Blaug, 1980; Weintraub, 1985a, 1985b. The best and original presentation of these ideas is Lakatos, 1970, 1978b.)

I have asserted in various writings (initially in *Microfoundations*) that there is a neo-Walrasian research program, and it is characterized by its hard core, its heuristics, and its protective belts of theory sequences. I claimed that the program is organized around the following theory generators:

HC1   There exist economic agents.
HC2   Agents have preferences over outcomes.
HC3   Independent agents optimize subject to constraints.
HC4   Choices are made in interrelated markets.
HC5   Agents have full relevant knowledge.
HC6   Observable outcomes are coordinated and must be discussed with reference to equilibrium states.

The positive and negative heuristics of the program consist of propositions like the following:

PH1 Construct theories in which economic agents optimize.

PH2 Construct theories that make predictions about changes in equilibrium states.

NH1 Do not construct theories in which irrational behavior plays any role.

NH2 Do not construct theories in which equilibrium has no meaning.

NH3 Do not test the hard core propositions.

The positive heuristic of the neo-Walrasian program organizes and restricts work in applied economics. The positive heuristic, in Lakatos's view, "consists of a partially articulated set of suggestions or hints on how to change, develop the 'refutable variants' of the research programme, how to modify, sophisticate, the 'refutable protective belt' " (1978, p. 50). In the neo-Walrasian program, the heuristic leads the analyst to construct restricted theories based on optimizing choice and equilibrium outcomes, and to explore the effect of giving different interpretations, in different models, to partially interpreted terms like "agent," "outcome," "knowledge," "equilibrium," and "market." The positive heuristic of the neo-Walrasian program defines the rules of the applied economics game. In what follows, I shall try to show how those rules work in actual practice.

A case study

One who claims that general equilibrium analysis is not explanatory understands neither applied economics nor applied econometrics. It is a nuisance that there are no detailed case studies of the development of empirical work in economics for methodologists to use as their touchstone. I need to develop my claim that the hard core of the neo-Walrasian program is the theory generator for applied work, and to allow the reader to evaluate my view that the program's heuristics shape the claims to progressivity made by the program's supporters. To allow a discussion of these points, I shall reconstruct (Lakatos, 1978a) three papers which form a distinct theory sequence; I shall examine "Nash-Bargained Household Decisions: Toward a Generalization of the Theory of Demand" (called in this section "paper 1"), "The Household Allocation Problem: Results from a Bargaining Model" ("paper 2"), and "The Joint Determination of Household Membership and Market Work: The Case of Young Men" ("paper 3"). The first two papers were written by Marjorie B. McElroy and Mary Jean Horney

(1981a, 1981b), and the third paper was written by McElroy (1985) alone.[1]

Consider the allocation of time spent by the female in the labor force, the amount of money spent on household goods, and the consumption patterns of households. There had been two distinct themes in the pre-1980 literature; first, demand was associated with an agent called a "person," so that demand for an automobile was the demand by a person for an automobile. Alternatively, one could specify that demand is generated by households as agents (Becker, 1981). In the former case, one has to perform aggregation to mesh joint demands by married couples, whereas in the latter case one must assume that household preferences are well defined. Both approaches are standard, though each has its difficulties, and, of course, each is only partially corroborated.

The models that each approach generates for testing are demand models, or demand systems, which are based on the agents, their preferences, their constraints, and the assumption of optimization. Each produces functions of the form $x_i = f_i(p_i, w, I)$, where x_i is the quantity of the ith good demanded, p_i is its price, and w and I are wage and nonwage income, respectively.

Suppose we are interested in the hours worked by married female nonheads of households, and let x_i be leisure for such a female. Whose wage is w and whose nonwage income is I? If f is a household demand function, so that both male and female wage incomes are combined, whose preferences are maximized?

Paper 1 sets up a model of individual preferences of males and females who choose $x = (x_0, x_1, x_2, x_3, x_4)$ with prices p_i, $i = 0, \ldots 4$. Here x_0 is a pure household good, a public good to the household, x_1 is the husband's market good, x_2 is the wife's, x_3 is the husband's leisure, and x_4 is the wife's. Thus the wife is concerned with $x_f = (x_0, x_2, x_4)$, for instance, and she is constrained by $I_f + p_4 (T - x_4) = p_0 x_{0f} + p x_2$, where T is total time available.

The issue is how the preferences and constraints of the husband and wife are interrelated in any household demand system that has testable implications. McElroy and Horney specify a Nash-bargaining theory in which the game theoretic structure of bargaining is used to model the interdependent optimization problem. They produce, in paper 1, a demand system of the form $x_i = h_i(p, I_m, I_f)$ with $i = 0, 1, 2, 3, 4$. The important point is that the functions h_i are restricted not by the usual

---

[1] I should declare my interest here. McElroy is a friend and colleague, and I served on Horney's doctoral examination committee. My reason for using these papers is that I am familiar with them and their origins, and I have had a chance to check my understanding of them with their senior author.

constraints and assumptions about preferences, but by the structure of the bargaining assumptions themselves; put another way, the form of h_i depends on the particular way that the Nash-bargaining model is associated with the optimization problem. The lesson is that interdependent optimization produces different restrictions on the demand system from those of the usual independent optimization analysis. Paper 1 is entirely concerned with the demand restrictions that result from the bargaining framework; a typical result is that the nonwage income of each spouse appears in the demand function of each member of the household.

Is this theory better, in some sense, than the simpler independent theory? The authors provide ways to test for progress.

For example, they develop a section with suggestions for a variety of tests: For example, test the hypothesis that "i) H_0: $X_{Im} = X_{If}$ versus H_A: $X_{Im} \neq X_{If}$, or the effect on the demand for x_i of a change in male non-wage income is identical to the effect of a change in female nonwage income" (p. 343). They conclude the section by noting that "Rejecting any of these hypotheses (such as i)) would be rejection of neoclassical (independent optimization) restrictions and would contradict the notion that the Nash demand model collapses to the neoclassical one" (ibid.).

Paper 1 thus presents a new theory and calls attention to the tests that would have to be performed to appraise the theory. Paper 2 performs these tests.

Paper 2 uses the 1967 National Longitudinal Survey (NLS) data to construct samples of married households by which the theory may be appraised. As usual, the data must be organized in sensible ways; this is a painstaking process in which openness and honesty are required. The data analysis is set out in both text and appendix. The demand system is linearized, specified, and estimated. The restrictions of the Nash theory, or "model," as the authors call it, are developed as hypotheses to be tested. Complicated statistical procedures are used and explained to perform the tests. The authors conclude that "we presented various tests that this Nash expenditure system collapses to a neoclassical one, and found evidence that it does not" (p. 16). They then go on to show the ways in which their tests may be inadequate. That is, they suggest that their analysis may not have been strong enough to reject the Nash theory, and they suggest other tests that should be done to appraise that theory (a theory of their own creation). They suggest, for instance, that "The lack of information on individual titles to nonwage income weakens our ability to produce powerful tests. This observation points to the critical need to obtain data on titles or property rights to income within the family" (p. 17).

In paper 3 McElroy extends the Nash framework to the joint determi-

nation of work (labor supply), consumption, and household membership. That is, in order to exploit the interdependent framework that the
Nash theory encourages, McElroy asks whether one can treat the decision of whether or not a teenager lives with parents as part of the
decision to supply labor services. In particular, it was known that the
work decisions of teenagers who live at home are different from the
work decisions of teenagers living apart from their families. Paper 3
seeks to embed, in the Nash theory, simultaneous analysis of those two
groups of teenagers. Thus paper 3 exhibits some excess content that is
present in the Nash theory and seeks to determine whether that excess
content is corroborated.

Instead of the usual models, which find no relation between household membership and work, McElroy finds that "except in special cases,
market work and household membership are jointly determined" (p.
312). The Nash theory allows interrelated decision analysis, and "the
interactions of these decisions are especially important for (1) youths of
both sexes, (2) women (where marital status replaces household membership), and (3) even prime-age males who, when facing temporarily
low wage rates, are ceteris paribus in a much better position to substitute
'leisure' for income when married to a worker" (ibid.). The major interpretation of the analysis is that "the family provides nonemployment
insurance to the son: parents insure their son a minimal level of utility
when he faces poor market opportunities" (pp. 312–13).

What is progress in applied economics?

From the perspective of a Lakatosian research program, appraising theories requires one to identify, in the program's belts, a sequence of models $\{M\}$ or theories and to show how each $M(t + 1)$ compares to its
predecessor, $M(t)$. Comparing $M(t + 1)$ to $M(t)$, did $M(t + 1)$ have
excess empirical content, some of which was corroborated? Were $M(t +
1)$ and $M(t)$ linked by shared features that were drawn from the hard
core of the program? The issue is one of progress. If $M(t + 1)$ has excess
content compared to $M(t)$ [that is, there is some implication of $M(t + 1)$
that is not an implication of $M(t)$] and $M(t + 1)$ explains as well as $M(t)$
the content of $M(t)$, then we say that the sequence of theories $\{M\} \equiv
\{M(t),M(t + 1), \ldots \}$ is theoretically progressive. If, in addition, some
of the excess content of $M(t + 1)$ is corroborated as well, then we say
that the theory (sequence) is empirically progressive. If a theory (sequence) is theoretically and empirically progressive, then we say that the
theory is progressive or that it represents a progressive problem shift.
Theories that are not progressive are said to be degenerating or to

represent a degenerative problem shift. Programs are themselves progressive or degenerative if, in comparison to other programs, their theories are (comparatively or relatively) progressive or degenerative. The role of applied economics is, in this framework, to develop and analyze theory sequences for progress or degeneration.

It is, of course, easy to construct seemingly progressive theories in a naive fashion. Consider the theory $M(t) \equiv P \rightarrow Q$. Let $M(t + 1) \equiv P \cup \Psi \rightarrow Q \cup \Psi$. Certainly this sequence is theoretically progressive, and if Ψ is a tautology, it would appear that the theory is empirically progressive as well, since the excess content Ψ is corroborated. Since, however, there is no potential falsifier of Ψ, there is no progress, for the idea of excess content requires that the implications of a theory be falsifiable. Thus the naive ploy does not produce a progressive problem shift; the theory sequence $\{M(t + 1)\}$ is degenerating.

Consider the standard independent optimizing model or theory of the decision of the female spouse to supply labor services and of the male spouse to purchase an automobile. The usual neoclassical demand system, individualistic and based on independent optimization, can explain these choices. Call this theory $M(t)$. Call the theory with a household utility function and optimization under a household budget constraint theory $M(t + 1)$. Call the McElroy–Horney theory of the Nash system theory $M(t + 2)$. At the simplest level, the supply of the wife's hours worked for $M(t)$ is given by function h_f, which has as arguments the wife's wage w_f and the wife's nonwage income I_f. Consequently $M(t)$ is associated with $h_f(p_f, w_f, I_f)$, where p_f is the vector of prices of goods of concern to the female spouse. For the theory developed from household choice, with the "agent" identified as the household, $M(t + 1)$ is associated with $\bar{h}_f(p, w, I)$, where p is the vector of prices faced by the household, w is the wage earned by the household, and I is household nonwage income. Certainly $M(t + 1)$ explains all that $M(t)$ explains and has excess content (predicts a "novel fact"[2]), namely, that variations in the husband's wage will be correlated with variations in the wife's hours worked. As this is at least partially corroborated, and is certainly falsifiable, the sequence $\{M(t), M(t + 1)\}$ is progressive.[3]

Considering $M(t + 2)$, the Nash system, $M(t + 2)$ is associated with $\hbar_f(p, w_f, w_m, I_f, I_m)$. In other words, there is an exact specification of the

---

[2] I have chosen to speak of excess content rather than novel facts, since the word "fact" seems to bring out the worst tendencies in economists and philosophers alike. There is, for example, the appalling view that the facts can be used to test theories for truth or falsity.

[3] This move is associated with Gary Becker and will, one suspects, result in Becker's being awarded the Nobel Memorial Prize some day.

way in which the demand system is restricted by the bargaining theory of Nash, so that there is less latitude in defining the function $\hat{h}_f$; $\mathbf{M}(t + 2)$ defines a restricted class of functions with respect to the class of functions associated with $\mathbf{M}(t + 1)$. The test for theoretical progress in this case is a more severe one than in the previous case, since $\mathbf{M}(t + 2)$ is a restriction of $\mathbf{M}(t + 1)$ that itself is a generalization of $\mathbf{M}(t)$. Thus it is a strong claim that "$\mathbf{M}(t + 2)$ explains what $\mathbf{M}(t + 1)$ explains," since what is at issue is the claim that all the predictions of $\mathbf{M}(t + 1)$ are generated from a restricted set of the functions $\hat{h}_f$. Even more important is the claim that $\mathbf{M}(t + 2)$ has excess empirical content with respect to $\mathbf{M}(t + 1)$. Such content results from the effects of changing the parameters of the interdependent Nash bargaining framework. For example, $\mathbf{M}(t + 2)$ requires there to be a parameter associated with the bargaining status quo, namely, the value to a spouse of being married as opposed to being single. Any change in this status quo point should change, for example, the wife's hours worked.

The creators of $\mathbf{M}(t + 2)$ in fact conclude their paper 1 as follows: "the Nash model provides for the first time an analytical framework for examining the effect of the 'marriage tax' on the joint labor supply of husbands and wives: her current married after-tax marginal wage rate is an argument of the full family income constraint; whereas her hypothetical unmarried after-tax marginal wage rate is an argument of her threat point. This is only one of a general class of applications where, due to taxes and transfers, the prices and nonwage incomes faced by an individual differ according to his or her marital status" (p. 346).

In the terms that we are using, the creators of $\mathbf{M}(t + 2)$ close their first paper by identifying excess empirical content associated with the move from $\mathbf{M}(t + 1)$ to $\mathbf{M}(t + 2)$. The substance of paper 1 demonstrates that the Nash demand system, $\mathbf{M}(t + 2)$, is a legitimate generalization of the neoclassical demand systems $\mathbf{M}(t)$ and $\mathbf{M}(t + 1)$. McElroy and Horney show, for example, that the properties of $\mathbf{M}(t)$ and $\mathbf{M}(t + 1)$ that are corroborated are also present in $\mathbf{M}(t + 2)$: "The Nash demand system retains the neoclassical properties of homogeneity and Cournot aggregation. It also exhibits what we call the Nash generalizations of Engel aggregation, of the Slutsky equation and of substitution symmetry" (p. 346). To put matters clearly, McElroy and Horney, in the conclusion to their paper 1, explicitly claim to have demonstrated what we have termed (in Lakatosian language) "theoretical progress."

Empirical progress requires that some of the excess empirical content be corroborated. It is frequently argued by philosophers and economic methodologists who have a Popperian mind set that finding corroborations is too easy and that the role of empirical work is rather to falsify theories (Popper, 1959, 1972). Those who hold this view are skeptical of applied economics. This skepticism is misguided. The issue of theoretical progress requires the development of excess content in theories. It is the role of applied empirical work to assess the nature of that content. Because it is, in contrast to the Popperian notion, so easy to falsify excess content, applied workers are legitimately wary of tests that theories do not pass. What is more difficult is to develop appropriate tests, using imperfect data, for appraisal of the theory's theoretical progress; or, put another way, the role of empirical work is to appraise the move from $M(t)$ to $M(t + 1)$ to $M(t + 2)$. Attempts to falsify the excess content of successor theories are but one thread of such appraisals. They must be joined with attempts to develop data sets on which the excess content can be identified, to present corroborations of some of that excess content, and to perform all such tasks from the point of view of one who does not believe that the excess content can be corroborated. That is, the empirical worker is bound by a belief that the excess content is false, and thus falsifiable, so that the claims of progress are false.

In the second McElroy–Horney paper, it is clear that months of work went into the job of finding and refining a data set adequate to frame an appraisal of the excess content of the Nash demand system. The NLS has an immense data file, and the authors had to restrict the set to married households with matched demographic characteristics. Their belief that there might be separate marriage gains for whites and nonwhites led to the development of separate white and nonwhite subsamples. They ended up with a white sample of 485 persons and a nonwhite sample of 186. Their Table A.1 presents descriptive statistics for the nineteen variables that are associated with the variables in $M(t + 2)$. Some of the variables could not be observed from the sample data, like the wife's nonwage income, and so that variable required the authors to impute its values from the available data set. In that particular case, McElroy and Horney used a different NLS subsample of 144 divorced women to impute a share of the family nonwage income to the wife, since that income is a variable important to the appraisal of excess content. Thus the stage of analysis associated with the construction of the data set is nontrivial; it is not sufficient to state, as some falsificationists do, that in "good science" facts falsify theories and economists do not look for falsifying facts, so economics is not good science.

McElroy and Horney develop the theory $M(t + 2)$, and $\hat{h}_f$, in such a way that it can be confronted with the data. Error and the stochastic nature of the theory require that there be a stochastic specification of $M(t + 2)$. Statistical tests require further simplifications, which the analysts make, about the distributions of the stochastic elements of the model. When this is done, the model is estimated and the hypotheses about the estimated parameters are tested. Note that stochastic specification, estimation, and testing are all done prior to falsification and corroboration, which is one reason why so many applied economists are bemused by philosophers who focus on such a limited point. *The idea that facts can falsify theories, and that the role of applied work is to produce the facts that falsify the theories that the theorists create, is simultaneously to misunderstand facts, theories, tests, and falsification. The activity of applied economic analysis is appropriately characterized as "developing evidence to appraise excess content."*

McElroy and Horney, in paper 2, do not falsify the theory $M(t + 2)$. Neither do they corroborate it. They instead indicate that there is some evidence that partially corroborates some of the excess content of $M(t + 2)$. This result itself is presented with extreme caution, however, since many modifications were required in the model to allow the available evidence to confront the excess content of $M(t + 2)$. The authors' conclusion to paper 2 is an exemplar of the best Popperian science, a point of view that is skeptical about claims of progress: "This paper . . . represents a start in evaluating the empirical payoff to a bargaining approach . . . [but] alternative data sources, bargaining models, systems of demand equations, and estimation techniques need to be examined before the empirical payoff on bargaining models can be judged" (p. 17).

In paper 3 a further step is taken in evaluating the bargaining approach. That is, the bargaining model is applied to a new problem, that of household membership. Specifically, where some earlier work had treated household membership as an exogenous dummy variable in studies of youth earnings, paper 3 examines the joint decision on wages, consumption, and household membership. "The estimated model agrees with the predictions of the Nash model and shows a strong interaction between household membership and the work behavior of youths. In contrast, at least for these data, if either household membership or work status is treated as exogenous one is led to the false conclusion that household membership and work behavior of youth are unrelated" (p. 294).

In short, the Nash model as $M(t + 2)$ has excess content compared with $M(t)$ and $M(t + 1)$, content associated with the household membership choice for young people; the first part of paper 3 explores that excess content, and the second part of that paper attempts to corroborate it by the use of maximum likelihood estimates of the implied model (a trinomial probit model) using matched samples of parents and sons from three NLSs. The results of that empirical analysis show that "at a sufficiently low offered wage the youth lives with his parents and does not work.

When the offered wage rises above his asking wage, the youth remains in his parents' household and works in the market. Finally, at a sufficiently high offered wage, the youth works in the market and also separates from his parents' household" (p. 294). From our perspective, the Nash model has allowed a regularity of the economy to be uncovered.

The heuristics in action

What has been the role of the heuristics in this progressive problem shift? How have the heuristics shaped the move to $M(t + 2)$? What is the relationship of the hard core of the neo-Walrasian program to this particular sequence of theories in the protective belt?

Let us examine each of the hard core propositions to see how they entered in the models in the sequence:

> HC1 "Agents" were single individuals in $M(t)$, households in $M(t + 1)$, and household members in $M(t + 2)$.
>
> HC2 Outcomes involve the disjunction between endogenous and exogenous variables. Exogenous variables for $M(t)$ included spouse income, household goods, and household membership; for $M(t + 1)$ spouse income and household goods were endogenous, but their interrelationships and household membership were exogenous. In $M(t + 2)$ all the previous variables are treated as endogenous.
>
> HC3 In $M(t)$, constraints were placed on an individual's choice by that individual's income and wealth. In $M(t + 1)$, the household faces constraints on joint income and wealth, but in $M(t + 2)$ the constraints are faced by the individuals in a household and are combinations of constraints associated with their individual resources and those resources held in common.
>
> HC4–HC6 There is no interpretive shift in these propositions as the sequence proceeds from $M(t)$ to $M(t + 1)$ to $M(t + 2)$.

The move to $M(t + 2)$ *involves extensions of the interpretations of the relevant hard core terms: Successor theories extend the hard core in such a way that the predecessor's interpretation* (of a term like "agent"), *although still appropriate, is encompassed by the successor's interpretation.*
Now consider the heuristics:

> PH1 Given $M(t)$ and/or $M(t + 1)$, several moves or shifts are immediately suggested. First, the injunction to create optimization-based theories forces attention to the interdependent

optimizing that occurs in households and predisposes the analyst to consider adopting a game theoretic model.

NH1   In asking that "sociology" be kept at bay, the heuristic demands that exogenous or independent "socio-variables" be embedded in optimization theories in which those variables can be treated as interdependent and endogenous (e.g., marriage forces interdependence on the husband's and wife's economic decisions), whereas common household membership forces parents and their children to live intertwined economic lives.

NH2   The move from $M(t)$ to $M(t + 1)$ was made by Becker, a Chicago economist. The move to $M(t + 2)$ could have been made only by a neo-Walrasian; Chicago–Marshallian price theory does not force attention to interrelationships among agents (Reder, 1982) or their decisions, but relies instead on judicious use of the *ceteris paribus* clause. Such a modeling strategy cannot "find" $M(t + 2)$.

NH3   There was no evidence, in this sequence, of "testing" for the presence of irrational behavior, or disequilibrium behavior, or incomplete knowledge as a response to the imperfect corroborations of $M(t)$ and $M(t + 1)$.

Conclusion

Critics argue that general equilibrium analysis fails to meet requirements for progress. Those critics do not specify with any clarity what tests it fails to meet. In contrast, I have suggested, using the case study, that there is, if not justice, at least meaning in the claim that the neo-Walrasian program is progressive in the Lakatosian sense.

One may believe that there is, in fact, a neo-Walrasian research program. Or one may believe that the program idea is a useful fiction by means of which a methodologist can organize appraisals of neoclassical economics. Or one may believe that the research program idea is a convenient framework to present histories of bits and pieces of economics. One may even believe that the program idea is a worthless artifact from philosophy intruding on the history of economic thought. No matter what one's position on research programs, a perusal of the relevant methodology literature leaves one with the impression that empirical economics is unimportant to the enterprise called "economics." Yet most of Kuhnian normal (economic) science is incomprehensible without a coherent view of the role of empirical work. My own suggestion here, that such work fits naturally into a research program vision, is an attempt to locate applied economics and its concerns in *some* context.

That the actual practices of serious applied economists need to be fitted into some scheme or other cannot be seriously questioned. That empirical work is respected by professional economists, even as it is ignored by methodologists, also cannot be doubted. Thus it is worth asking why appraisals of empirical work have been outside the methodological pale.

My own answer is that Popper's influence has been too large; the role of empirical work has been understood, by Popperian methodologists, as that of "developing falsifications of theories"[4] But it is known by anyone who cares about empirical economics that no falsifications of theories are sought, nor are any desired. This tension leaves the Popperian methodologist two options: (1) Economics can be vilified as unscientific or (2) methodology can avoid the issue by concerning itself with "high theory" alone.

Whatever its defects, the research program idea allows two related points to be aired: A *sequence* of models is the unit in which applied economics is in fact appraised within the economist-community, and empirical work is associated with partial corroborations of theories, and not falsifications.

I assumed here that general equilibrium analysis is associated with a Lakatosian research program called the "neo-Walrasian program." I have shown how the hard core of that program, and the heuristics, have generated theories in the belts of that program. Analysis of the case study suggests that theoretical progress can be appraised by attention to those heuristics. I have also tried to show that empirical work, applied economics, is not an activity in which facts falsify theory but is rather associated with bringing evidence to bear on the excess content of theory sequences.

References

Becker, G.S. (1981). *A Treatise on the Family*. Cambridge, Mass.: Harvard University Press.

Blaug, M. (1980). *The Methodology of Economics*. New York: Cambridge University Press.

Coddington, A. (1975). "The Rationale of General Equilibrium," *Economic Inquiry* 13:539–58.

---

[4] As de Marchi notes in his own chapter in this volume (chapter 4), Popper was never really understood by economists; what practical economists took from Popper was the position that Lakatos called "naive falsificationism" (Lakatos, 1970). Thus it is a bit misleading to put the blame, if there be blame, on Popper.

De Marchi, N. (1985). "Popper and the LSE Economists." Chapter 4, this volume.

Hahn, F.H. (1973). *On the Notion of Equilibrium in Economics*. Cambridge: Cambridge University Press.

Handler, E.W. (1980). "The Logical Structure of Modern Neoclassical Static Microeconomic Equilibrium Theory," *Erkenntnis* 15:33–53.

Hands, D.W. (1984a). "The Role of Crucial Counterexamples in the Growth of Economic Knowledge: Two Case Studies in the Recent History of Economic Thought," *History of Political Economy* 16:59–67.

(1984b). "What Economics Is Not: An Economist's Response to Rosenberg." Unpublished working paper, Department of Economics, University of Puget Sound, Tacoma, Wash.

(1985). "Second Thoughts on Lakatos," *History of Political Economy* 17:1–16.

Hausman, D.M. (1981). "Are General Equilibrium Theories Explanatory?" in J.C. Pitt, ed., *Philosophy in Economics*. Dordrecht: Reidel, pp. 17–32.

Klant, J. (1984). *The Rules of the Game*. New York: Cambridge University Press.

Kotter, R. (1983). "General Equilibrium Theory: An Empirical Theory?" in W. Stegmuller, W. Balzar, and W. Spohn, eds., *Philosophy of Economics*. Berlin: Springer-Verlag, pp. 103–17.

Lakatos, I. (1970). "Falsification and the Methodology of Scientific Research Programmes," in I. Lakatos and A. Musgrave, eds., *Criticism and the Growth of Knowledge*. Cambridge: Cambridge University Press, pp. 91–196.

(1978a). "History of Science and Its Rational Reconstructions," in I. Lakatos, ed., *The Methodology of Scientific Research Programmes: Philosophical Papers*, Vol. 1, ed. J. Worrall and G. Currie. New York: Cambridge University Press, pp. 102–38.

(1978b). *The Methodology of Scientific Research Programmes: Philosophical Papers*, Vol. 1, ed. J. Worrall and G. Currie. New York: Cambridge University Press.

Leijonhufvud, A. (1976). "Schools, 'Revolutions', and Research Programmes in Economic Theory," in S. Latsis (ed.), *Method and Appraisal in Economics*. Cambridge: Cambridge University Press, pp. 65–108.

McElroy, M.B. (1985). "The Joint Determination of Household Membership and Market Work: The Case of Young Men," *Journal of Labor Economics* 3:293–316.

and Horney, M.J. (1981a). "Nash-Bargained Household Decisions: Toward a Generalization of the Theory of Demand." *International Economic Review* 22:333–49.

(1981b). "The Household Allocation Problem: Results from a Bargaining Model." Discussion Paper, Department of Economics, Duke University, Durham, N.C.

Popper, K. (1965 [1959]). *The Logic of Scientific Discovery*. New York: Harper Torchbooks.

(1972). *Conjectures and Refutations: The Growth of Scientific Knowledge.* London: Routledge & Kegan Paul.

Reder, M. (1982). "Chicago Economics: Permanence and Change," *Journal of Economic Literature* 20:1–38.

Rosenberg, A. (1980). "A Sceptical History of Microeconomic Theory," *Theory and Decision* 12:79–93.

(1983). "If Economics Isn't Science, What Is It?" *The Philosophical Forum* 14:296–314.

(1986). "The Lakatosian Consolations for Economics," *Economics and Philosophy* 2:127–39.

Stegmuller, W., Balzar, W., and Spohn, W., eds. (1982). *Philosophy of Economics.* Berlin: Springer-Verlag.

Weintraub, E.R. (1979). *Microfoundations.* New York: Cambridge University Press.

(1985a). "Appraising General Equilibrium Analysis," *Economics and Philosophy* 1:23–37.

(1985b). *General Equilibrium Analysis: Studies in Appraisal.* New York: Cambridge University Press.

PART V

Non-Popperian perspectives on economics

CHAPTER 9

The case for pluralism

BRUCE J. CALDWELL

Introduction, acknowledgments, and dedication

This is a revised version of a paper delivered at the conference, The
Popperian Legacy in Economics, held in Amsterdam in December 1985
to honor the retirement of J.J. Klant.

I apologize in advance for writing what is bound to be perceived as a
very egocentric chapter. In it I trace the development of some of my
ideas on methodology, and I attempt to construct a case for pluralism. In
constructing my case, I try to answer some of the objections I have heard
most often concerning pluralism. Most of these objections were raised
by a number of people who commented on earlier drafts of this chapter.
I am indebted to Neil de Marchi, Wade Hands, Uskali Maki, Bob Coats,
Roy Weintraub, Dan Hausman, Mark Blaug, Larry Boland, and members of Neil de Marchi's workshop in the history of economic thought at
Duke University for their thoughtful comments and criticisms. Finally, I
would like to dedicate this chapter to J.J. Klant. I suspect that he will
feel some ambivalence about this, since many of the ideas expressed
here will not meet with his full approval. However, it should be clear
that I share his desire to understand better the "rules of the game" in
economics.

My road to pluralism

As a good Popperian might, I begin with a problem. The problem may
be posed as a question: How should we do economic methodology?
When it is stated in this form, it should be clear that this question is a
normative one and a meta-methodological one. Popper would not like
the question because it appears to be an essentialist one. I therefore
emphasize that I am asking it pragmatically.

In order to answer the question, we must first figure out what the
purpose of methodological work is. Many answers suggest themselves.

I first became interested in economic methodology in graduate school
because I thought that studying it would help me *to understand what
economists were up to*. This, of course, was a fundamental mistake. The

writings of methodologists, particularly in the positivist era, usually did not have much to do with the actual practice of economics. It is perhaps appropriate to note at this point that figuring out what economists are up to is not particularly easy. One can learn how to *do economics,* of course, by simply training to become an economist. But as Thomas Kuhn points out, this process is anything but a self-conscious one. It occurs through a sort of mental osmosis as one learns the paradigmatic solutions to various well-established normal science puzzles. By becoming an economist, one learns how to do economics, but this does not answer the question of what economists are up to.

Another naive notion that was soon dispelled was that methodology would tell me how to proceed; it would show me *how to do economics scientifically.* I now feel a little better about my naiveté, having read Neil de Marchi's contribution to this volume, where he describes the flirtation with Popperian thought that took place among economists at the LSE in the early 1960s. Apparently I was not the only one to make the mistake of thinking that philosophers held the key to how to do science, and that makes me feel better. Naiveté, like misery, loves company.

Later, as I read more deeply in the philosophy of science, I entertained two other possible answers to the question of the purpose of methodological work. One of these was that methodology tells us what science is; it allows us to distinguish science from nonscience; *it solves the demarcation problem.* The other answer was that methodology tells us how to choose among competing theories; it instructs us how to go about selecting the best theory; *it solves the theory choice problem.*

These answers were promising on one level, because they helped me to make sense of some of the methodological writings by economists that I encountered. Friedman's famous essay, "The Methodology of Positive Economics," for example, may be read as a prescriptive pronouncement on how to solve the choice problem: Choose the theory that predicts best and use simplicity as a tie-breaker. But on the philosophical level, these answers were problematical. Though there was no dearth of philosophers who claimed to have solved the demarcation problem (e.g., Popper, 1972; Lakatos, 1974), I found their critics to be more persuasive, particularly when I thought about applying their solutions of the demarcation problem to economics. Regarding the theory choice problem, I felt that Kuhn (1970) was closest to the truth when he argued that the search for a universally applicable, objective algorithm of choice is chimerical.[1] So, I did not find philosophy of science

---

[1] I review some of the arguments that led me to these conclusions in *Beyond Positivism*, chapters 5, 11, and 12. I should emphasize that I am now, and have always been, far less interested in these purely philosophical questions than I am in the pragmatic task of

to be very helpful in answering the question: What is the purpose of methodological work?

That the question has not yet been adequately answered has had an effect on the status of methodological work within the economics profession. Its position as a subfield is certainly an ambiguous one. Some economists openly disparage methodological work, because they consider it a waste of time. Yet many of the profession's most well-known members (e.g., among Nobel laureates, the list includes Hicks, Samuelson, Friedman, Myrdal, Hayek, Simon, Stigler, and Buchanan) have tried their hand at methodological writing. Certain groups within economics but outside of the mainstream (e.g., Austrians, Marxists, institutionalists, post-Keynesians) display an active interest in methodology. Their view of methodology is that it provides a framework for launching fundamental critiques of mainstream practice. However, most mainstream economists do not take these fundamental criticisms seriously. Indeed, the fact that heterodox economists engage in methodological work is taken as further evidence that methodological study has little importance. Paradoxically, even as they disparage methodological work, orthodox economists employ methodological arguments (albeit rather unconsciously) all the time. Arjo Klamer's recent book on the rational expectations revolution in macroeconomics, *Conversations with Economists,* makes this point very well. Note too that the usual dismissive argument made by mainstream economists against their heterodox critics (that the theories propounded by rival schools are "unscientific") is a methodological one.

It seemed to me that if methodological work was ever to be taken seriously within the profession, its purpose required clarification. But before such a task could be started, two other problems had to be addressed. My readings in philosophy convinced me that much methodological debate in economics was needlessly confusing. The first task was to acquaint economists with twentieth-century developments within the philosophy of science, with an emphasis on the current problems facing that field. The second was to use the philosophy of science to clarify various methodological debates among (mostly) mainstream economists. In these debates, economists usually viewed methodology as offering a set of prescriptions concerning legitimate scientific practice, and most had borrowed rather haphazardly from various philosophical positions (almost all within the tradition I labeled loosely as "positivism") in making their arguments. A knowledge of the philosophy of

trying to figure out how to apply them within economic methodology. I am not a philosopher; my demand for philosophical discourse is a derived one. This was my point when I subtitled my concluding section of chapter 5 on contemporary philosophy of science "A Dilettante's Review and Commentary."

science was helpful in clarifying language, in eliminating semantic de-bates, and in dismissing arguments from authority when economists had misread the philosophical authorities. These were my goals in writing *Beyond Positivism*. Of course, my insights were not unique. Both Mark Blaug and J.J. Klant approached the subject in much the same way in their books on methodology. That three independently executed at-tempts at surveys of the field should be so similar in approach is evi-dence that this work was needed and had to be accomplished first.

Of course, there are also differences in how we approached our sub-ject. Without wishing to caricature their positions, I think it is safe to say that both Blaug and Klant adhere to some variant of sophisticated meth-odological falsificationism. This lends a coherence to their books that is absent in mine. Whether one is examining alternative methodological views (e.g., instrumentalism, a priorism) or particular research pro-grams in economics (as Blaug did in the third section of his book), if one is a falsificationist one has a consistent set of criteria against which other positions may be judged. Of course, one need not be a falsificationist to be consistent. A good a priorist, or, for that matter, a good Marxist, or Freudian, or Christian, also has consistency on his or her side.

For me, *Beyond Positivism* is a very preliminary work. Its title is meant to suggest these questions: What lies beyond positivism? How are we to do methodological work in the postpositivist era? Obviously, this brings us back to the question of the *purpose* of methodological work. I tried to answer that question in the last section of my book, and the approach I took was labeled "methodological pluralism." In the remain-der of this chapter, I develop that position more fully and try to show its strengths and weaknesses.

Pluralism defined

On the most general level, the pluralist believes that the primary pur-pose of methodological work in economics is to enhance our *understand-ing* of what economic science is all about and, with luck, by so doing, to *improve* it. I employ the term "understanding" in its everyday, common-sense usage, and I will speak more about the term "improve" later. To accomplish these goals, the pluralist undertakes *critical evaluations of the strengths and limitations of various research programs in economics and economic methodology*. In addition, our *understanding* of econom-ics may be enhanced by various descriptive studies, for example, histori-cal studies of the development of ideas, analyses of the sociological milieu in which a research program or discipline develops, and studies of the rhetoric of economics. Whether one wishes to consider such studies as methodological or not seems to me to be a matter of personal taste. Finally, both *novelty* and *criticism* are important to the pluralist. An aphorism that nicely captures the pluralist position is, "Seek novelty, and continually try to reduce it through criticism."

At this very high level of generality, there is little in my description of pluralism that should cause strenuous objection, but also little that distinguishes it from other views. The specific ways I would put my program to work are perhaps more controversial. In what follows, I will explore some of the details of pluralism and attempt to answer some of the more important questions raised by my critics.

Pluralism does not attempt to answer the demarcation question

One attractive feature of Popper's falsificationism, Lakatos's Methodology of Scientific Research Programmes, and certain other approaches in the philosophy of science is that they give clear answers to the demarcation question. One is able to distinguish scientific theories from nonscientific ones because only the former are capable of being measured against a well-defined set of criteria of theory appraisal. Sometimes, though not always, those that pass this test can be further evaluated, so that at a given point in time one theory may be chosen provisionally as the best one.

As we will see, the critical appraisal of theories plays an essential role in methodological pluralism. However, criticism is undertaken for the purpose of *understanding,* and with the hope that with understanding will come improvement. But criticism is *not* undertaken for the purposes of either discovering or applying some universal criterion of demarcation.[2] Of course, the majority of the profession may find the criticisms against a given research program to be compelling, with the result that few economists will work within it. That is a separate matter. The role of the methodologist is to discover the strengths and weaknesses of research programs. This is a categorically different endeavor from searching for a universally applicable answer to the demarcation question.

My position raises another question: How are we even to know what

---

[2] I hope that it is clear that it is the quest for a *universal* criterion of demarcation, or worse, the application of some such alleged criterion, that I find most objectionable. I believe that there are differences between science and nonscience. But at this point in time, we are very far from understanding what these differences are. The differences are subtle, and they may not even be capable of articulation: We may know more than we are able to say. As such, our past preoccupation with the search for a criterion of demarcation seems misguided. I must add that the view that we cannot discuss criticism without first solving the demarcation problem seems to me to be a particularly short-sighted form of obstructionism.

counts as "economics" if we do not try to solve some sort of demarcation problem? Methodological pluralism looks to the practitioners of economics to see what economics is.[3] Now, of course, the practitioners disagree among themselves about this. Even a casual observer of the discipline will discern a huge and amorphous mainstream that is surrounded on all sides by the heterodoxy, a group so diverse that it sometimes seems that the only bond among them is a dissatisfaction with mainstream analysis. Which groups should be included? The pluralist answers: *all of them*. Even further, the pluralist encourages and applauds both novel approaches to theorizing in economics *and* defenses of orthodoxy against the attacks that such novelty brings. There is no perversity in this. The point is that it is only through the constant clash of a diversity of ideas that positions become sharply defined, intelligible, understandable. In short, I am contending that much is to be gained by shifting our focus of attention away from the philosophical question of demarcation and toward the more practical concern for forms of criticism.

Does pluralism lead to anarchy?

This complaint is frequently voiced. The argument usually runs as follows: Failure to solve the demarcation problem implies an absence of standards, and an absence of standards leads to anarchy. Thus Mark Blaug, in a review of my book, equates pluralism with the doctrine "let a hundred flowers bloom," and comments, "To me this seems to be the abandonment of all standards, indeed, the abandonment of methodology itself as a discipline of study" (1983, p. 3). In *The Politics and Philosophy of Economics*, T.W. Hutchison speaks darkly about the outcome of the abandonment of standards:

it would be disastrous to collapse into the kind of obscurantism which refuses to recognize, or try to uphold, *any* common epistemological criteria or standards which should be shared by natural and social scientists alike (as Popper has always insisted). That way lies the permissive chaos in which the principle that "anything goes" will ripen into the dogmas of mob rule, and so usher in the dictatorship of some genocidal popular or "proletarian" boss, such as "the great scientist," Stalin. (1981, p. 218)

Because the charge that pluralism is anarchic is so frequently heard and so important an objection, I will answer it at length. Three counterarguments are offered. I will argue, first, that the fear of anarchism

---

[3] The absence of a criterion of demarcation makes the circularity of this definition unavoidable. However, the definition as stated does serve the purpose of emphasizing the important role of the scientific community in defining the domain of discourse.

misunderstands science, which is basically a traditional and conservative enterprise. Next, it misunderstands the role of the methodologist in science. And finally, it misunderstands the pluralist position, in which criticism plays a crucial role.

1. The fear of anarchy, or of a totalitarian response to anarchy, is not based on a correct perception of science as it is currently practiced in free societies. There already exist a number of powerful constraints on scientific practice today. Because these constraints are so powerful, the pluralist is less worried about *anarchism* than about *dogmatic demarcation.* These constraints are multifarious; a few will be briefly mentioned.

First is the important role played by *tradition* in science. Traditional ways of viewing the world, of approaching problems, and of solving them exist at any given point in time in the development of a particular science. As Kuhn has pointed out, the role of tradition is strongest during periods of normal science, and is weakest during revolutionary periods. But as some of Kuhn's critics (e.g., Toulmin, 1970) have pointed out, no revolution is ever absolute and complete; even after a revolution, many things remain the same. Second – and again the insight is Kuhn's – science takes place within a *scientific community;* it is a shared, communal endeavor. As in other communities, there exist *norms* of behavior within scientific communities. Such norms, though they are seldom explicitly articulated, are nonetheless potent constraints on behavior. Third, science involves the free exchange of ideas; it is an *interpersonal* enterprise. It involves *communication* among individuals, attempts at mutual *persuasion,* the use of *criticism* and of *rhetoric.* It is because pluralists recognize these sorts of constraints that they welcome studies in the history of science, sociology of science, and rhetoric, all of which illuminate the roles played by such constraints, and which lead to a deeper understanding of science.

I will grant to my critics that what I have just said presupposes that science takes place in a free society. One can surely imagine certain types of political, theological, or nationalist revolutions that would change all of that, and force science to come up with "ideologically correct" answers to its questions. I share with my critics an abhorrence of such an outcome, and it is my belief that it is the duty of every citizen to oppose such changes. But crucially, this is the duty of the *citizen,* or even the *citizen-scientist,* not of the *methodologist.* This brings me to my second line of defense.

2. Those who view the purpose of methodology as the enunciation of a universal criterion for distinguishing science from nonscience often argue that such steps are necessary to keep science free. Because advocates of this approach to methodology generally choose one criterion of

demarcation to distinguish science from nonscience, I will call this sort of approach *monism*. In my view, monist approaches to methodology misconceive the role of the methodologist and have caused much mischief in the field. I will briefly mention some of the dangers associated with monism; it should be clear that each point could be treated at greater length.

First, monist approaches have motivated the quest for a single set of immutable standards of legitimate scientific practice, a quest that most observers now recognize as chimerical.

Next, monism forces its advocates into the untenable position of clinging to *some* set of standards anyway, even when those standards cannot be applied. One is reminded of the reprise of the popular song, "Even a bad love is better than no love at all." If one's job is to protect science, even bad standards are better than no standards at all.

Third, monism fails to appreciate the richness of science, the diversity of theories that exist, and the diversity of ways of criticizing them that scientists actually employ.

Fourth, monist approaches put the methodologist in the position of telling scientists how to proceed. This breeds resentment among practitioners of science who, used to arguing in the languages of theory and econometrics, discover from their more philosophically oriented colleagues that they are not doing proper science. Thus, I place much of the blame for the second-class status of methodology within the economics profession squarely at the door of those who advocate prescriptive monist approaches to methodology. Such approaches are also responsible for the embarrassing gap between economic science as actually practiced and the writings of methodologists.

Finally, it is certainly questionable whether monist approaches to methodology provide any real defense against totalitarianism. The logical positivists were not fuzzy-minded anarchists, but they had little success against Hitler.

The role of the methodologist is not to be a guardian of science. Nor does studying methodology *teach one how to do economics;* one learns that by becoming an economist, and different economists learn different things. Studying methodology may help one to understand *what it means to be an economist.* An apt analogy is that the study of such fields as theology, or the philosophy or sociology of religion, helps one to understand religious phenomena. Clearly, such study is neither necessary nor sufficient to guarantee that one is a religious person.

3. The charge that pluralism leads to anarchy fails to recognize that criticism plays a crucial role in pluralism, because it is through criticism

that the strengths and weaknesses of various research programs are revealed.

There are many roads to criticism, and as such, I use the term "criticism" in its broadest terms. Such an approach may be contrasted with the approaches of those who believe that theories should be appraised according to some universally applicable standard of theory choice: for example, only falsifiable theories are acceptable; only fully axiomatized theories are acceptable; only theories that are fully verified are acceptable. Such approaches lead to the kinds of sterile debates in methodology that have caused many to turn their backs on the field; one group favors axiomatized theories, another prefers falsifiable ones, and the interminable debates between them lead nowhere. But even more important, such universalist approaches to criticism blind the methodologist to the richness of scientific practice.

For example, when falsificationists look at economics as currently practiced, they are forced to conclude that little in economics passes the test. This is fine if one is criticizing a particular research program that one dislikes, be it Marxism or Austrian economics or general equilibrium theory. And for programs for which one has more sympathy, one can always urge them to try harder. But neither response gets one very far in terms of understanding economic science. Matters are only a little bit better for someone like Milton Friedman, for whom predictive adequacy and simplicity are the ultimate criteria to be considered in the appraisal of theories. At least there exist some theories that pass this test in economics. Perhaps not surprisingly, these theories (perfect competition rather than monopolist competition, single-equation monetarist models rather than multiequation Keynesian models) are also the ones that Friedman prefers in terms of their policy implications.

Finally, such approaches often fail to recognize the important point that theories are attempts to solve problems. Theories are often best assessed according to how well they solve the problems they attempt to address. Given this perspective, the choice of one's tools of assessment often depends on what kinds of problems a theory purports to answer; in Larry Boland's (1982, ch. 12) apt summary, methodology is problem dependent.

What criteria of appraisal are open to pluralists? There are, of course, the traditional ones: empirical criteria of various sorts; structural criteria like logical consistency and the ability to be axiomatized; aesthetic ones like elegance, simplicity, or Machlup's "ah-ha-ness"; dynamic considerations like generalizability, fruitfulness, and the ability to encompass previous theories; heuristic criteria like having analogies in other fields, usefulness for pedagogic purposes, realism.

Next, there is internal criticism, in which the purposes, goals, and methodology of a particular approach are taken as given, and then the research program is evaluated on its own terms. This type of criticism is especially useful when one is evaluating the claims of nontraditional groups in economics. For example, this was the direction I took in my assessment of praxeology (Caldwell, 1984).

Next, one might assess the evolution of a theory (or set of theories) through time, using Lakatosian or some other criteria for purposes of evaluation. Roy Weintraub does this, both in an earlier paper (1984) and in his contribution to this conference.

One might wish to differentiate the various types of theories that are commonly encountered in economics (e.g., axiomatic, normative, predictive, explanatory, and descriptive theories), and to evaluate a given research program to see which characteristics it possesses and which it lacks. This approach is especially useful if one wishes to emphasize the problem dependence of methodology.

One might explore other areas of inquiry – jurisprudence, literary criticism, new developments in Bayesian econometrics – to see what modes of criticism are used elsewhere, and with what effect.

There are many roads to criticism. Pluralists employ as many as they are able to find. Their purpose is not to demarcate, nor to find the "best" theory by comparing rival theories against a set of immutable standards, but to find the strengths and weaknesses of whatever program they are investigating. If they do their job well, we will all have a better understanding of what economic science is, and with luck that will lead to its improvement.

If everyone was a pluralist, what positions would be left to criticize?

This important question deserves special attention. Note first that pluralism is a *meta-methodological* position. It offers no specific methodological advice to economists. Indeed, what economists do is taken as given by the pluralist.

What economists do, whether they are part of the mainstream or part of the heterodoxy, is to work on a specific research topic. Such research takes place within a specific research tradition (e.g., neoclassical, Marxist, Austrian) and, as such, presupposes a methodology. Further refinements within traditions are also frequently encountered: A priorism has been challenged by an interpretive, hermeneutical turn in the Austrian camp; neo-Walrasians follow a methodology that is quite different from that employed by empirically oriented applied microeconomists.

The traditional methodological article is written by someone within one of these research traditions. Its purpose is to defend the methodological approach used within the tradition or to attack rivals. Given the diversity of research approaches in economics, such work will continue. Furthermore, such methodological work is beneficial, for it helps clarify the specific procedures, the hard cores and heuristics, used by researchers in the various traditions.

But this traditional approach to methodology is *not* very useful for fostering communication across paradigms; it does not lead to enhanced understanding. It is here that pluralist methodologists have a contribution to make. Pluralist methodologists do not embrace a particular tradition; their goal is the evaluation of all traditions. In a sense, pluralist methodologists attempt to practice *value-free evaluations:* Their assessments are critical, but they do not presuppose some ultimate universal grounds for criticism.

If everyone was a pluralist, there would be no positions left to criticize. But a consistent pluralist would not advocate that everyone become a pluralist! This underlies the pragmatic (as opposed to universalist) nature of my plea for pluralism. In the current environment, pluralism makes good sense. I suspect that this situation will continue. But more important, I *hope* it will continue. The emergence of a single universalist methodology is anathema to the pluralist, but so is the emergence of a single universalist nonmethodology. This is a point that Feyerabend rather remarkably failed to see.

Will pluralism lead to the discovery of true theories?

Methodological pluralism makes no epistemological claims; it is not grounded in any theory of truth. For this reason, philosophers like Dan Hausman, and philosophically astute methodologists like Wade Hands, will have difficulty in considering it a serious position. Without a theory of truth, we cannot speak meaningfully about understanding (for it may be an "understanding" of false beliefs), and we cannot talk about "improvement" or "progress" without defining what we are progressing toward.

This is probably the most serious criticism of my position. Note that it is not a problem for Popper. (Though if Dan Hausman's thesis in his paper in this volume is correct, it is a problem for Popper.) As Lakatos (1974) has pointed out, Popper discovered truth via Tarski in the early 1960s, and this saved him from skepticism. That falsificationism eliminates error is Popper's major claim in this regard. Though his fallibilism forces him to claim that we can never know if we have reached the truth, we can know that we have eliminated error. His theory of truth makes not one whit of difference *operationally,* of course, but it does solve the problem philosophically.

I took my cues from Feyerabend, another pluralist who in his early work (e.g., 1962, 1970) tried to show how pluralism could lead to an expansion of true knowledge. He argued that because all facts are theory laden, the multiplication of theories multiplies empirical content, or knowledge. He was crucified for the initial premise of his argument, the strong theory dependence thesis, and as a result he turned to anarchism, and ultimately to Dadaism (Feyerabend, 1975). As a philosopher he had little choice.

Luckily, I am not a philosopher; I have choices. But even so, I recognize this as a very serious criticism of my position. I can think of a number of responses to this criticism, but I doubt that any will convince my critics.

I could try to use a pluralist argument to defend pluralism by arguing that a commitment to a particular theory of truth narrows one's approach to questions of methodology. But such an argument is clearly circular.

I could offer pragmatic arguments. For example, I could argue that my concern is to make methodological discourse more useful, and as such, I am not concerned with the philosophical question of truth. Or I could simply claim that my approach should be measured by its effects, and that I think the effects would be good. This seems sensible enough to me, but I fear my critics would see little sense in it.

I could point out that others have supplied very helpful analyses while still falling into the same trap as me. Kuhn, for example, is forced to use the weasel word "evolution" rather than "progress" in the final pages of *The Structure of Scientific Revolutions* for the same reasons: One cannot talk of progress without some conception of what we are progressing toward. Larry Laudan attempts to define progress without having recourse to the notion of truth in *Progress and Its Problems.* Though both Kuhn and Laudan have helped us to understand science better, both have been criticized on this point.

I could take the offensive and cite the antifoundationalist philosophers who play so prominent a role in McCloskey's "rhetoric of economics" approach. Thus I too could capitalize Truth in order to ridicule it. But I must say, this seems to me to be the least satisfactory approach. Look what it's done for McCloskey. Five years after publishing his important article in the *Journal of Economic Literature,* in which the rhetoric approach was trumpeted, he's still trying to figure out the arguments of philosophers in order to answer his critics. He has very little time left over to actually do any work using the rhetoric approach.

Perhaps the best argument I've heard was suggested by philosophers. Dan Hausman told me to argue that, given the present disarray in philosophy, I am forced to recommend pluralism as an interim position. There is a modesty to this argument that is appealing. But on the other hand, it may be a bit too modest. Uskali Mäki noted that pluralism need not be incompatible with a theory of truth and held out the possibility that some day, someone may be able to link the two together. I certainly agree with him that it would be foolish to rule out such a possibility. But that is a task for a philosopher, and one for which I have no comparative advantage. Perhaps the best position for me to take now is to invite anyone who would like to try to show how pluralism can be linked with a theory of truth.

Conclusion

The pluralist believes that the primary goal of methodological work is to reveal the strengths and weaknesses of various research programs in economics. Many tools of criticism are employed, and the focus is on the practice of economists.

In this chapter I have tried to offer a pluralist appraisal of pluralism. I have outlined the strengths and weaknesses of pluralism, I have tried to address the many arguments that have been brought against it, and I have focused on how to practice the trade of economic methodology. I hope that this will lead to a better understanding of the pluralist position.

The goals of pluralism *are* modest. Methodologists are not set up as experts offering advice to economists on how to do their science. Methodologists do not try to solve the demarcation problem, or the theory choice problem, or the problem of truth. Rather, methodologists try, together with their colleagues in the history, sociology, and rhetoric of science, to enable us to reach a better understanding of the science of economics. This is a modest goal. But it also is an achievable one. And it finally provides an answer to the question that has gone too long unanswered among methodologists: What is the purpose of our work?

References

Blaug, M. (1980). *The Methodology of Economics: Or How Economists Explain*. Cambridge: Cambridge University Press.
  (1983). "Book Review: *Beyond Positivism*," *The Wall Street Review of Books* (Winter):1–6.

Boland, L.A. (1982). *The Foundations of Economic Method*. London: Allen & Unwin.

Caldwell, B.J. (1982). *Beyond Positivism: Economic Methodology in the Twentieth Century*. London: Allen & Unwin.

(1984). "Praxeology and Its Critics: An Appraisal," *History of Political Economy* 16(3):363–79.

Feyerabend, P.K. (1962). "Explanation, Reduction and Empiricism," in H. Feigl, G. Maxwell, and M. Scriven, eds., *Minnesota Studies in the Philosophy of Science*, Vol. III. Minneapolis: University of Minnesota Press, pp. 28–97.

(1970). "How to Be a Good Empiricist – A Plea for Tolerance in Matters Epistemological," in B. Brody, ed., *Readings in the Philosophy of Science*. Englewood Cliffs, N.J.: Prentice-Hall, pp. 319–42.

(1975). *Against Method: Outline of an Anarchistic Theory of Knowledge*. London: New Left Books, 1975.

Hutchison, T.W. (1981). *The Politics and Philosophy of Economics*. New York: New York University Press.

Klamer, A. (1983). *Conversations with Economists*. Totowa, N.J.: Rowman and Allanheld.

Klant, J.J. (1984 [1979]). *The Rules of the Game: The Logical Structure of Economic Theories*. Trans. I. Swart. Cambridge: Cambridge University Press.

Kuhn, T.S. (1970). *The Structure of Scientific Revolutions*, 2nd enlarged ed. Chicago: University of Chicago Press.

Lakatos, I. (1970). "Falsification and the Methodology of Scientific Research Programmes," in I. Lakatos and A. Musgrave, eds., *Criticism and the Growth of Knowledge*, Cambridge: Cambridge University Press, pp. 91–196.

(1974). "Popper on Demarcation and Induction," in Paul Schilpp, ed., *The Philosophy of Karl Popper*, Vol. XIV, Book I, *The Library of Living Philosophers*. La Salle, Ill.: Open Court, pp. 241–73.

Laudan, L. (1977). *Progress and Its Problems: Towards a Theory of Scientific Growth*. Berkeley: University of California Press.

McCloskey, D. (1983). "The Rhetoric of Economics," *Journal of Economic Literature* 21(2):481–517.

Popper, K. (1972). "Conjectural Knowledge: My Solution to the Problem of Induction," in *Objective Knowledge: An Evolutionary Approach*. Oxford: Clarendon Press, pp. 1–31.

Toulmin, S. (1970). "Does the Distinction between Normal and Revolutionary Science Hold Water?" in I. Lakatos and A. Musgrave, eds., *Criticism and the Growth of Knowledge*, Cambridge: Cambridge University Press, pp. 39–47.

Weintraub, E.R. (1984). "Appraising General Equilibrium Analysis," *Economics and Philosophy* 1(1):23–37.

CHAPTER 10

Thick and thin methodologies in the history of economic thought

DONALD N. McCLOSKEY

Outsiders make the same complaint about philosophers as they do about economists, saying, These writers thin down the question so. And so they both do. The economist thins the question of the good society right down to matters of price and marginal cost. The philosopher thins the good argument right down to matters of modus tollens and infinite regress. Precision comes from the conversational thinness, as does employment and other goods. But even after such achievements, we should not be surprised if outsiders want to get back to the main and fatter point.

The trouble with using Karl Popper's thinking for a history or methodology of economic thought is not mainly some flaw in its technique, though Daniel Hausman has made the pervasiveness of the flaws clear. The main problem, even in this the richest of philosophies, is its thinness. Rich as Sir Karl's thinking is, supplemented by Lakatos, elaborated and applied with wonderful ingenuity by their followers, it looks thin beside the actual conversation of science. A conversation begun in the primeval forest, as Michael Oakeshott once said, extended and made more articulate in the course of centuries, is probably not going to fit easily into a few lines of philosophy. Or rather, since the issue is empirical, it might – it might be that a philosophy could describe well what goes on in the conversation of science – but it hasn't. One can imagine a world, perhaps, in which the growth of knowledge was interestingly philosophizable. But it doesn't seem to be our world (cf. Rorty, 1982, p. xiv).

A methodology of economics "based" (that hopeful word) on philosophy, especially on philosophy as construed in the English-speaking world, is too thin to work. Such a remark is not to be taken as antiintellectual, antirational, antiphilosophical, or even antianalytic. Thinking is good, even when thin, and so is thinking about thinking. No one wants to abandon first-order predicate logic, even though it might not be a complete model of sound thinking. Nor is the remark to be taken as one of those sneers at methodology, the sort that grace the exordia of methodological papers by Paul Samuelson and George Stigler. Thinking about thinking about thinking is good, too.

245

Yet even those of us who, from time to time, make use of philosophy of science complain about its thinness. Roy Weintraub, for example, complains rightly that Popper reduces the rich conversation of empirical work down to a falsifying "fact." Lakatos's philosophical work was an extended complaint about the lack of thickness in Popper's work, as Popper's was a complaint about earlier and still thinner philosophies of science. None of it works. Mark Blaug, J.J. Klant, and Lawrence Boland accept Lakatos's program, the "rational (which is to say, philo-sophical) reconstruction of research programs," as what methodology should do, but strain at its limits when applying his program to real work in economics. Boland, for one, skirts the edge of an economic literary criticism (e.g., 1982, pp. 116–17). And Weintraub notes in *General Equilibrium Analysis: Studies in Appraisal* (1985, p. 142) that his case study "raises several other problems that rest uneasily in a Lakatosian bed."

The thinness of the philosophy comes from the thinness of the ques-tion it asks. The question in a rational reconstruction of a piece of science is: Does the discourse fit, say, a Lakatosian model? What is the hard core, the protective belt, a typical negative heuristic? Can it be made to lie down on the bed, with suitable trimming at head and feet?

The question will strike the outsider as odd. A study that verifies or falsifies the fit of such a simple notion as sophisticated falsificationism to a part of economics does not ask very many questions. The one question it does ask would not strike a working scientist as interesting. At the end of the day, you are led to ask what has been accomplished.

Consider again Roy Weintraub's recent work, the brilliant imitation of Lakatos just mentioned and his elegant paper for this conference, "The Neo-Walrasian Research Program Is Empirically Progressive." All right, suppose that by the Lakatosian definition the neo-Walrasian pro-gram is empirically progressive. (Weintraub certainly persuades on the point: His work exhibits precision and candor well beyond the call of duty in intellectual history.) But what follows? What at the end of the day has been accomplished? We are now persuaded (set aside the prob-lem of induction in talking about the problem of induction) that neoclas-sical economics can be rationally reconstructed to correspond with a pattern adumbrated by a certain philosopher. Well, so what?

The question is pragmatic, but not in a vulgar sense. It will be per-fectly satisfactory if the cash value of the Lakatosian categories shows up merely in their value for further thinking: for setting economics in con-text, for making economists more self-aware, for telling persuasive sto-ries about the history of economics, for understanding why economists go on as they do. Among professional intellectuals these should count as good reasons. There is no vulgar demand here for "better economic predictions" from the philosophy, or some market test.

This is fortunate, since philosophical formulas for science have failed to yield vulgar cash rewards in other fields. The lack of correspondence or coherence between the history of science (as written over the past couple of decades) and the philosophy of science (as thrown into confusion over the past couple of decades) is epistemologically striking. Near enough, the philosophy of science has been falsified. Though working scientists will occasionally use a philosophy for a rhetorical purpose, no one seems actually to have carried out a Baconian program, much less a Popperian or Lakatosian program.

But whether there is any practical payoff or not, professional intellectuals can reasonably require that ideas have at least intellectual consequences. If you explain that the orbit of the moon arises from the "orbital character" of the moon you have a handsome turn of phrase, applicable to other moons as well, but not rich in consequences and not answering human questions. If, on the other hand, you explain that the orbit has to do with $F = ma$, the consequences are many, answering questions that people might ask: Why is a moon like an apple? Where did the moon come from and where is it going? How do you get to the moon from here?

The Lakatosian character of some piece of economics has no consequences. It does not answer a question that an economist, or even a non-Lakatosian philosopher, would ask.

The question it does ask is one of the nature-of questions that Popper explicitly spurned. Problem situations, not natures, he said, are the proper subject of science. Popper and Lakatos have emphasized repeatedly that new questions – in other words, a continuity in the conversation – characterize progressive science. One is led to ask: Is the program of applying Popperian or Lakatosian or other philosophical ideas to the history of economic thought itself empirically progressive? What is the problem of which the Methodology of Scientific Research Programs is a progressive solution?

The answer seems to be that it is considered important for economics to be adjudged "empirically progressive" (in Lakatos's sense), just as a little earlier the talk of economists was abuzz with the importance of Popperian falsifiability; and before that of Bridgemanian operationality; and before that of Millsian methodicalness; and before that of Baconian inferentiality. Around 1980 the task of the Lakatosian methodologist or historian of thought was to check out this Lakatosian virtue in economic science. Yet Lakatos might alternatively have called a science "scientific" or "free of false consciousness" instead of "progressive"; and these, without further argument, would amount to synonyms for "Lakatos-beloved" (compare Euthyphro, Stephanus 10e–11b). But why, in turn, would we care that economics would be beloved of Imre Lakatos?

We might indeed care about economics being "empirically progressive" if "progressiveness" in Lakatos's sense were shown historically to correspond to progress. But this is doubtful, and is indeed explicitly denied by both Popper and Lakatos. They do not pretend to give persuasive histories of how science actually did progress. Theirs is rational, not historical, reconstruction. As I just said, if their appeal rested on a claimed fit to science, they would be in serious trouble with present-day historians and sociologists of science, not to speak of Paul Feyerabend, Michael Polanyi, and Stephen Toulmin.

To take another possibility, we might care about Lakatos-belovedness if a "progressive" scientific research program could be shown to lead to Truth. But it is reliably reported that there is a problem with Truth. The problem is not with lowercase truth, which gives answers to questions arising now in human conversations, requiring no access to the mind of God: On a Fahrenheit scale, what is the temperature in Iowa City this afternoon? On a historical scale, what is the quality of the President's decisions in foreign affairs? You and I can answer such questions, improving our answers in shared discourse.

The problem comes when trying to vault into a higher realm, asking whether such and such a methodology will lead ultimately to the end of the conversation, to the final Truth about economics or philosophy. This is the question asked by Plato and reiterated by Descartes and Bacon. The modesty of the sophist Protagoras, that man is the measure of all things, was not pleasing to Plato, Descartes, and Bacon: "For it is a false assertion that the sense of man is the measure of all things. On the contrary, all perceptions as well as of the sense as of the mind are according to the measure of the individual and not according to the measure of the universe. And the human understanding is like a false mirror, which, receiving rays irregularly, distorts and discolours the nature of things by mingling its own nature with it" (Bacon, 1965, ch. XVI).

The "measure of the universe," however, cannot be taken direct; it can only be taken from the sublunary mirrors we have. Questions such as "What will economics look like once it is finished?" are not answerable on this side of the Last Judgment. Wolfgang Pauli used an economic metaphor to scold physicists for anticipating the physics that would arise once judgment was ended, claiming "credits for the future." Economists, with their dismal jokes that lunches are not free and $500 bills do not lie about unclaimed, should have no trouble seeing that little can be hoped for prescience in such matters. The problem is that it is precisely prescience, knowing before knowing.

What then? If methodology – Popperian, Lakatosian, or whatever – is not a guide to the history of thought or to the completion of science, one may ask what it is a guide to. What, really, is the philosophy of economic science about? The answer appears to be that it is about morality. And there is no sin in this.

Popper and company are not so much concerned to tell a persuasive story or lead a march to the godhead as to persuade scientists to be good. The sneering and name calling and good-guy identifying and horrified-viewing-with-alarm that characterize methodological discourse fit a program of goodness. We berate and banish the criminal, the bad person. The rules of the game give us a way of classifying scholars as citizens or as thought criminals. If we can tag the nasty descendants of Nietzsche as "irrationalists," for example, we can shut them up, or at any rate protect innocent students from their words. Again, if we can identify the Freudians and Marxists as aliens, we can conveniently deport them from our open intellectual society. (An unhappy side effect of such a policy, strictly enforced, would be the deportation of most economists forthwith, pleading from the back of the truck their falsification credentials.)

A moral purpose explains the strength of feeling against John Dewey, Milton Friedman, Richard Rorty, and other harmless pragmatists. Moral and political purposes are not always denied by advocates of the received view. At certain moments they will admit to them. In 1938, for example, before it was fully received, the father of us all wrote thus in favor of neopositivism in economics:

The most sinister phenomenon of recent decades for the true scientist, and indeed to Western civilization as a whole, may be said to be the growth of Pseudo-Sciences no longer confined to hole-in-corner cranks . . . but organized in comprehensive, militant and persecuting mass-creeds. . . . [Testability is] the only principle or distinction practically adoptable which will keep science separate from pseudo-science. (Hutchison [1938], 1960, pp. 10–11)

One can agree with a purpose here of attacking Nazism without agreeing that some method of Science will achieve it. One can argue in fact the other way around. After all, the Nazis were gloriously Scientific in their experiments. Victorian and even British Science, with its elaborate ceremony of testability (most skillfully practiced by the psychologist Sir Cyril Burt), was a major source of racist theories (cf. Gould, 1981). And on the other side it is not easy to blame, say, Jewish numerology or Gypsy legerdemain for the rise of Nazism.

There is little doubt, however, that a desire to defend liberal values against the barbarians feeds methodology. The unargued moral and political message in positivism and its offshoots explains perhaps the fascination with the demarcation problem. When you consider it, it's not clear why it should matter whether economics is or is not a science. Of course, there are certain material advantages: a place under the National Science Foundation's tiny budget for social sciences; a Nobel Prize in Economic science; a few memberships in the National Academy of Science. The label gives economists license to sneer at sociologists and philosophers. But the main reason for demarcation seems to be that astrologers and parapsychologists are thought to be bad people, touchie-feelies from Santa Monica perhaps. It is taken as given that such intellectual criminals, violators of the rules of the game, are not to be tolerated in the open society. The appeal of methodology is moral and political.

These moral and political fears of the methodologists are not scrutinized. If they were, they would take a more realistic form. As Bruce Caldwell notes wisely, "The fear of anarchy [by which he means "chaos," the war of all against all], or of a totalitarian response to anarchy, cannot be based on a correct perception of science as it is currently practiced in free societies" (1985, p. 5). To solve the German problem between the wars, or the Slavic problem after them, some rigid rules might make sense, the more rigid the better – the better to defend a conversation from the state. When the party man in charge of the scientist's soul detects some deviation, the scientist can pull out a sheaf of computer paper and ask mildly, "Yes, perhaps I have made a mistake; please show it to me, comrade." But this ploy (which is more than an armchair possibility) is not nearly so sweet in an open, plural, and pragmatic society. The appeal to the character of the Scientist in such a place more often supports authoritarianism in the Department of Defense or the National Aeronautics and Space Administration. The barbarians against which philosophical methodology should fight are inside, not outside, the gates.

It would be good to see the defenders of the fact–value split scrutinize their moral agenda. They might find enlightenment in the long conversation among philosophers about virtue. If they knew that their methodologies were about virtue, they could start with the Old Testament and the Gorgias and work forward.

The psychological literature on moral development is worth reading, too. This very conference and the wider discussion beyond it of the rules of the game have notably few women participants. Carol Gilligan, in *In a Different Voice: Psychological Theory and Women's Development* (1982), quotes Janet Lever's study of the games of boys and girls–

"[B]oys were seen quarreling all the time, but not once was a game terminated because of a quarrel" – and explains that "it seemed that the boys enjoyed the legal debates as much as they did the game itself, and even marginal players of lesser size or skill participated equally in these recurrent squabbles. In contrast, the eruption of disputes among girls tended to end the game" (p. 9). The parallel with methodological disputes is suggestive. Gilligan reports on Piaget's observation of "boys becoming through childhood increasingly fascinated with the legal elaboration of rules . . ., a fascination that, he notes, does not hold for girls" (p. 10). The girls stressed community, conversation, solidarity, and the other nonrule values of those known affectionately as the "new fuzzies" (Rorty, 1987). Arjo Klamer and I can be viewed therefore as presuming to bring a feminine perception to the matter.

I suggest, with Klamer, that the good that lies behind methodological thinking is the goodness of community, solidarity, openness to ideas, educated public opinion, and a better conversation of humanity. By their moral fervor the methodologists reveal their values. Their values are fine, and not much different from those of the terrible fuzzies they fear.

The word is *sprachethik,* speech morality, the ethics of conversation. That the word comes from a hive of Marxist fuzzies in Frankfurt-am-Main should not be alarming, for it is liberalism incarnate: Don't lie; pay attention; don't sneer; cooperate; don't shout; let other people talk; be open-minded; explain yourself when asked; don't resort to violence or conspiracy in aid of your ideas. These are the rules adopted by the act of joining a good conversation. Socratic dialogue – flowing first from a pen devoted to finishing conversation – is the model for Western intellectual life. An American philosopher put the point well. What is crucial, writes Amelie Oksenberg Rorty, is "our ability to engage in continuous conversation, testing one another, discovering our hidden presuppositions, changing our minds because we have listened to the voices of our fellows. Lunatics also change their minds, but their minds change with the tides of the moon and not because they have listened, really listened, to their friends' questions and objections" (1983, p. 562). Good science is not good method but good conversation.

We know when conversations are going well among our own intellectual friends. Most economists would agree, for example, that the conversation about international trade since 1950 has been through a bad stretch, relieved only temporarily by a burst of creativity fifteen years ago on the financial side. They would agree, too, that economic history improved radically after 1958 and has flourished ever since. Working economists do not need the advice of a philosopher – least of all an economist in philosopher's clothing–to know when things are going well or badly in their neck of the woods.

It is a crucial point about the conversational view of intellectual life that conversations overlap. You are almost as sure about neighboring conversations as about your own, which is what research panels, editorial boards, and tenure committees depend on. If good conversation is maintained in one part of the conversation of humanity, the overlap provides standards for others. The overlap of the overlap spreads good standards, such as care in reading earlier work (and bad habits, too, such as the mechanical use of statistical significance). This free market–not the central planning proposed in the official methodologies–gives the only promise worth having that the economy of intellect will continue to run as well as can be expected.

The argument replies to certain monists, who insist that other people stick to what they call "standards." They exempt their own conversation from such rhetorical scrutiny: They reckon that Plato's beard or Descartes's cogito will suffice for serious men. The alleged standards of philosophical empiricism (distinct from empirical work, which no reasonable person speaks against) have persuaded some scientists to spurn whole classes of evidence: Economists have spurned surveys, psychologists the evidence of their own minds, and policymakers the moral reasoning necessary for the making of policy. It is hard to take the claim of philosophically imposed standards seriously. The real standards, after all, reside where they should, on the lips of men and women of science conversing together.

The methodologists, then, accept the *sprachethik* of the fuzzies even as they attack what they think it is. So also more directly do Bruce Caldwell, Husain Sarkar, and other pluralists. As human conversationalists they can hardly avoid doing so. The methodologists are drawn thus into the "cultural sensitivity" of which Klamer speaks, though they do not like it and will not admit it and grow cross when it is mentioned. While having a culture-bound conversation about whether knowledge is culture bound, they insist that conversation is not culture bound. They think they can assume an Archimedean point with which to lever the world of conversation. They do not want rhetoric, but rules of perfect knowledge for all time. They are not discouraged by the failure of 2,500 years of the epistemological conversation to find a single one.

The question is how to converse about this culture-bound conversation of humanity. We know how to make the conversations lie down on the guest beds of philosophers, but agree that the result is unhelpful. Science doesn't fit well on a bed of science-is-modus-tollens or science-is-positive-heuristics. It has to be trimmed to fit.

Happily, there exists alternative thinking about how to do the thinking, thick and rich. It is called the humanities. The humanistic tradition of the West can be used to understand the scientific tradition. What historians and methodologists of economic thought mainly do anyway, without knowing it, is literary criticism. Sophisticated criticism is merely understanding how the texts of economists produce their effect, as one criticizes poetry. Criticism in this sense is neither "assault" nor "ranking." It is not a murder trial or a beauty contest – it is not, as Northrop Frye puts the point, "the odious comparison of greatness," a "pseudo-dialectics, or false rhetoric," "an anxiety neurosis prompted by a moral censor" that has "made the word critic a synonym for an educated shrew" (1957, pp. 24–7). The usual philosophical criticism lets in the shrewishness: thin, bad-tempered, superficially judgmental. By the standards of good literary criticism, a philosophical criticism – Lakatosian, say – seems thin and harshly normative, unattractive stuff. The literary model can lead to a better way of examining the conversations of economists.

Its merits show up when placed side by side with some of the other alternatives to philosophical criticism. They are all at least as thick as philosophy. For example, the history of economic thought can be written as biography. George Stigler has attacked this tradition persuasively, though doubtless it will survive even his pen (1976). The biographical approach is certainly thick: One can know all about Ricardo's businesses and Keynes's love affairs, yet still have more questions to ask. The conversation may be irrelevant to matters of import, as Stigler would argue, but there is at least nothing thin about it. This probably explains its vitality in the face of much lofty methodological sneering.

Another thick alternative is the Whiggish theory, advocated by Stigler and practiced by Mark Blaug, that the progress of science can be viewed as successive approximations to the right answers. Eventually we'll get it right. In the meantime, we can look on the history of the field as a dawning of enlightenment. This is history of science as examination question: Quick, Ricardo: would it matter to your argument if labor was only 93 percent of costs? Quick, Malthus: How would you draw your theory in the wage–population plane? Most history of thought taken seriously by most economists (Schumpeter a while ago, Blaug et alia nowadays) takes this line and has done great service. Though more useful for enriching economic thinking, the Whiggish approach is not so thick as the biographical. As with slow students disfiguring their examination scripts, one runs out of patience with the errors of the past.

Another thick alternative to philosophical criticism has again been advocated by the polymorphous Stigler. It is to turn economics on itself and view the history of the field as itself a consequence of economic forces. Here again, as America's leading vulgar Marxist, Stigler shows a characteristic openness to left-wing thought. The program is as rich as is empirical economics (Diamond, 1984; 1987). It amounts to an especially narrow version of the next and better alternative to philosophical criticism.

The better alternative is sociology of science, advocated for economics most prominently by A.W. Coats (1984). It is attractively thick. There is little limit to what one can ask about the sociology of the economics profession in England c. 1900 or the sociology of journal editing c. 1987. Furthermore, it is relevant to what we wish to know: If knowledge is social, as it is, the growth of knowledge will be a social growth.

I should like to argue at the end, however, that the thickest parts of the so-called Strong Program in the Sociology of Science overlap with a specifically rhetorical criticism. Sociology and rhetoric are one.

An illuminating example of the Strong Program is a book by Harry Collins, *Changing Order: Replication and Induction in Scientific Practice* (1985). It is about physics; the Strong Program has not had much of a trial in economics yet. Collins, a sociologist at the Science Research Centre at the University of Bath, calls his approach "sociological," which is fair enough: Science is social, Collins is a sociologist, and sociological phenomenology has played a part in his thinking. But it is not sociological in the sense that earlier sociologists of science, such as Robert Merton, would recognize. He does not, for example, collect biographical data on the scientists, though he could have done so with less trouble. He did not because the scientists are not his subjects.

His subjects are controversies, debates, words, argumentative ploys – that is, the rhetoric of science. The quantified gossip that constitutes sociology of science in the Mertonian or Stiglerian vein is missing. This is notable because Collins has elsewhere done Mertonian tasks (Collins and Pinch, 1982). What interests Collins in *Changing Order* is not the resumés of his people but the course of the debate among them. He speaks repeatedly of the "argumentative strategy" of this or that scientific remark. He never attributes a move in the argument to party or passion. Toward the end of the book he rejects the usual social correlates in favor of a definition of his subject that focuses attention on debate:

> The set of allies and enemies in the core of a controversy are not necessarily bound to each other by social ties or membership of common institutions. . . . If these enemies interact, it is likely to be only in the context of the particular passing debate. This set of persons does not necessarily act like a "group." They

are bound only by their close, if differing, interests in the controversy's outcome. (1985, p. 142)

Collins treats the debate among physicists about gravity waves, for example, as just that: as a debate, showing how one or another rhetorical move led to the result. At its turning point, for instance, the chief proponent of gravity waves, Joseph Weber, "in accepting . . . electrostatic calibration . . . accepted constraint on his freedom to interpret results" (p. 105). Collins notes that Weber did not have to accept the calibration (which itself, by the way, is a rhetorical turn common to many fields: the selection of a quantitative standard). It was a rhetorical choice. But having made it, Weber was constrained by rules of debate, rules that can themselves be studied and partially understood, and have in fact been studied and partially understood since the time of the Greeks.

The varied rules of human debate, not godlike tests, decide the outcome. "It is control on interpretation which breaks the circle of the experimenters' regress [Collins's phrase for Duhem's dilemma], not the 'test of a test' itself" (p. 106). That is to say, it is rhetorical considerations, the workings of a human conversation, not mechanical applications of rules within a closed system, that end a scientific debate. Scientists do not commit a crime when they argue beyond the constricted realm of formal logic. "Scientists do not act dishonourably when they engage in the debates . . . ; there is nothing else for them to do if a debate is ever to be settled and if new knowledge is ever to emerge from the dispute" (p. 143). It is not the logic of inquiry that allows scientific progress, but the rhetoric of inquiry (cf. p. 153, note 5).

I am asserting that Collins and other observers of scientific controversy contribute unawares to the rhetorical tradition. Rhetorical criticism is the thickest approach. It draws on an immensely long tradition from the Sicilian sophists to the present, running parallel to philosophy, though spurned by philosophy in every age. At present the tradition lives in law schools, in the literary world (Booth, 1974; Fish, 1980), and in writings on argument emanating from specialists in rhetoric (Scott, 1967). Occasionally it can be seen half-conscious in a philosopher gone wrong (Toulmin, 1958; Steiner, 1975; Rosen, 1980; Rorty, 1982; Walton, 1985).

It is not "mere" rhetoric, and not an ornament to be distinguished from the substance of argument. It is rhetoric in the ancient and honorable sense:

the art of probing what men believe they ought to believe, rather than proving what is true according to abstract methods . . . , of discovering good reasons, finding what really warrants assent, . . . of discovering warrantable beliefs and improving those beliefs in shared discourse. (Booth, 1974, pp. xiii, xiv)

It is, in brief, the art of argument, argument not confined to syllogism or meter reading. It includes arguments from pure logic and simple measurement, to be sure, but includes the other 90 percent of scientific argument, too – the ubiquitous "models" of scientific thinking, for example, which are arguments from analogy, and the ubiquitous appeals to the reputation of the scientist, which are arguments from authority.

Scientists, even economists in the grip of philosophy of science, argue with all the means their culture makes available, honestly if they have the will and thoroughly if they have the energy. Their official rhetoric does not admit this, because the officials have been enchanted since the time of Plato with a thin quest for certainty. They have hidden most of the argument, uncertain as it is, in hallway conversation and conference room retort, in what is implied rather than stated. An economic criticism and literary sensibilities can bring economic arguments out into the light.

The rhetorical concern, in sum, is how we really do convince each other, not "what is true according to abstract methods." The point is that it is also the concern of the scientists; they couldn't care less what is true according to abstract methods; they want to persuade, to bring a particular debate to a conclusion. Scientists in all fields, psychology and economics as much as physics and biology, talk incessantly about rhetorical matters. They talk as though engaged in a debate at the Oxford Union or a case at law or an important business judgment. The scientific conversation is not governed by rules convenient for a pocket-sized card. It is a thick and complex rhetorical matter. It is a matter of listening, really listening, to what our fellows say; then answering, really answering.

References

Bacon, F. (1965 [1620]). *The New Organon*, in S. Warhaft, ed., *Francis Bacon: A Selection of His Works*. Indianapolis: Bobbs-Merrill.
Boland, L.A. (1982). *The Foundations of Economic Method*. London: Allen & Unwin.
Booth, W.C. (1974). *Modern Dogma and the Rhetoric of Assent*. Chicago: University of Chicago Press.
Caldwell, B. (1985). "The Case for Pluralism." Paper for this conference.
Coats, A.W. (1984). "The Sociology of Knowledge and the History of Economics," in W. Samuels, ed., *Research in the History of Economic Thought and Methodology*, Vol. 2. Greenwich, Conn.: JAI Press.

Collins, H.M. (1985). *Changing Order: Replication and Induction in Scientific Practice*. London and Beverly Hills, Calif.: Sage.

and Pinch, T.H. (1982). *Frames of Meaning: The Social Construction of Extraordinary Science*. London: Routledge & Kegan Paul.

Diamond, A.M. (1984). "An Economic Model of the Life-Cycle Research Productivity of Scientists," *Scientometrics* 6:30–6.

(1987). "The Determinants of a Scientist's Choice of Research Projects." Working Paper, Department of Economics, University of Nebraska–Omaha.

Fish, S. (1980). *Is There a Text in This Class? The Authority of Interpretive Communities*. Cambridge, Mass.: Harvard University Press.

Frye, N. (1957). *An Anatomy of Criticism*. New York: Atheneum.

Gilligan, C. (1982). *In a Different Voice: Psychological Theory and Women's Development*. Cambridge, Mass.: Harvard University Press.

Gould, S.J. (1981). *The Mismeasure of Man*. New York: Norton.

Hutchison, T. (1960 [1938]). *The Significance and Basic Postulates of Economic Theory*, 2nd ed. New York: Kelley.

McCloskey, D.N. (1985). "Sartorial Epistemology in Tatters: A Reply to Martin Hollis," *Economics and Philosophy* 1:134–7.

1986. *The Rhetoric of Economics*. Madison: Vol. 1 in the Series on the Rhetoric of the Human Sciences. Madison: University of Wisconsin Press.

Rorty, A.O. (1983). "Experiments in Philosophic Genre: Descartes' Meditations," *Critical Inquiry* 9:545–65.

Rorty, R. (1982). *The Consequences of Pragmatism*. Minneapolis: University of Minnesota Press.

(1987). "Science as Solidarity," in J. Nelson, A. Megill, and D.N. McCloskey, eds., *The Rhetoric of the Human Sciences*. Madison: Wisconsin University Press.

Rosen, S. (1980). *The Limits of Analysis*. New York: Basic Books.

Scott, R. (1967). "On Viewing Rhetoric as Epistemic," *Central States Speech Journal* 18:9–17.

Steiner, M. (1975). *Mathematical Knowledge*. Ithaca, N.Y.: Cornell University Press.

Stigler, G. (1976). "The Scientific Uses of Scientific Biography, with Special Reference to J.S. Mill," in J.M. Robson and M. Lane, eds., *James and John Stuart Mill: Papers of the Centenary Conference*. Toronto: University of Toronto Press.

Toulmin, S. (1958). *The Uses of Argument*. Cambridge: Cambridge University Press.

Walton, D.N. (1985). *Arguer's Position: A Pragmatic Study of Ad Hominem Attack, Criticism, Refutation, and Fallacy*. Westport, Conn.: Greenwood Press.

Weintraub, E.R. (1985). *General Equilibrium Analysis: Studies in Appraisal*. Cambridge: Cambridge University Press.

1985. "The Neo-Walrasian Program Is Empirically Progressive." Paper for this conference.

CHAPTER 11

Economics as discourse

ARJO KLAMER

What I am doing is also persuasion. If someone says, "There is not a difference" and I say, "There is a difference" I am persuading. I am saying, "I don't want you to look at it like that."

The theme

The determination to speak of economics as discourse signifies interest in the problems of communication in economics. The preferred image is that of economists involved in conversations. Rather than reducing these conversations to a series of statements – the prevalent tendency in talk about economics – we want to observe the multiformity of economic discourse and explore the various arguments, analogies, metaphors, stories, argumentative strategies, and other rhetorical devices that economists use in their conversations. These explorations are intended to illuminate the tensions and conflicts that keep economic discourse alive. They may also uncover different modes within economic discourse and disagreements as problems of communication.

This interest in the communicative aspects of economics implies a paradigmatic shift in the discourse about economics. Issues such as the logical properties of economic theories, criteria for their appraisal, and the scienticity of economics, which have been until now the dominating concern of economic methodologists, lose much of their relevance once we alter our discussion as I am advocating.[1] The leading questions change and so do major concepts.

In this chapter, I am addressing myself primarily to those who got me interested in talking about economics – J.J. Klant, T. W. Hutchison, and Mark Blaug. Their work represents the currently dominant tradition in economic methodology.[1] I now propose to alter that tradition, but I

Paper presented at the conference in honor of Professor J. J. Klant, Amsterdam, December 1985. This paper was written with the financial support of the National Endowment of the Humanities. Thanks to Robert Fischer, Will Mason, and Neil de Marchi for their comments.
[1] Caldwell (1982), Boland (1982), and Hausman (1981) are some of the other works that bolster this tradition, each in its idiosyncratic ways. Caldwell (1985) and Hausman (1985) are collections of the main writings that constitute conventional methdological discourse in economics.

hasten to say that their work played a critical part in the development of my argument. It is with deference to their insights that I disagree.

The following discussion presents philosophical reasons for changing our talk about economics. It could be interpreted as an indication of what happens when we replace Karl Raimund Popper as the central character in our conversations. I shall have little to say about economics per se; that has been and will be my concern elsewhere.[2]

Let the argument begin with a story.

A story

When I came to the United States as a graduate student, I experienced a variety of "culture shocks." Not only did I have to think and talk in another language, but I also had to discover the cultural dimensions of things like humor, human relationships, and doing economics. One striking discovery was the fascination of students and professors with baseball. Conversations on baseball were frequent and endless, and baseball metaphors were ubiquitous in other conversations.

I was puzzled by this fascination. Baseball looked like a boring game to me, with very little action, few hits, long periods without a score, and much hanging around. It was not my type of game, and I did not understand that it could be such a popular game in an allegedly action-oriented society that appears to celebrate toughness, aggression, and immediate gratification.

My fellow students, bothered by my indifference to their game, began to explain the rules to me. So then I knew that "RBI" stands for runs batted in and three strikes means "out!" I was still bored with the game and the endless conversations about it.

One student persisted in his attempts to convince me and finally dragged me to a local game. The experience was an eye-opener. I found myself on the stands amid a heterogeneous group of Americans—construction workers, doctors, intellectuals, men, women, blacks, and whites—and I heard them talking with each other, commenting on the plays and the players, citing statistics, exchanging stories about players and games. I watched their reactions at the playing of whatever song it is that they play at the beginning. I noticed that organ that tried to get the fans going; we ate clammy hot dogs, they sipped beer, and we all stood up in the middle of the seventh inning "to stretch the legs." No one had ever told me about this folklore, the stories, and the statistics, all of which clearly are a critical part of the baseball experience. I subsequently was persuaded to participate in the Friday afternoon softball games.

After this I understood why American intellectuals like baseball meta-phors. (I also came to realize that the possibility of quantification – you can count the number of RBIs, hits, home runs, stolen bases, and so on – befits the American love for numbers. The success of soccer in the United States will undoubtedly be partly determined by the possibility of quantifying that game as well.) I still am not enthused with baseball, but I can now endure the conversations about it.

The story as analogy

An analogy is used to illuminate one phenomenon by suggesting similari-ties to another, familiar phenomenon. The experience of entering the world of economists is analogous to the cultural experience in this story. At first, it is hard to understand what economists talk about and what gets them interested or why what they say is interesting or meaningful. Students often comment that learning economics is like learning a new language. Aspiring economists are going through what we may call initia-tion rituals that precede membership in the economic tribe. These initia-tion rituals comprise doing exercises and exams, as well as socializing with the members of the tribe.

The story works as an analogy in various other ways.

> Like baseball fans, economists and economic methodologists have conversations;
> A conversation is like a game. Each participant in a conversa-tion has to respect certain rules in order to be taken seri-ously. (Wittgenstein's notion of a language game reflects this analogy, too.)
> Just as there are different ways of playing a game, there are different ways of conducting a conversation. (It stands to reason that such different ways constitute distinctive conver-sations. Accordingly, Keynesians, new classicals, Marxists, and Austrians would be involved in different conversations.)
> Just as successful participation in the game of baseball requires particular skills, so does participation in a conversation about baseball or economics. Accordingly, the art of playing base-ball is analogous to the art of talking well about baseball or the art of talking well in economics. The art of talking well we could also call "the art of persuasion."
> Knowing the rules of baseball proved to be insufficient for me to

understand and appreciate the game; experience of how the
game is played and in which ambience was indispensable. A
similar experience befalls a beginning economics student who
has the idea that large government deficits are bad for the
economy but does not know how to talk about the idea. That
student will be helped little when she learns the methodological rules by which economists play.

Following through on the preceding point, we conclude that
"knowing" any activity well, in the sense of knowing how to
play the game well or how to talk well, requires intimate
involvement. Playing baseball, doing economics, or doing
economic methodology is a "way of being." We could also
talk of "cultural activities," since the game or the conversation presupposes a set of shared beliefs that can be learned
only through intimate involvement.

Academicians tend to be wary of stories and analogies (even though,
as we are beginning to discover, they use them in their discourse all the
time). The discipline of scholarly conversations requires the construction of arguments and the serious comparison of those arguments with
already established arguments.

Therefore, let me clarify some terminology and specify a model that
can discipline and direct the conversation about the observations just
made.

Some terms and a model

I use "discourse" to indicate the processes by which economic ideas are
communicated. These processes involve the writing and reading of economic texts (articles, books, dissertations, course papers, reports, letters, etc.), as well as informal conversations. I use "conversation" as a
less formal expression for discourse. Its drawback is the association
with chitchat, an association that I do not want to encourage. But it has
various benefits: "Conversation" refers not only to the "interchange of
thought and words" but also to the "action of consorting with others"
and "manner of life" and even "sexual intimacy."[3] Accordingly, the
notion of conversation alludes to the sense of community that we encounter among people talking about baseball, ballet, economics, or
methodology.

The notion of a game is a useful metaphor for a scientific conversation, as it indicates that such a conversation is disciplined through a set

---

[3] According to the *Oxford English Dictionary*.

of explicit and implicit rules, just like a baseball game. The implicit rules deserve emphasis: Participation in the economics game requires not only knowing the methodological rules, but also how to talk with economists, what questions to ask, which names to know.

For our study of economic discourse we can choose to confer with semioticians, rhetoricians, communications theorists, literary critics, linguists, philosophers of science, cognitive psychologists, ethnographers, sociologists, anthropologists, or information theorists. The possibilities are too many, so we are compelled to choose an entry point.

The following simple model of communication is a useful start.

vehicle

sender   receiver

signal

We usually think of the sender as a person or a group of persons, but it can also be a machine, typescript, or any other thing. The vehicle is the physical medium through which a signal is transmitted and can be anything from a telegraph pole to waving hands. The signal is the content of the message. The receiver could be a machine or animal, but as our interest is human communication, it will be one or more human beings.

The model can be easily extended. For example, we may want to add the element of "expression" between the sender and the signal and that of "interpretation" between the signal and the receiver. The expression involves the translation, or coding, of a thought into a signal. Interpretation, then, is the decoding of the signal by the receiver.

This model is like the equation for the quantity theory of money: Without further hypotheses, it merely classifies different elements in the communication process. But it can channel our discussion.

Rhetoric as one approach among others to study communication

The study of rhetoric is one way of delineating a specific domain for the model of communication. Here Aristotle's *Rhetoric* points the way.

Aristotle defines rhetoric as "the faculty of discovering in the particular case what are the available means of persuasion." Rhetoric, to him, is the art of public speaking and is distinct from dialectic, or the art of logical discussion. Accordingly, Aristotle's rhetoric is a form of communication that takes place in the courtroom (deliberative oratory), in the political arena (forensic oratory), and at celebrations (epideictic oratory). Translated in terms of his rhetorical triad, the communication model reads: speaker – discourse (or *logos*) – audience.

However, Aristotle carved out too small a domain for the application of rhetoric. Besides the courtroom and the political arena, the novel, the street, and scholarly seminars and writings can be considered the domain of rhetoric. Aristotle's rhetorical triad has already turned out to be useful for students of literature, colloquial discourse, and academic disciplines such as mathematics, psychology, history, and economics.

Aristotle's discussion of the rhetorical process has psychological overtones. He invites us to think of the emotions of the audience (*pathos*) and points at the *ethos* or moral character of the speaker as significant factors in the process. Translated into contemporary terms, the rhetorical model compels us to consider the authority of the speaker (in economic discourse, the name of a Robert Solow or Robert Lucas on an article is likely to have a stronger rhetorical effect than the name of any other intelligent but little-known economist) and the role of the reader(s). The point is that the signs of the rhetor are never self-evident or complete and require decoding or interpretation. The art of persuasion is therefore the art of being able to induce the intended interpretation.

Characteristically rhetorical arguments are, according to Aristotle, the *enthymeme,* which is a deduction that omits a premise or contains premises that are merely plausible. An example of the *enthymeme* is the economic statement: If the price of a good falls, the quantity demanded will increase. The statement has the form of a syllogism but clearly leaves out various assumptions, such as the assumptions that individuals maximize their utility, that indifference curves are convex, that the substitution effect is greater than the income effect, and that preferences are constant. The user of the *enthymeme* presumes a critical contribution of the audience, as the missing links have to be filled in. Decoding of the statement, then, requires the application of information and knowledge that is not contained in the statement itself.

The use of so-called *topoi,* or lines of argument, is a critical factor in bringing about the decoding that the speaker intends. *Topoi* are assumptions or arguments that are not necessarily true, but are reasonable and generally accepted by the audience. For example, an audience of neoclassical economists is likely to accept the *topoi* that individuals are rational and their preferences constant. They understand what the speaker means when he or she uses these *topoi,* that is, they can imagine the appropriate diagrams and are familiar with the literature in which these *topoi* are developed.

Another characteristically rhetorical device is the *example.* When economists, for instance, argue that government deficits do not necessarily inhibit economic growth, they may offer the case of West Germany in a particular period as an example that confirms their argument. (Another example is this example.)

Delivery and style, the elements that are primarily associated with rhetoric, are secondary in Aristotle's instruction, but they are important "since it is not enough to know *what* to say – one must also know *how* to say it" [p. 182]. As Aristotle talks about oral suasion, he considers the use of voice critical in delivery. Literary critics have pointed out that voice is important in a written text, too. This may be why academics are taught to use "we" rather than "I," and to refrain from cute phrases, so that we capture the voice of objectivity and scholarly seriousness.

The issue of style gets us into the use of language, the role of metaphors, analogies, narration, and all that. McCloskey's work has done much to bring out the ubiquitous presence of metaphors and analogies in economic discourse.[4] Aristotle considers the main role of the metaphor to be to give "clearness, charm, and distinction to style," but students of the metaphor have recently come to the conclusion that metaphors play a crucial part in the creative process in the expression and interpretation of signs. We are now coming to recognize that models are metaphors or analogies (which are the sisters of metaphors). As most economists will affirm, models of a complex reality (read: analogies) are indispensable in the probing and grasping of that reality; the creative contribution of the model occurs when it gives the model builder new insights into that reality, such as unsuspected relationships or interactions between variables. The same could be said about the analogy between the talk about baseball and economics or between playing baseball and doing economics: Such an analogy draws our attention to previously unnoticed or ignored features of economics as a discipline.

The importance of metaphor in our conversations, as well as examples, *enthymemes,* and *topoi,* indicates that we cannot say "it" all or write "it" all down. Writing and talking are rhetorical activities in which we overcome the limitations of language through the use of its peculiar power to communicate a perspective to an audience that may or may not be disposed to accept that perspective.

From economic rhetoric to economic discourse

As the examples indicate, the rhetorical model that is a specific interpretation of the communication model can serve as a first guide in the study of economics as discourse. Yet, I believe that its usefulness is limited

---

[4] See McCloskey (1985). See also Mirowski (1984), which is an interesting discussion of physics analogies in economics.

and suggest that thinking of "discourse" and "conversations" is an important next step. Let me clarify my reservations.

McCloskey's argument, which has been the major application of the rhetorical model to economics so far, is limited to the middle of the rhetorical model, the signs that economists transmit. He *identifies,* in his studies of Fogel's book, Muth's article and econometrics, the rhetorical devices with which economists give their signs the aura of "Science." The argument targets those who still maintain that economics is a Science ruled by one Method, the Scientific Method. Asking *"Why Is Economics Not Yet a Science?"*, as do Eichner and other post-Keynesians, becomes senseless in the light of McCloskey's argument.

Elsewhere I contributed to the rhetorical project when I attempted to identify different types of argument, each to be located on a particular level of economic discourse (Klamer, 1984a, 1984b). The argument endorses McCloskey's insofar as his criticism of the notion of economics as a Science is concerned. Not only theories are arguments, but also empirical tests, which therefore function very much as rhetorical examples (Klamer, 1983).

However, these discussions make only partial use of the model of communication. They are strictly limited to the identification and categorization of the signs that make up economic discourse. More questions can be asked and new insights gained about these signs when we seriously consider the context in which they are uttered, what they signify, and in what ways they can signify different things.

Speaking about economics as discourse or conversation, rather than about the rhetoric of economics, produces various possibilities. First of all, it encourages us to imagine a different situation. Instead of the rhetorical situation, which is that of an individual facing an audience (the I-versus-them situation), we think of a group of conversing people, a speech community, or the I-among-others situation. Thinking in that way emphasizes the interaction and bond or, as Kenneth Burke (1969) would say, identification between those who speak and those who listen: An academic audience, after all, presumedly consists of active participants.

Second, the literature on discourse makes us aware of questions concerning the conditions that render a discourse possible and sustain it. Such questions, among others, occupy Foucault in the *Archeology of Knowledge* (1972). He describes his work as

an attempt to reveal discursive practices in their complexity and density; to show that to speak is to do something–something other than to express what one thinks; to translate what one knows, and something other than to play with the structures of language (*langue*); to show that to add a statement to a pre-existing series of statements is to perform a complicated and costly gesture, which involves conditions (and not only a situation, a context, and motives), and rules (not the logical and linguistic rules of construction); to show that a change in the order of discourse does not presuppose "new ideas," a little invention and creativity, a different mentality, but transformations in a practice, perhaps also in neighbouring practices, and in their common articulation. (p. 209)

The focus on "discursive formations," to use Foucault's term, makes sense especially when different conversations (or discursive practices) make up the talk about economics. McCloskey takes seriously the difference between academic and colloquial talk about economics but leaves aside the difference within academic discourse.[5]

My third point concerns the issue of interpretation. Identifying metaphors is one thing; exploring what they do, what they mean, and how they allow different interpretations is another. The opening story illustrates the complexity of interpretation and the possibilities for misinterpretation: It shows that what is meaningful and interesting in one conversation may leave someone outside that conversation indifferent.[6] Likewise, metaphors or *topoi* that may be meaningful for one group of economists possibly do not work for other economists. The neoclassical formulation of the optimizing individual, for example, is an ineffective *topos* for Austrian economists who cannot recognize in its image their heroic individual, or for psychological economists who miss the psychological dimension, or for Marxist economists who question the usefulness of the individual as an analytic entity. McCloskey deemphasizes differences *within* economic discourse, and that may be the reason why interpretation is not a relevant issue in his work.

In the following section, I present an illustration of the way in which we can uncover differences in discourse. The differences that I want to show are between seemingly similar philosophical arguments, namely, those of Karl Popper and Richard Rorty. I chose their arguments as an illustration because their differences correspond to the differences between the conventional methodological argument and the argument that I am developing here.

---

[5] The framework that I set up in Klamer (1984b) is intended to deal with differences in economic discourse.

[6] This phenomenon was once again striking when Franco Modigliani was asked about the reasons why he had just won the Nobel Prize. He explained his contribution as the idea that people save for old age, and not because they are wealthy. Only those who are acquainted with macroeconomic discourse in the 1950s, or the condition of the game at the time, could have understood why such an obvious idea is worth recognition.

One and many: a reading of a discussion

"How do we determine which theory or, if you wish, which conversation to choose? What are the criteria?"

"Are you suggesting that there is no truth, that everything we do is relative to the context in which we do it? You advocate the rule of mobs!"

These recurrent questions and criticisms that are directed against the conversation on economics as rhetoric or as discourse betray the expectations and aspirations of the dominant discourse about economics. They reflect the *topoi* of traditional Western philosophy.

Karl Popper and Richard Rorty are two contemporary philosophers with a critical perspective on traditional epistemology. Many of their views seem similar, but whereas the preceding questions maintain their natural place in the conversation that Popper encourages, they are of little interest in the context of the conversation that Rorty wants to conduct.

The backdrop for both of their conversations is traditional philosophy. Ever since Socrates, through the mediation of Plato, rebuffed Gorgias, the sophist, dominant philosophical discourse has endorsed his commitment to the pursuit of the Final and Absolute Truth in opposition to the sophistic preoccupation with the realm of the plausible, intermediate, and relative, or the realm of rhetoric. The quest is for certain knowledge, the foundations for which some philosophers sought in the structure of things (i.e., observations), others in the structure of the mind (i.e., mental categories). The preoccupation is with *identity,* or the sameness of all things, which is to be determined through deduction (the application of logic) or induction (repetition in observation).[7] The language used alludes to the possibility of an objective knowledge that transcends the intervention of emotions and social force. The talk is about universals, logic, facts, verification of meaning, the problem of induction, and so on. The underlying belief is that disparate beliefs about things will ultimately converge to the identification of their physical characteristics.

Popper's break with this tradition is best represented by his distinction of three worlds in the process of knowing (Popper and Eccles, 1977; Popper, 1979). He defines world 1 as the "universe of physical entities" (which we attempt to know); world 2 represents "mental states" (which feature in the process of knowing); world 3 is the "world of the products

---

[7] The separation of modes of thinking in accordance with the emphasis on identity, difference, and similarity was suggested to me by Barend v. Heusden, a Dutch semiotician.

of the human mind, such as stories, explanatory myths, tools, scientific theories (whether true or false), scientific problems, social institutions and works of art" (1977, p. 38).

Through his interpretation of these worlds, Popper tells us how he wants to discipline the conversation about the process of knowing. First, he tells us that we cannot talk directly about world 1. "I believe," Popper lets us know, "that 'What is?' or 'What are?' questions or, in other words, are verbal or definitional questions, should be eliminated. [. . .] So I think that we should also discard the question, 'What is truth?' " (1979, p. 309). Then, expressing his antipsychologistic stance, he admonishes us to stop worrying about world 2. He proposes the elimination of the knowing subject and the banning of the traditional question "How do we know?" from our conversation. (This reflects his opinion that the problem of induction is unsolvable.) "We should realize," he argues, using an economic metaphor, "that the study of the products [pertaining to world 3] is vastly more important than the study of the production [pertaining to world 2], even for an understanding of the production and its methods."

Popper's next invention is that we select among the rich arrangement of human products (signs in the communication model) statements as the subject of inquiry. When he calls those statements "objective knowledge," he means that they exist independently of the knowing subject. We might kill off the people who know, he argues through an allegory, but their knowledge would survive through, say, their books stored in libraries.

The punchline of his argument is: All statements are fallible, so we should seek the truth through a process of conjectures and refutations. The argumentative strategy, at least in intention,[8] is that of a logical analysis of scientific statements.

Popper's conversation, although not very influential in academic philosophical discourse, has persuaded many social scientists, including economists. Each methodological work cited previously refers to Popper more often than any other philosopher. Klant refers to Popper on thirty-nine pages versus Hempel on twenty. The comparisons for the others are as follows, Blaug: Popper forty-six, Nagel eighteen; Boland: Popper forty-one, Agassi eighteen; Caldwell: Popper twenty-seven, Feyerabend and Khun twenty-one; Hutchison (1977): Popper twenty-three, Lakatos twenty-one.

Their discussions bear out the discipline that Popper advocates. The

[8] Likewise, accepting the importance of logical studies, as I am quite willing to do, does not imply that my version will be like Popper's or that of any other conventional philosopher.

overriding question is "How do we choose between competing theories?" In accordance with Popper's prescription, economic methodologists tend to seek the answer in the logical properties of economic theories. Klant, for example, proposes that "we analyse the logical structure of economic theories to find a solution to our decision problem" (1984, p. ix). The concomitant strategy involves the reduction of all the signs that economists communicate to statements, that is, sentences that represent hypotheses and theories. This reduction can be a "rational reconstruction," that is, the reduction of all signs to a logically coherent series of statements in which the logic is usually provided by a Lakatosian framework. E. Roy Weintraub (1985) implements such a reconstruction for the neo-Walrasian program; Rob Fisher (1986) reconstructs the work of Walras, Menger, and Jevons, using the Lakatos of *Proofs and Refutations* as his guide; Bruce Caldwell also proposes the rational reconstruction, though without endorsing a Lakatosian framework.

The exercises along these lines have produced interesting insights into the logical properties of such reconstructions. But those who hoped to find universally acceptable criteria for the appraisal of theories have been disappointed. Popper's falsification criterion in particular is inadequate. Klant, for example, uses Papandreou's distinction between basic and specific theories (Papandreou, 1958) to show that falsification is more an ideal than a reality in economics. Specific instantiations of a theory may falsifiable, but the basic theory need not be. Caldwell and Boland study various proposed criteria for theory appraisal only to conclude that none suffices.

Negative conclusions are not a reason for rejecting the discourse that produced them, but they can be a reason for discontinuing that discourse. A project that is inspired by the conviction that logic and fact can unify all people in their knowledge of their world loses its interest when logical criteria do not live up to their assigned role. It seems to run out of steam when its protagonists abandon the quest for a methodologically unified approach and defend pluralism (cf. Boland, 1982, and Caldwell, 1982) or when extensive work produces the lamentation: "Fundamentally, I do not understand what is going on" (Rosenberg, 1985).

Definite reasons for the dismissal of a particular discourse do not exist. But there are good reasons for doing so. One such reason is that we consider issues that are not talked about too important or interesting to leave out. The contrast with other conversations can bring out those issues. Therefore, let me introduce Richard Rorty and the conversation that he propagates.

Richard Rorty's philosophy has much in common with Popper's. Like Popper, he has as direct opponents analytical philosophers; like Popper, he dismisses the question "How do we know?" as uninteresting for the same reason as Popper, namely, that we cannot expect to find final authority in mental categories. Both Rorty and Popper are antifoundationalist and antipsychologistic.

Rorty's major work, *Philosophy and the Mirror of Nature* (1979), is a philosophical (read: not easily accessible to nonphilosophers) argument to expose the mind as an invention and, concomitantly, the fruitlessness of the notion of truth as correspondence with reality. Even though Rorty does not refer to Popper in this book, elsewhere, in a footnote, he claims to be Popper's comrade (Rorty, 1985). But this claim is implausible and misleading. The beginning of the footnote reads:

The [i.e., Rorty's] attitude toward truth, in which the consensus of a community rather than a relation to a nonhuman reality is taken as central, is associated not only with the American pragmatic tradition but with the work of Popper and Habermas. (p. 17)

Popper's argument with Kuhn (Popper, 1979) quickly exonerates him from this association. Even though Popper considers the problem of induction insoluble and speculations on foundations that rest in his world 2 uninteresting, he holds up the banner of "identity," of the rational scientist whose commitment to the criterion of falsifiability transcends cultural and historical boundaries and promises and convergence to the truth through a process of elimination. Conventional economic methodologists gather under his banner.

Rorty, on the contrary, rejects any banner with such a systematic message for the reason that such a banner is inevitably ethnocentric. Whereas Popper provides a solution to the epistemological problem, Rorty denies that there is a solution. He considers his writing "therapeutic" in the sense that it weans us of our addiction to the search for "criteria of rational choice" and objective, or acultural and ahistorical, knowledge. He proposes that we "set aside" the problem of "correspondence with reality" and "see knowledge as a matter of conversation and of social practice rather than as an attempt to mirror nature" (Rorty, 1979, p. 171). Popper dismisses the historical perspective; Rorty advocates its merits. Popper holds up the image of the hard sciences as an example; Rorty imagines a culture "in which neither the priests nor the physicists nor the poets nor the Party were thought of as more 'rational,' or more 'scientific' or 'deeper' than one another. No particular portion of culture would be singled out as exemplifying (or signally failing to exemplify) the condition to which the rest aspired" (1984, p. xxviii).

Rorty is part of a broad movement that is highly critical of modernism, the approach in the human and physical sciences and the arts that emphasizes the universal, the rational, structure, uniformity, Identity. "Postmodernism" is the label that may be attached to this new movement. It persuades us to acknowledge and probe "differences" in our experiences and to seek ("similarities" rather than "identity." It is responsible for bringing back concern with meaning, culture, and thus interpretation into our conversation.

Further implications of the differences between Popper and Rorty

A characteristic question of identity seekers to observers of difference is whether two people who are involved in two different conversations can sit down and come to agree. We could imagine a Keynesian and a radical economist talking about the reasons for the productivity slowdown in the 1970s. If they are reasonable people who are committed to clear definition and respect the results of empirical tests, Popperians presume, agreement is only a matter of time.

Following Rorty, I do not consider this situation of much interest. Two particular people may reach agreement with some goodwill, but the impact on the conversations is what really matters. The Keynesian may accept conflict between workers and supervisors as an explanatory factor,[9] but the important question will be whether the exploration of such a conflict will be put on his research agenda and, very importantly, that of other Keynesians. The radical economist may accept the Keynesian modeling technique, but will she and other radicals sustain a conversation that respects that technique?

The problem in such a situation is that the differences between economic conversations do not necessarily pertain solely to the use of tools. The pluralists among economic methodologists[10] appear to argue that economists choose tools or, more generally, a methodological approach to fit the purpose of their project; they do not discuss the consequences of that choice for the way economists see and understand the world. In the conversation that I favor, we talk about the involvement in different conversations that represent, in the terms of Nelson Goodman, different "ways of world making."

Nelson Goodman, like Richard Rorty, Alisdair MacIntyre, and Hilary Putnam, an analytic postpositivist philosopher,[11] is not "speaking in terms of multiple possible alternatives to a single actual world but of

---

[9] I have in mind the work of David Gordon, Thomas Weisskopf, and Samuel Bowles. See, for example, *Beyond the Wasteland* (New York: Doubleday, 1984).

[10] Like Bruce Caldwell.

[11] They adhere to the analytical style but reject the major tenets of positive philosophy.

multiple actual worlds" (1978, p. 2). He rejects the vision of identity that is pivotal in Popper's conversation. "The uniformity of nature we marvel at or the unreliability we protest," Goodman asserts, "belongs to a world of our own making" (1978, p. 10). Accordingly, we could think of monetarism and Keynesianism as two different versions of world making. It is possible that elements in one version, such as the emphasis on money in the monetarist version, are adopted by the Keynesian version, but that does not make those versions identical. We are bound to find persistent differences in the weighing of the role of money and other factors, the ordering, composition, deletions in their discourse, that is, processes that, according to Goodman, go into world making.

Reality and truth, then, are densely related to a particular version of world making. Goodman has the following to say about truth:

Truth, far from being a solemn and severe master, is a docile and obedient servant. The scientist who supposes that he is single-mindedly dedicated to the search for truth deceives himself. He is unconcerned with the trivial truths he could grind out endlessly; and he looks to the multifaceted and irregular results of observations for little more than suggestions of overall structures and significant generalizations. He seeks systems, simplicity, scope; and when satisfied on these scores he tailors truth to fit. He as much decrees as discovers the laws he sets forth, as much designs as discerns the patterns he delineates. (1978, p. 18)

This position concurs with the incommensurability hypothesis, the critical hypothesis in Kuhn's work. The notion of discourse or conversation is significant in this context. A statement in one conversation can be commensurable with or translatable in the context of another conversation – the notion of conflict can be translated possibly into terms Keynesians will understand – but what matters is the conversation as a whole. Participation in another conversation requires more than translation; it is like learning to play another game. The person will be different because of it.

The project, then, becomes the study of differences and similarities between versions of world making or conversations. In Foucault's words:

It is a task that consists of not – of no longer – treating discourses as groups of signs (signifying elements referring to contents or representations) but as practices that systematically form the objects of which they speak. Of course, discourses are composed of signs; but what they do is more than use these signs to designate things. It is this *more* that renders them irreducible to the language (*langue*) and to speech. It is this "more" that we must reveal and describe. (1972, p. 49)

The finding and articulation of this "more" begs for interpretation and thus consideration of the meaning of the signs economists and economic methodologists communicate.

Further differences: on interpretation and politics

The issue of meaning is taboo to Popper, who "avoids, like the plague, discussing the meaning of words" (1979, p. 309). He does, however, discuss the problems of understanding, in particular the understanding of problems. Using Galileo's theory as an example, he argues that understanding of problems is "a matter of handling third-world structural units, [of getting] familiar with these units and their logical interrelations" (1979, p. 182). He thus disentangles our understanding of the phenomenon "understanding" from the common association with a mental activity (his world 2).

This perspective makes sense but only in a limited way, as the contrast with Wittgenstein's discussion of understanding and meaning may indicate. Wittgenstein, like Popper, rejects the reference to mental activities, but he creates a much larger discursive domain for interpretation and meaning. The meaning of a word is, according to Wittgenstein, its use in the context of what he calls a "language game" (or "discourse," or "conversation"). The meaning of "money," "conflict," and other economic terms, therefore, is to be understood through the use in conversation. From this perspective, Popper's discussion is restrictive for two major reasons. Firstly, Popper's interpretation of world 3 represses the possibility that one term has many incommensurable interpretations, a possibility that is invoked through the metaphorical use of the "game" and "conversation." Secondly, whereas Popper wants us to believe that understanding is a matter of recognizing the problem at hand – and not the meaning of words – Wittgenstein urges us to consider the appropriate cultural context, or the language game, when we want to understand the meaning of words.

Popper's restrictions on interpretive discourse are an immediate corollary of his three-worlds analogy. He constructs his world 3 to be the set of human products. The "meaning" of world 3 is indicated by the use of the expression "objective knowledge": It makes us think of the components of world 3 as being independent of knowing subjects, or his world 2. For further clarificiation he presents a story – a "thought experiment," he calls it:

All our machines and tools are destroyed, and all our subjective learning, including our subjective knowledge of machines and tools, and how to use them. But *libraries and our capacity to learn from them* survive. Clearly, after much suffering, our world may get going again. (1979, p. 108)

The adverb "clearly" in his description tempts us to sidestep the problems of interpretation (which are problems of communication.) But what happens if the "we" in his experiment are illiterate people who come out of the bushes after all literate people have been eliminated in a series of neutron bomb explosions? For all they know, the meaning of library books is that they burn well.[12]

The problem with Popper's analogy is that world 3 is like world 1. Both are a complex whole of things and relationships among things that are to be known; in the postmodernist manner of speaking, both are a collection of texts to be read. Any of its elements, whether a particle or an article, becomes real only through conversation, that is, by virtue of an interpretive community. Before the bush people can "read" the particle or article the way any of "us" does, they need to learn how to participate in the appropriate conversations. In that sense, their experience would be similar to the experiences of novices in the games of baseball and economics. Accordingly, they need to learn not only the proper language, the necessary jargon, but also the reasons why it is good to be interested in nuclear physics and text analysis. Like my learning about baseball, their learning involves a cultural experience that will change them.

Let me give one final argument. Popper tells us that understanding a theory is a matter of understanding the problem that it attempts to solve. But do we understand his epistemological theory when we recognize that it attempts to solve the problem of induction? If so, how do we understand the tenacity with which Popper clings to his theory in spite of logical and historical difficulties? How do we understand the differences between Rorty and Popper in spite of the similarities? These questions inevitably expand the interpretive domain.

A significant extension is the political connection. Both Rorty and Popper make the connection explicit in their writings. Popper writes in his *Logic of Scientific Discovery:* "I hope that my proposals may be acceptable to those who value not only logical rigour but also freedom from dogmatism" (p. 38). The dogmatists he has in mind are the Marxists, fascists, and Freudians, as he makes explicit in his other writings. He favors the open society in which people are willing at all times to submit their ideas (conjectures) to the strongest tests available. Rorty shares Popper's liking for a democratic society that allows individual expression, but his assessment of the most important features is different. Whereas Popper stresses criticism, Rorty talks about solidarity. In Popper's world we seek peaceful coexistence through respect for objectivity; in Rorty's world the sense of community is crucial and is threat-

---

[12] The movie "The Gods Must Be Crazy" is a humorous portrayal of such a learning process. The story is about a bushman who tries to return to the gods a coke bottle that dropped from heaven (an airplane) and is confronted with a Western culture for the first time in his life.

ened by the pursuit of objectivity, which values a relationship with something outside the community above relationships within.

For pragmatists [like himself], the desire for objectivity is not the desire to
escape the limitations of one's community, but simply the desire for as much
intersubjective agreement as possible, the desire to extend the reference of "us"
as far as we can. (Rorty, 1985, p. 5)

Rorty wants us to participate in a conversation rather than contribute to
an "inquiry." Our commitment should be to sustaining the conversation,
for it is through conversation, rather than argument, that we maintain a
sense of loyalty to the community.

   Those who follow Popper or Rorty in their philosophical conversations do not have to make these political connections themselves, but
the point is that we all make various similar connections that render our
conversations meaningful and of interest. Understanding what we say
requires recognition of those connections. And that is the process of
decoding or interpretation. It is the process I was engaged in when I
tried to understand the American fascination with baseball.

So what?

Why is a long chapter necessary when the title "Economics as Discourse" plus one or two sentences could have said it all?

   The answer is the title itself, which is an argument that we go beyond
the singular statement and consider the discursive practice, the conversation in which a statement is communicated and receives its meaning.

   Why is the chapter as short as it is? Not everything can be said, and
to communicate the complex whole of ideas and images that make the
title meaningful, rhetorical devices are indispensable. Through the composition of arguments, a story, various analogies, contrasts with alternative arguments, quotations and footnotes, and so on, I have attempted
to make a case for cultural sensitivity in talk about economics. The
proposal to consider economics as discourse entails a conversation that
is different from the prevalent one, the main difference being that it
respects differences among conversations. Once we relinquish our preoccupation with identity and respect that people and their conversations are different, we are ready to seek similarities that bond us
all.

References

Aristotle. (1932). *Rhetoric,* trans. Lane Cooper. New York: Appleton-Century-
   Crofts.

Blaug, M. (1980). *The Methodology of Economics: Or How Economists Explain*. Cambridge: Cambridge University Press.

Boland, L. (1982). *The Foundations of Economic Method*. London: Allen & Unwin.

Burke, K. (1969). *A Rhetoric of Motives*. Berkeley: University of California Press.

Caldwell, B. (1982). *Beyond Positivism: Economic Methodology in the Twentieth Century*. London: Allen & Unwin.

   ed. (1985). *Appraisal and Criticism in Economics: A Book of Readings*. London: Allen & Unwin.

Eichner, A. (1983). *Why Economics Is Not Yet a Science*. New York: M.E. Sharpe.

Fisher, R. (1986). *The Logic of Economic Discovery*. Brighton, Sussex: Wheatsheaf.

Foucault. M. (1972). *The Archeology of Knowledge*. New York: Harper Colophon Books.

Geertz, C. (1983). *Local Knowledge*. New York: Basic Books.

Goodman, N. (1978). *Ways of Worldmaking*. Cambridge: Hackett.

Hausman. D. (1981). *Capital, Profits, and Prices: An Essay in the Philosophy of Economics*. New York: Columbia University Press.

   ed. (1985). *The Methodology of Economics*. Cambridge: Cambridge University Press.

Hutchison, T. W. (1977). *Knowledge and Ignorance in Economics*. Chicago: University of Chicago Press.

   (1978). *On Revolutions and Progress in Economic Knowledge*. Cambridge: Cambridge University Press.

Klamer, A. (1983). "Empirical Arguments in New Classical Economics," *Economie Appliquée* 36:229–54.

   (1984a). *Conversations with Economists: New Classical Economics and Their Opponents Speak Out on Current Controversies in Macroeconomics*. Totowa, N.J.: Rowman and Allenheld. Published in England under the title *The New Classical Macroeconomics: Conversations with New Classical Economists and Their Opponents*. Brighton, Sussex: Wheatsheaf.

   (1984b). "Levels of Discourse in New Classical Economics," *History of Political Economy* 263–90.

   (1987). "As If Economists and Their Subjects Were Rational . . . ," J. Nelson et al., eds., *The Rhetoric of the Human Sciences*. Madison: Wisconsin University Press.

Klant, J.J. (1988). *The Rules of the Game*. Cambridge: Cambridge University Press.

McCloskey, D.M. (1985). *The Rhetoric of Economics*. Madison: Wisconsin University Press.

Mirowski, P. (1984). "Physics and the Marginalist Revolution," *Cambridge Journal of Economics* 8:361–79.

Papandreou, A. (1958). *Economics as a Science*. Chicago: University of Chicago Press.

Popper, K. (1975 [1959]). *The Logic of Scientific Discovery,* 8th impression. London: Hutchinson.

(1979 [1972]). *Objective Knowledge,* rev. ed. Oxford: Oxford University Press.

and Eccles, J.C. (1977). *The Self and Its Brain.* London: Springer-Verlag.

Rorty, R. (1979). *Philosophy and the Mirror of Nature.* Princeton, N.J.: Princeton University Press.

(1985). "Solidarity or Objectivity?" in J. Rajchman and C. West, eds., *Post-Analytic Philosophy.* New York: Columbia University Press.

Rosenberg A. (1987). "Methodological Diversity in Economics," in Bruce Caldwell, ed. *Research in the History of Economic Thought and Methodology,* Vol. 5. Greenwich, Conn.: JAI Press, pp. 207–42.

Weintraub, E.R. (1985). *General Equilibrium Analysis.* Cambridge: Cambridge University Press.

Index

279